Journey Through the Twelve Forests

JOURNEY
THROUGH THE
TWELVE
FORESTS

An Encounter with Krishna

David L. Haberman

New York   Oxford
OXFORD UNIVERSITY PRESS

Oxford University Press

Oxford   New York   Toronto
Delhi   Bombay   Calcutta   Madras   Karachi
Kuala Lumpur   Singapore   Hong Kong   Tokyo
Nairobi   Dar es Salaam   Cape Town
Melbourne   Auckland   Madrid

and associated companies in
Berlin   Ibadan

Copyright (c) 1994 by David L. Haberman

Published by Oxford University Press, Inc.
198 Madison Avenue, New York, New York 10016-4314

Library of Congress Cataloging-in-Publication Data
Haberman, David L. 1952–
Journey through the twelve forests :
an encounter with Krishna /
David L. Haberman.
p.   cm.   Includes bibliographical references and index.

ISBN 978-0-19-508478-8 ; 978-0-19-508479-5 (pbk.)

1. Hindu pilgrims and pilgrimages—India—Mathura (District)
2. Krishna (Hindu deity)—Cult—India—Mathura (District)
3. Mathura (India : District)—Religious life and customs.
I. Title.   BL1239.36.M37H33   1994
294.5'35'09542—dc20   93-3269

For Anna, Meagan,
and especially Sandra,
my fellow sojourners.

And for Anjuli,
who joined us for
all too brief a time
on another Braj adventure.

Pilgrimage experience is radical experience—exposure to trial and peril, the making of perilous passage from a world grown comfortable and too confining into a world whose vastness we had only dimly surmised. Pilgrimage experience deports us from home; it exports us abroad into a hitherto unimaginable reality.

RICHARD NIEBUHR

Preface

Krishna, one of the most popular deities in India today, is typically encountered through story. His stories are seldom encountered in the passive reading of a book, but are more often heard, sung, danced, or enacted. They are also celebrated through pilgrimage activity in a land called Braj, a distinctive cultural region in north-central India. My travels in this region have taught me that the physical geography of Braj is itself a kind of text, and that the preeminent way of "reading" this text is by means of pilgrimage. This book, the result of my own wanderings in Braj, focuses on a pilgrimage known as the Ban-Yatra, the journey through the twelve forests, and is designed to take the reader on a journey around Braj and through the stories told in this locale, with the intent of providing a glimpse of Krishna and his companions as they are encountered there by a Ban-Yatra pilgrim.

A great deal can be learned from the stories told on this pilgrimage. They give a vivid sense of the manner in which the divine is conceived in the culture of Braj. Moreover, an analysis of these stories within a specific ritual context can serve as an entry point into the religious world of Braj Vaishnavism. Few previous scholars have mined the incredible wealth of information these stories contain in the particular context of the Ban-Yatra pilgrimage for better understanding the complexities of the unique religious traditions of Braj. In this book such an analysis will be employed to highlight the religious strategy developed in Braj Vaishnavism to deal with the human struggle with the tumultuous nature of desire. As we shall see, these stories give expression to a way of life that is in conscious tension with the position of many ascetics in South Asia.

With the increasing availability of mass transportation, pilgrimage activity in India has become one of the most visible and popular forms of Hindu practice; more people are visiting the sacred places of India than ever before. The increase in the number of pilgrims in India is matched by an increase in published studies on pilgrimage activity in recent years.[1] In most of these works pilgrimage is typically assumed to be a temporally limited experience of Hindu asceticism. For example, William Sax has remarked in a recent study of a Himalayan pilgrimage that pilgrimage space in India is commonly thought to be a field of and for asceticism, and that the particular form of asceticism known as pilgrimage is performed in pursuit of specific "fruits": "By journeying to these powerful places and performing certain actions in them, pilgrims obtain what are called 'fruits,' usually transformations of themselves or their life situations."[2] Pursuit of this "fruit" is the motive for the journey. Sax supports his reading of Indian pilgrimage as fruitful journeys which embrace asceticism by referring to several well-known studies, most notably Ann Gold's *Fruitful Journeys*. It would be absurd to dispute this scholarly characterization of Indian pilgrimage—in the great majority of cases it is true—but one must be careful not to let this weighty analysis obscure other instructive possibilities. Gold partially recognizes this by acknowledging the existence of a kind of journey that is executed without a specific motive (her Rajasthani informants call this a *yatra* in contrast to a *jatra*, a journey performed as work with a specific goal in mind).[3] Though she does not call it this, Gold suggests that there exists a "fruitless journey" in which the goal is not some concrete benefit but rather *moksha*, the highest aim of the ascetic renouncer. But in the interest of gaining a fuller understanding of South Asian pilgrimage, one might ask whether there is a type of sacred journey that is purposeless or "fruitless" and that eschews even the ascetic's goal of moksha. If so, what might such a goalless journey look like?

I here contend that the Ban-Yatra provides an example of such a situation. What makes this pilgrimage unique among many previously studied journeys is that it is self-expressedly purposeless and subordinates the ascetic goal of moksha to something higher. Here even the paradigmatic ascetic Shiva must undergo dramatic transformations to enter into the forests of Braj, where all pursuit of purposeful gain is abandoned.

The path of the Ban-Yatra is circular; in the end it goes nowhere. Walking the goal-less circuit of Braj, hearing and living the stories of Krishna's play, has a particular effect: it opens up a new perspective, namely, that all life is *lila*, or purposeless play. The subjective experience of this realization, the theologians of Braj tell us, is *ananda*, or limitless joy. A major concern of this book is to explore the experiential effects of the Ban-Yatra and to weigh the implications of this circular journey for current theories about pilgrimage.

Another aim of this book is to introduce the reader to the cultural history of Braj and the Ban-Yatra. For the most part the Ban-Yatra is a product of the sixteenth century, but it has continued in a vital way to the present day due to the support of the material culture of Braj, which has come from a variety of patronage sources. The story of this shifting patronage is tracked throughout the book. Examination of the historical events which produced the culture of Braj, however, reveals something else: it helps us understand how the various kinds of stories told in this region are related. We do not find here a hard line of distinction between history and myth. Historical figures reveal myth through their lives and actions, and mythical stories determine historical perspectives and developments. In Braj, history becomes another layer of the same old story; or rather, the same old story manifests in new form. We will see that most of the historical figures involved in the development of Braj are understood to have alter egos in the very stories they reveal. This conflation of myth and history seems to account for much of the paradigmatic appeal these figures have for the present-day pilgrims following in their footsteps.

Most of what is contained in this book I learned while following the footsteps of Ban-Yatra pilgrims, past and present. The tracks I followed varied greatly—from written texts, to conversations with those who were making footprints in the soil of Braj as we spoke, to a land mapped out with sacred shrines. Following these tracks required a twofold methodology: textual research and ethnographic field research.

We are today witnessing the erosion of many academic boundaries. In years past the fields of anthropology and the comparative study of religion or history of religions were fairly divided along methodological lines. Anthropologists—initially defined as those who studied preliterate societies—relied almost exclusively on the ethnographic methods of field research. Historians of religions researched written texts. The great father of the comparative study of religion, Max Müller, forbade his students from going to India and never made the journey himself. The real India, he insisted, was to be found in texts. All this is changing; the licenses held by both disciplines which allowed each of them to ignore much of the territory of the other have been revoked. Anthropologists are now working with written texts and historians of religions are going to the field; it appears that these two sometimes make creative bedfellows. As a historian of religions, I am a child of Max Müller, but I am a disobedient child, for in addition to engaging in textual research, I have made the long trek to India to conduct field research. This book is an attempt to offer the reader some of the results of my transgression by exploring the interaction between pilgrimage literature and ethnographic research conducted at the site described in such literature.

Many early Western studies of Hinduism, particularly those conducted by British Orientalists, insisted that a proper understanding of Hinduism must be based on the right set of authoritative, written texts.[4] In the effort to define the essential nature of Hinduism, the Orientalist as "expert" in effect usurped the role of cultural agency.[5] Medieval and modern texts, living traditions, and contemporary forms of Hinduism (such as pilgrimage) were often regarded with suspicion from the interpretive environment within which the true or "essential" tradition was constructed. The innocence of this move has now been exposed as being related to the politics which helped undermine the power of existing religious authority in India, assert the superiority of the Orientalists' own scientific methods, and legitimize the British Raj.[6]

The Orientalist project involved a concern for *authenticity*. Whereas those involved in this project privileged certain texts and rejected others in their search for the authentic, more recent moves within the academy have questioned the cultural assumptions driving the quest for the authentic and have examined the political forces involved in privileging certain kinds of texts in the study of another culture. I want to add my voice to those who resist the privileged and authoritative reading of Hindu traditions by abandoning the search for the real or essential and replacing it with an effort to give voice to the multitude of agents involved in the production of culture. This is one case in which I believe more is better: we must be prepared to engage in complex readings of multiple texts.

The move to multiple texts, however, does not absolve us from the responsibility of critical work. This move demands that careful attention be given to the specific nature and function of each kind of text with which one works. All texts deserve open examination, but they are not the same. Victor Turner, the father of the comparative study of pilgrimage, has led anthropologists into fruitful explorations of written texts, but he seems to have been confused on this point. In his famous article "The Center Out There: Pilgrim's Goal" and in his later work *Image and Pilgrimage in Christian Culture*,[7] Turner fails to ask the question of genre and confuses ethnographic descriptions of pilgrimages with idealized evocations written by priests and popular historians to promulgate and advocate pilgrimages.[8] The resulting conclusions of his pilgrimage studies have been questioned by many.[9] This highlights the need for extreme care in reflecting on and contextualizing the use of multiple texts. Each text represents a distinctive style of discourse, is written for a distinctive purpose, operates within distinctive criteria of production, and appeals to a distinctive type of cultural authority. Each text, therefore, must be read in a very particular way.

The culture of Braj has involved a vast proliferation of texts; in studying this culture I have encountered literally hundreds of them. To give a sense of the range of texts that constituted the voices I labored to hear, let me discuss eight (a sacred number in Braj) kinds of texts. The first four types I worked with were written texts composed by those involved directly in the production of the religious culture of Braj. First among these was the Mahatmya literature—Sanskrit texts that extol the greatness of a place and identify the benefits of visiting particular sites within that place. The land of Braj is described in a genre called the Mathura Mahatmya, located in several of the Vaishnava Puranas, the most important of which is found in the *Varaha Purana*. The latter focuses on the city of Mathura, suggesting that it is the product of the Chaturvedi brahmans of Mathura—the traditional pilgrimage priests of that city—before they had been influenced by the theological developments which occurred in Braj later in the sixteenth century. What I gained specifically from reading the *Varaha Purana* was a sense of how pilgrimage in Braj was conceived on the eve of the extraordinary developments that transformed the region's culture in the sixteenth century. In this text pilgrimage is viewed primarily as a technique for cleansing oneself and achieving merit. The text also provides a sketchy map of an early itinerary of pilgrimage in Braj. The Mathura Mahatmya appears to have been a propagandistic tool of the Mathura brahmans, and since no texts survive which give us access to direct observations of the time, it is difficult to determine what it tells us about actual pilgrimage behavior and existing sites in Braj; therefore, it should be used for this purpose only with extreme caution.

The next type of text I worked with was produced by those involved in the early formulation of the Braj pilgrimage as it has been conceived since the early sixteenth century. A prime example is the *Vraja Bhakti Vilasa*, written by an influential figure named Narayan Bhatt, who came to Braj in the mid-sixteenth century from his hometown of Madurai in southern India. More than any other figure he was responsible for the intricate mapping process whereby the mythical realm of Braj as expressed in Vaishnava literature and oral tradition was physically imprinted on the topographical region of Braj. For these accomplishments Narayan Bhatt is remembered as the great Acharya of Braj. The *Vraja Bhakti Vilasa* describes an overwhelming number of sacred sites in the area, including all the major forests and shrines of the contempo-

rary pilgrimage. This text identifies the story associated with each
site and provides a description of the appropriate ritual action for
participating in it. The *Vraja Bhakti Vilasa* also maps out a detailed
procedure and itinerary for the performance of the pilgrimage through
the twelve forests of Braj, which is called for the first time the Ban-
Yatra. Narayan Bhatt's framework significantly influenced the written
accounts of the Braj pilgrimage performed by the inspirational and
exemplary saints associated with the area, such as Chaitanya and Vallabha, and thereby still determines the basic structure for many who
perform the Ban-Yatra today. What I have learned from this genre of
texts is the nature of the activity that was responsible for the explosion
of sites in Braj, transforming it from a sacred place focused on Mathura
and known mainly for its merit-producing sites to the land of Krishna's
playful activities where pilgrims come to participate in its purposeless
play and experience its ananda. This group of texts also provides an
indication of what the pilgrimage might have been like in the formative
years of the mid-sixteenth century.

The third group of texts I consulted consists of contemporary pilgrimage guidebooks. Inexpensive paperbacks written in Hindi, Bengali, and Gujarati are available for purchase in the bazaars of Braj and
make up the most prolific category of pilgrimage-related texts being
produced in Braj today. For the most part these books contain accurate
descriptions of the sites in Braj, telling what can be found at a particular site, such as temples and natural forms associated with some story,
the distance and direction from other sites, length of the circumambulatory path, and so forth. The authority operative in this kind of text
is a keen knowledge of the physical landscape of Braj and is typically
embodied by the modern-day *panda*s, the local guides who steer pilgrims through the network of shrines in Braj. These texts are more
reliable sources of information about actual existing shrines than the
more ideal maps of the Sanskrit Mahatmyas, and are tested for their
accuracy by those who purchase them to accompany a journey through
the forests of Braj. They also almost always contain some account of
the stories associated with many of the shrines visited by the pilgrims.
As their function is to serve as practical and informative guides for the
performance of the Ban-Yatra, they are invaluable for one studying the
pilgrimage, and I have learned much from them about the structure
and modern-day conception of the pilgrimage in Braj.

The fourth and last category of texts written from within the tradition is the genre of poetic literature. A wealth of poems have been
produced in Braj since the sixteenth century which portray ideal de-

scriptions of some feature of Braj. I have found that examination of these texts is essential for gaining access to the realm of cultural imagination, or *bhavana*, so important to Braj culture. These poems are usually composed from and for worship of Braj. They are products of and for visualization and create what Kenneth Bryant has called a "verbal icon";[10] they make available to the culturally sensitive listener an image of Braj that is not ordinarily visible—what the tradition calls *aprakrita*, or unmanifest Braj. The type of authority recognized in the production of these texts is meditative accomplishment. The signature line in the poem is important since it validates the vision that the poem evokes. What I learned from these texts is that there is an important dimension of Braj for the pilgrims that is not available to the visual observations of the field researcher.

I also found historical documents useful, particularly for reconstructing some of the important historical developments which took place in the early sixteenth century whereby the land of Braj was transformed into what it is today. Most specifically, it helped me understand the kind of patronage that supported the creation of the physical culture of Braj that has been so vital to its survival. I had always been puzzled by the fact that Braj—located midway between Delhi and Agra—sprang up in the very heart of the Muslim Empire. Surviving imperial orders, or *farmans*, administered by the Mughal court in Delhi proved particularly useful for helping me understand the relationship between the Muslim rulers and those involved in the development of Braj culture. These documents were produced for court records and for maintaining the legal rights of those involved in the development of temples and shrines in Braj. By these documents I came to know which temples were in existence in the sixteenth century, how the Mughal court viewed the Hindu buildup in Braj, and which figures had developed a working relationship with the court in Delhi. These texts are an invaluable source for understanding the institutional history of the creation of a sacred space.

But if one were to stop with the rather idealized pictures of Braj available in much of the written literature, many voices would go unheard, with misleading results. The first time I ever visited Braj, wandering into the town of Vrindaban with a Fulbright grant in my pocket, my initial reactions were feelings of great disorientation and fright at the realization that I had signed up to live here for a year. I had first learned about the land of Braj in libraries on the other side of the world, examining the wonderful eighteenth-century Kangra paintings of Krishna and reading the poetry with which they are associated.

Although in some sense I knew better, I was still shocked by the great incongruity I experienced between the representations of Vrindaban in the paintings and poetry and the Vrindaban bazaar where I found myself. The experience showed me that I was fixated on one particular voice within the traditions of Braj and had to get moving. I have now spent more than two years in Braj and see it differently. That difference has to do with the slow process of listening to more voices and reading a variety of texts, many of which are available only through ethnographic research. The ethnographic method is justified in a general way by the claim that there are certain aspects of cultures that can be gotten at only by means of direct observation. In this age when all is in question, I would not want to privilege the ethnographic text more than any other kind of text—where, after all, are we to stand for judgment if we take seriously the cultural anthropologist's claim that all perceptions are determined by particular symbolic systems? However, I certainly would not want to ignore the ethnographic texts either. They are invaluable texts which seem to have added greatly to my own understanding of the pilgrimage culture of Braj. I cannot imagine writing about this pilgrimage and its land without ever spending time there.

Thus the three remaining types of texts involved in the production of this book were not written from within the tradition but are texts read only by conducting field research. The first is the ethnographic text that became available to me by talking with and observing pilgrims in Braj. I spent close to two months walking with two different groups of Ban-Yatra pilgrims. While sharing the trials of the trail with a large number of pilgrims, I had much opportunity for conversation and the chance to ask many of them about themselves and their performance of the pilgrimage. I found the information that they offered crucial to understanding the pilgrimage as actual religious practice. This ethnographic research allowed me the opportunity to observe rituals and other behavior unavailable in the written texts. It gave me access to texts other than those produced by the priests who maintain and benefit from this pilgrimage, and ear to voices of the living tradition. This is something that I, in contrast to the early Orientalists, find vital in constructing my own texts about another culture.

Another kind of text I found to be important to an understanding of the Ban-Yatra and the land of Braj is the oral tradition maintained by the priests who attend the temples and shrines scattered throughout the region. After spending two months walking with pilgrims, I passed the rest of that year living in Braj, wandering its sites and talking further with these priests. Each of the sites in Braj has a particular story associated with it, many of which are not found in the great Vaishnava scriptures. I learned some of these stories when a temple priest gathered a group of pilgrims together and narrated the episode which occurred on the site of his shrine. Others I learned through direct interviews with the priests during the remainder of my year. These stories told me a great deal about the religious strategies of Braj, as well as how Krishna is conceived there.

The final category of "texts" I want to discuss is the text of my own bodily experience. Accepting the advice of Bronislaw Malinowski and other anthropologists, who insist that the best way to learn about the rituals of another culture is to participate in them as directly as possible, I performed the pilgrimage myself. The culture of Braj is playful, and I gave myself permission to play with it. Paul Connerton, in his book *How Societies Remember*, demonstrates that much of culture is transmitted through bodily exercises and highlights the importance of paying close attention to bodily experience when trying to understand another culture.[11] By traversing the path of the pilgrims, I was able to read the texts of the Ban-Yatra with more than my eyes. My own experience recognizably differed from that of an individual raised in Hindu culture, but there was much that would have remained inaccessible to me if I had not performed the pilgrimage myself. Moreover, pilgrimage is a physically demanding activity, and I found my own body most valuable as a research tool when I was suffering. For example, the sight of my bleeding feet—and this is true serendipitous research—provoked many interesting conversations which told me much about cultural conceptions of intentional suffering. Specifically, it granted me access to important cultural concepts about the relationship between asceticism and desire and the way these seeming opposites relate to the stated goal of the pilgrimage, which is expressed by the technical term ananda, bliss. My own bodily experience also taught me that pilgrimage is not ethereal religion, not refined intellectualism, but concrete bodily experience of the material. The pilgrims of Braj get down and dirty; they worship not in immaculate temples but in open landscapes, dark forests, flowing rivers, dusty plains, muddy fields, still ponds, and rocky mountains. Since the body is the vehicle of such experience, I could not have written about the pilgrimage in the way I have if I had not put my own body on the line.

To repeat, no single text represents the real Braj; rather, all these texts give voice to the multivalency that is Braj. They demonstrate that Braj is a series of sacred sites for acquiring merit, the playground of Krishna, a space for temples marking special features and events, a glorious land visualized in meditation, the site of a material culture that was the result of a political compromise between the different forces ruling northern India, a place peopled by living pilgrims, a circle of stories, and a physical terrain to be encountered with one's body. The Braj that appears depends on the text being read. In my own writing on the Ban-Yatra, I have tried to avoid the monocular and judgmental reading of the "real" and give voice to all the various texts I have encountered, while keeping in mind that there are important differences between them. The object of this study is not "true" Hinduism—whatever that might be—but the Hinduism that is practiced by Hindus. I am not necessarily saying that my product is better, for that lapses back into the Orientalist's search for the real; what I am saying is that the process by which I go about my work strives to be more open to the variety of voices involved in the production of Indian culture, and that, I would argue, is our business.

The eminent Indian psychoanalyst Sudhir Kakar has observed that the story of Krishna and his intimate companions "is less a story remembered than a random succession of episodes. . . . [It] is not a story in the sense of an orderly narrative."[12] I have found this to be particularly true of the story told on the Ban-Yatra. To honor the nature of the story as told in this context, I have allowed the structure of the pilgrimage to determine the structure of this book. Therefore, the various episodes will be presented not as a progressive narrative—chronological time is somewhat alien to Krishna's play—but in the order in which they are encountered on the pilgrimage.

The path of the journey through the twelve forests is circular. This circular path can be visualized as a *jap-mala*, a wooden-beaded rosary used in India to meditate on a deity. Each site visited on the circular journey represents a "bead" to be fingered and provides an occasion to learn or remember an episode connected with a particular site. Many of these episodes have been imbibed since childhood by the participants in this pilgrimage. Since I assume no knowledge of Indian culture on the part of the reader, I recount the episode associated with each site in detail. Many of the episodes have a basis in Hindu scriptures, many do not. There are a number of ways to tell a story; the primary sources for those which follow are the versions I heard while walking the land of Braj. These were supplemented by pilgrimage guidebooks written in Bengali, Hindi, and Sanskrit, and sometimes by the important Vaishnava scripture, the *Bhagavata Purana*. I have tried to preserve the free narrative style of the Ban-Yatra even when translating an episode from Vaishnava scripture.

The episodic beads of this book are strung together on several strands of thought. I will be tracking four main strands as I proceed around the circular path of the Ban-Yatra. One consists of the history of the development of Braj and the Ban-Yatra. I will recount the history of the cultural region of Braj as it is evoked through the various monuments encountered on the Ban-Yatra. Following a second strand, I have explored the process of the Ban-Yatra, and the experiences of those who undertake it. I have tried in the following pages to give a sense of the structure of the pilgrimage and what it means for those who journey from afar to perform it. This leads to the third strand: the Ban-Yatra provides a favorable opportunity to explore theories of pilgrimage and to learn something about Indian religions in particular and religion in general. By paying close attention to the movements of the god Shiva in Braj, I found that one can learn much in the Ban-Yatra about various and competing religious strategies in Hindu culture for dealing with the tumultuous nature of desire. The fourth strand is my own bodily experience. I have related personal incidents from my own pilgrimage when I deemed them useful either for giving a more vivid sense of the physical performance of the Ban-Yatra or for better understanding the place of intentional suffering in the pursuit of bliss.

Finally, it is my individual perspective that ties this episodic jap-mala together. Its beads were threaded in a particular way. No two Ban-Yatras are alike; this pilgrimage, like everything in Krishna's lila, is ever changing. The journey described in the following pages, then, is a particular journey undertaken at a particular time and recorded in a particular way. I therefore try to make clear the kinds of questions and perspectives which I bring to this study. Furthermore, I am sure that my own experiences differed significantly from those of my fellow pilgrims. I attempt to relate something of their experiences as expressed in numerous conversations, but in the end much of my own experience also finds its way onto the pages that follow. Besides being the best way I know to give the reader a vivid sense of what it is like to perform this pilgrimage, a self-reflective style strikes me as being the best way of making explicit the fact that all ethnographic truths are limited, and that they consist of the fragmentary records of partial and multiple discourses.[13] The culture of Braj, like every culture, resists final summation. Any culture based on a playful and unpredictable god could never be pinned down or fully known. At best we catch

only limited glimpses. By including an autobiographical voice in my
range of voices, I have tried to give a sense of how and where I stood
to catch the glimpse I received.

Much of this book was written in Vrindaban, the spiritual heart of Braj
for many worshipers of Krishna; this has certainly flavored the resulting work. Part of my research method involved the attempt to
submerge myself in the playful world of stories and related experiences
available in the pilgrimage culture of Braj. I first undertook a twenty-
one-day journey with pilgrims who were predominantly from a Hindu
denomination known as Gaudiya Vaishnavism. I then spent an additional two weeks wandering with pilgrims from a denomination known
as the Vallabhacharyas, or the Pushti Marg. This was followed by several months' residence in Vrindaban and peripatetic research, exploring further the stories and history of the various sites in Braj.

I received valuable assistance from many individuals during my wanderings in Braj. Let me first thank the many residents who took the
time to tell me their stories; without them this book would not have
been possible. I would also like to offer a special thanks to the following: I am grateful to Shrivatsa Goswami and Maganlal Sharma; both
made my entry into the Gaudiya Ban-Yatra possible. Krishna Gopal
Shukla and Umesh Chandra Sharma accompanied me throughout
much of my wandering, helping me gain access to the world of the
Braj-lila and entertaining me with their antics whenever my spirits
flagged. I would like to thank Goswami Indirabetiji for graciously opening her Pushti Margi camp to me and Sunder C. Parikh for nurturing
me with his delicious Gujarati food. I have learned much by wandering
Braj with Shyam Das and Madan Mohan. The American Institute of
Indian Studies made possible my year of research in India (1988–89)
with a Senior Research Grant and helped look after my family when I
abandoned them to follow the pilgrim's trail. Williams College provided
the funds for a month of follow-up research during January 1991. The
staff at the Vrindaban Research Institute deserves a hearty thanks for
their support of this project. I also want to acknowledge a debt to Alan
Entwistle, whose detailed work on Braj proved to be an immense help.
I am grateful to Margaret Case for taking the time to read an early
manuscript of this book in Vrindaban and offer her insightful editorial
comments. John S. Hawley read a penultimate account of my journey;
I benefited greatly from his careful reading, encouraging words, and
detailed contributions. Karen Kane provided the artwork for the two
maps that follow. I want to thank the students who shared their inter-

ests in sacred journeys with me in my courses on pilgrimage at Williams College; in many ways this book was written for them. Finally, I thank my wife, Sandra H. Ducey, for reading early drafts, making vivid suggestions, and pushing me to write in a manner that better evokes the spirit of Braj. She and my children were true troopers throughout this project, and this book is dedicated to them.

It says in the Mathura Mahatmya of the *Varaha Purana*: "Those dwelling far from Braj, who only listen to the accounts of the pilgrimage from a man who has accomplished the journey, will be freed from all troubles and will attain the highest goal" (158:80). I would not want to promise the highest goal, but I do hope this book expands the reader's awareness of human experience and contributes to an appreciation of a fascinating culture on the other side of our diverse planet.

Vrindaban, Uttar Pradesh   *D.L.H.*
Bloomington, Ind.
August 1993

NOTES

1. See, for example, Agehananda Bharati, "Pilgrimage in the Indian Tradition," *History of Religions* 3, no. 1 (1963): 135–67, and idem "Pilgrimage Sites and Indian Civilization," in *Chapters in Indian Civilization*, ed. Joseph W. Elder (Dubuque, Ia.: Kendall-Hunt, 1970), 85–126; Surinder M. Bhardwaj, *Hindu Places of Pilgrimage in India* (Berkeley: University of California Press, 1973); Diana L. Eck, *Banaras: City of Light* (Princeton, N.J.: Princeton University Press, 1982); Ann G. Gold, *Fruitful Journeys: The Ways of Rajasthani Pilgrims* (Berkeley: University of California Press, 1988); Irawati Karve, "On the Road: A Maharashtrian Pilgrimage," *Journal of Asian Studies* 22 (1962): 13–30; D. B. Mokashi, *Palkhi: An Indian Pilgrimage* (Albany: State University of New York Press, 1987); E. Alan Morinis, *Pilgrimage in the Hindu Tradition: A Case Study of West Bengal* (Delhi: Oxford University Press, 1984); William S. Sax, *Mountain Goddess: Gender and Politics in a Himalayan Pilgrimage* (New York: Oxford University Press, 1991); and E. Valentine Daniel, *Fluid Signs: Being a Person the Tamil Way* (Berkeley: University of California Press, 1984).

2. Sax, *Mountain Goddess*, 13.

3. Gold, *Fruitful Journeys*, 136–46. Also relevant is Diana Eck's distinction between a purposeful *(sakama)* journey and a purposeless *(nishkama)* journey; see her *Banaras*, 221.

4. Many of the nineteenth-century British Orientalists claimed that true Hinduism was based solely on the Vedas and judged existing traditions that

strayed from their interpretation of these texts as corrupt. Many of the Krishnaite traditions of Braj were condemned in this move.

5. Ronald Inden makes this point in *Imagining India* (Oxford: Basil Blackwell, 1990).

6. See my "On Trial: The Love of the Sixteen Thousand Gopees," *History of Religions* 33, no. 1 (1993): 44–70.

7. Victor Turner, "The Center Out There: Pilgrim's Goal," *History of Religions* 12, no. 3 (1973): 191–230; and, with Edith Turner, *Image and Pilgrimage in Christian Culture* (New York: Columbia University Press, 1978).

8. Glenn Bowman makes this point in "Anthropology of Pilgrimage," in *Dimensions of Pilgrimage: An Anthropological Appraisal,* ed. Makhan Jha (New Delhi: Inter-India Publications, 1985), 4–5.

9. See chapter 2, note 59.

10. Kenneth Bryant, *Poems to the Child-God: Structures and Strategies in the Poetry of Surdas* (Berkeley: University of California Press, 1978), especially chapter 3.

11. Paul Connerton, *How Societies Remember* (Cambridge: Cambridge University Press, 1989).

12. Sudhir Kakar, "Erotic Fantasy: The Secret Passion of Radha and Krishna," in *The Word and the World,* ed. Veena Das (New Delhi: Sage Publications, 1986), 75.

13. Many contemporary anthropologists support this position. See, for example, the collection of essays in James Clifford and George E. Marcus, eds., *Writing Culture: The Poetics and Politics of Ethnography* (Berkeley: University of California Press, 1986). The introductory essay by James Clifford is particularly appropriate.

Contents

A Note on Translation and Transliteration

The translations that appear in this book are mine unless otherwise attributed. In an effort to make this study more accessible to a wider audience, I have eliminated the use of all diacritical marks. Combining transliterations of three Indian languages (Hindi, Bengali, and Sanskrit) leads to a certain amount of inconsistency. I have transliterated words from these languages in a manner that attempts to represent actual pronunciation, following the standard system as closely as possible without making use of diacritics (thus "*lila*" instead of "*leela*," although in this case the long *i* will not be differentiated from the short *i* of "Shiva"). Consonants have been selected and medial and final vowels have been dropped when such practice more closely reflects local pronunciation in Hindi and Bengali (thus "Braj" instead of "Vraja"). The final vowel, however, has been retained in a few words that have become familiar to English-speaking readers in such spellings (e.g., yoga, kama, Shiva). Medial and final vowels have also been retained in Sanskrit titles to indicate which texts were written in that language (thus the Hindi "Braj" but the Sanskrit title "*Vraja Bhakti Vilasa*"). For the sake of continuity, I have tried to make my transliteration of geographical place-names in Braj reflect standard romanized forms similar to those used by others writing on Braj today. A glossary of frequently used names and Indian terms, designed as a quick reference for the general reader, can be found at the end of this book.

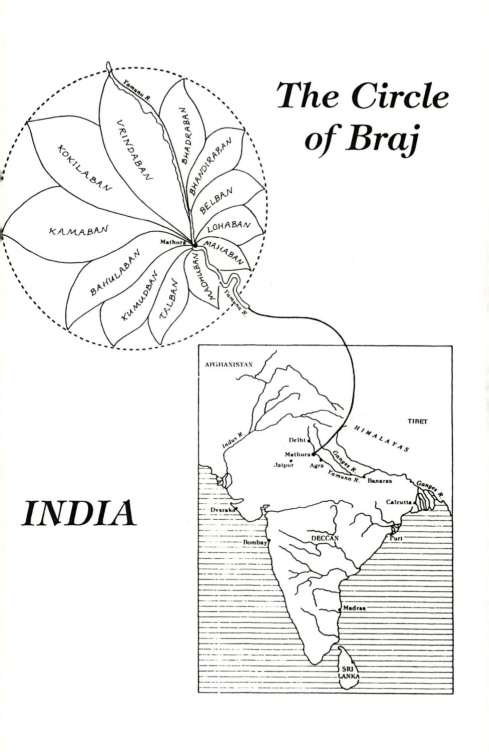

The Circle of Braj

Yamuna R.

VRINDABAN
BHADRABAN
KOKILABAN
BHANDIRABAN
BELBAN
LOHABAN
KAMABAN
MAHABAN
Mathura
BAHULABAN
MADHUBAN
TALBAN
KUMUDBAN
Yamuna R.

INDIA

AFGHANISTAN

TIBET

HIMALAYAS

Indus R.

Delhi
Mathura
Jaipur
Agra
Ganges R.
Yamuna R.
Banaras
Ganges R.
Calcutta

Dvaraka

Bombay
DECCAN
Puri

Madras

SRI LANKA

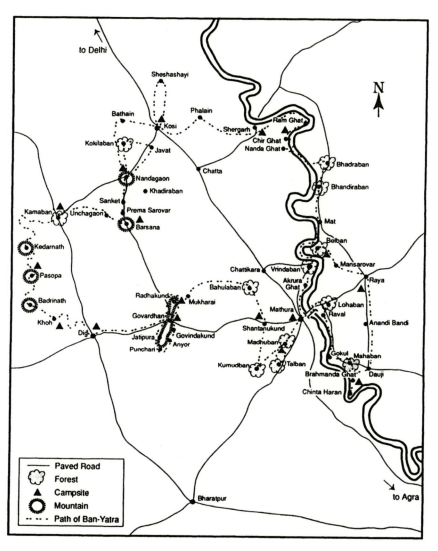

Map of Braj

Journey Through the Twelve Forests

1

Beginnings

If I am to be a man, then let me, Rasakhan,
live as a cowherd in the village of Gokul.
If I am to be an animal, then let me live
always grazing among the cows of Nanda.
If I am to be a rock, then let me be one
upon the very hill that Krishna used as
an umbrella against Indra's storm.
If I am to be a bird, then let me live
in the branches of a kadamba tree
on the banks of the Yamuna.[1]

RASAKHAN

In the middle of a dark night on the eighth day of the waning moon in
the month of Bhadon (August–September), jagged bolts of lightning
pierced the thick black clouds covering the sky as the monsoon raged
outside the prison cell. From deep within came the cry of a newborn
baby, the eighth child born to Devaki and her husband, Vasudeva.
Years before, Devaki's wicked cousin Kansa had jailed the couple on
their wedding day because he had heard a voice telling him that he
would die at the hands of their child.

King Kansa, the unhappy result of the rape of a queen by a demon,
controlled the rich and glorious kingdom of Mathura. He had usurped
the throne from the rightful king Ugrasena, who was now languishing in
the palace dungeon. A host of oppressive demons were among Kansa's
closest friends. His rule was so tyrannical that Mother Earth was unable to bear the burden any longer. Taking the form of a distressed
cow, she sought the divine aid of the gods. The gods quickly discerned
the monstrous nature of Mother Earth's calamity and led her to the

3

shore of the cosmic ocean, the abode of the supreme Lord Vishnu. Standing on the edge, Mother Earth appealed to Vishnu. Vishnu assured her that her affliction would soon be relieved and plucked two hairs from his head, one light, one dark; by means of these he would deal with the demonic Kansa. Vishnu then told the gods to proceed to Braj and prepare for a unique manifestation.[2]

The wedding of Devaki and Vasudeva was celebrated in the court of Mathura soon after, but the grand ceremony suddenly ceased when Kansa heard the voice telling him that he would be killed by the couple's eighth child. Greatly alarmed, King Kansa grabbed hold of Devaki and was about to slay her when Vasudeva intervened and promised to yield him all their offspring. In the following years the first six children of Devaki were slaughtered at birth.

Then came the time for Vishnu to act. His light hair manifested as the seventh child of Devaki, who was transferred by Vishnu's creative power to the womb of Rohini, a second wife of Vasudeva, who was hiding across the river in the cow encampment of Vasudeva's trustworthy friend, Nanda. While Kansa assumed that Devaki had miscarried, Rohini joyously gave birth to Balarama, an incarnation of Vishnu's cosmic serpent, Ananta.

By means of the dark hair Vishnu manifested himself as the eighth child of Devaki and Vasudeva. On the night this child was born, Vishnu caused the prison guards to fall asleep and Vasudeva's chains to loosen. Placing his newborn son in a basket on his head, Vasudeva escaped and ran toward the Yamana River. As he stepped into the raging river the monsoon-swollen waters subsided momentarily and the serpent Ananta sheltered Vasudeva and his precious cargo from the pouring rain with the mighty hoods of his five heads till they arrived unharmed at the encampment of Nanda on the other shore. There he quietly exchanged his son with the seemingly stillborn daughter of Nanda's wife, Yashoda, and returned across the river to his prison room. When Kansa heard that Devaki had once again given birth he rushed to her cell, seized the baby, and dashed it to the stone floor. From the tiny crushed body rose the goddess Yogamaya, a manifestation of Vishnu's creative power, who announced to Kansa that the real child of Devaki and Vasudeva remained alive and would one day return to kill him. Meanwhile the dark one, Krishna, was quite safe in the loving arms of Yashoda.

Thus Krishna entered the land of Braj, the area surrounding the royal city of Mathura. This is the beginning of a story, a story celebrated in the pilgrimage known as the Ban-Yatra, a journey through the twelve forests associated with Krishna's activities in Braj.

Krishna is the favorite deity of many Hindus in India. He is a mischievous, youthful lover who turns the world upside down with his unpredictable play. He is a joker, a thief, a prankster with a bottomless bag of amusing tricks; one who delights in foiling established order. Krishna's playful ways reveal an indifference toward rules and a disregard for social convention. His behavior belongs to the joyous realm of pointless play. One of his popular epithets is Banke Bihari, the "Crooked Lover." This can be understood as referring to the erotic pose Krishna assumes while playing the flute, a pose he frequently takes to attract his lovers; but more often it refers to his crooked ways in love affairs. One devotee of Krishna told me that you have to get yourself straight before you approach the dutiful Lord Rama, but Krishna himself is crooked. Far from being a sober and judgmental god, Krishna is an unpredictable, mischievous boy who likes to romp in the forest, playfully teasing all he encounters. With the irresistible call of his flute, he lures his players into the forest to experience his essential nature, which is declared to be ananda—"joy" or "bliss." Krishna is Ultimate Reality assuming unexpected forms. His ways are ultimately unknowable; only those who can surrender the desire for mastery and let go in a world of uncertainty are free to dance with him.

The history of the cult of Krishna is long and complex and need not detain us here.[3] Krishna belongs to the oldest layer of Hindu beliefs, having roots reaching back into the religious prehistory of India, though he does not enter the Brahmanic mainstream until the Gupta period (4th–6th cen. C.E.). From this time onward Krishna increasingly becomes the most important theological form for those Hindus designated throughout India as Vaishnavas, that is, those who worship some form of Vishnu as the supreme manifestation of divinity. It is likely that Krishna the divine cowherd was first a minor deity associated with the pastoral castes living in the vicinity of Mathura, but if this is true, he was soon carried by these pastoralists to southern India, where he became absorbed into important Vaishnava theological reflections.[4] With the eighth-century mystical poems of the southern Indian Vaishnavas known as the Alvars, Krishna the playful cowboy became a central object of Vaishnava devotion.

Although the cult of Krishna has always been linked to the area around Mathura, and although archaeological evidence indicates the presence of Krishna worship in the vicinity of Mathura during the early centuries of the first millennium C.E., much of the theological development took place outside the geographical area in which the cult began. The Braj scholar Charlotte Vaudeville remarks: "If the cowherd god comes from the banks of the Yamuna, if he is the 'child of Mathura in the north,' it is in Southern India nevertheless that he prospered and that his legend, highly charged with its primitive origins, was progressively refined by and assimilated into Vaishnava *bhakti*. This process comes to an end, in the South, towards the end of the tenth century, with the compilation of the *Bhagavata Purana*, a real Krishnaite Bible, which becomes the starting point for the development of medieval and modern Vaishnavism throughout India."[5] Nonetheless, whether in religious imagination or in physical cult, Krishna and his playful activities have always been associated with the area surrounding Mathura, a region which later came to be known as Braj.[6]

Braj is located along the Yamuna River about ninety miles south of Delhi. It lies in the middle of that fertile heartland of northern India created when the South Asian subcontinent crashed into the continent of Asia some 50 million years ago, forming a huge ditch to be filled in with the rich alluvial soil from the rapidly rising Himalaya Mountains. The area of Braj is somewhat circular, with a diameter of roughly sixty miles, and is situated in the cultivated river valley of the western Mathura district in the modern state of Uttar Pradesh, extending into the desert terrain of the Bharatpur district of eastern Rajasthan. It is very likely that Braj was first and foremost a mythical land, a meditative space in the mind, or a place in the heart.[7] Much of this book explores the developments that resulted in the transformation of Braj from a meditative space to a physical land of pilgrimage.

I traveled to Braj with my family during the summer months of 1988 to join in the festivities that precede Janmashtami, the celebration of Krishna's birth. I had spent a period of time in Braj seven years earlier, and had discovered new and unexpected things about Krishna in Braj. I came to realize that Braj was a kind of text all its own; there were many wonderful stories told about Krishna at various sites in Braj that did not appear in the famous Vaishnava scriptures. I learned eventually that the Ban-Yatra is the preeminent way of reading the text of Braj. I therefore returned eager to journey with Ban-Yatra pilgrims on the trail through the twelve forests associated with Krishna and "read" these intriguing tales for myself.

I had a strong, if inexplicable, desire to make this pilgrimage. In part I wanted to push and test myself physically, to place myself in a demanding situation to see what I could do, to see what I might learn. But there was more. The theme of the journey had captured my imagination. Why is it that we move? Why do we search? Why do we travel to distant lands? What are we looking for? What do we want? What is the nature of the desire I share with so many on the road?

Pilgrims are restless, discontent, dissatisfied, on the move, looking for something. Pilgrims take to the road in search of some object, often quite vague, which promises to provide something to fill the painful holes in their lives. This object of yearning is difficult to pin down; it is experienced as that which is missing, some unnamed object lost long ago; it is that haunting lack which engenders the incessant flight from one thing to another. The promise of fulfillment, of wholeness, of perfection, of completion lures us out onto the road to begin a quest.

In Delhi we boarded a bus bound for Vrindaban, the spiritual heart of Braj for a denomination of Hindus known as Gaudiya Vaishnavas, who identify Vrindaban as the location of Krishna's nighttime activities with his favorite lover, Radha. Even before we left the crowded station of the Inter-State Bus Terminal of Old Delhi it was clear that this would be no ordinary ride. The conductor, dressed in Western clothes, motioned us in an official manner to the few remaining empty seats at the back of the bus. His magisterial motions, however, did not distract our attention from the gaping hole in the steel floorboard near the driver's seat; nor did they prepare us for the array of passengers who filled the bus. Women wrapped in brilliant saris bounced babies on their laps; dark, mustached men spouted mouthfuls of bright red betel juice out the windows; and holy men draped in ocher cloth, whose foreheads were painted with variously stylized footprints of Krishna and who wore heavy wooden beads around their necks, gazed sternly at our American apparel. Yet smiles flashed all around us as we stowed our bags and plopped onto the hard seats.

Everyone in the crowded green-and-yellow bus was extremely excited. The hot August sun beat on the roof, heating the interior like a furnace. My wife was pressed next to a fat man dressed in a sweaty T-shirt and dripping with perspiration. Some of the moisture sliding off the man's face was absorbed by a towel slung around his neck; the remainder he flicked unaware in the direction of my wife, who looked annoyed. We lurched out of the station through the swarming streets of Delhi, eventually leaving the polluted industrial air of the city far behind. The hot breeze coming in through the open windows provided some relief, but not much. Two brothers, who farmed a small plot of land just north of Vrindaban, occupied the seats next to me; they were curious about our presence. Offering me a small hand-tied cigarette called a *bidi*, they began asking me questions about my family and life in America. As we passed through fertile farmland, the two of them took turns identifying crops for me: millet, wheat, barley, and sugarcane. In the winter months these fields would be dominated by the brilliant yellow blossoms of mustard plants.

After driving for three and a half hours down the ancient Agra road, lined with green fields and trees, we turned off the highway for Vrindaban. A sign welcoming us to the "Land of Krishna" marked the turn. As we approached the town of Vrindaban, temple towers suddenly poked through the trees and the fat man sitting next to my wife burst into jubilant song. Several women on the bus responded with a heartfelt refrain: "Radha! O Radha! All glory to the Beloved of Krishna!" The joyous mood of their songs was infectious. I looked over and noticed a smile on my wife's face.

The songs continued as we entered the narrow, twisting lanes of Vrindaban, dodging cows, pigs, dogs, and bicycle rickshaws. Swarms of pilgrims were everywhere. Large, multi-colored tents had been erected in empty lots to create space for the crowds attending religious plays and talks by well-known saints. Temporary restaurants were set up alongside the road; the sun glittered brightly off rows of neatly stacked stainless steel plates. Tea stalls and small souvenir shops which catered to the pilgrims were bustling with activity. I experienced a rush of ambivalent emotions. I was excited to be back; I felt that I was somehow coming home, to a home on the other side of the planet. And yet an old familiar feeling of apprehension returned. How was I to act in a world which seemed so alien, so different? How would I be able to manage during the time of the pilgrimage where everything—people, language, land, interests, values, expectations, clothing, daily schedule, food, and even toilet habits—would be so different?

Thousands of pilgrims make the roughly two-hundred-mile circuit of Braj every year. Some do it alone, some do it in small groups, but most do it in large parties organized by local pilgrimage guides. There are many ways to perform this pilgrimage and much variety among itineraries. I had elected to walk the pilgrimage circuit with a group mainly made up of Gaudiya Vaishnavas, Hindus associated with a denomination of Krishna devotionalism that has roots in sixteenth-century Bengal. I left the task of finding an appropriate pilgrimage party to our current host, Shri Shrivatsa Goswami, a traditional Gaudiya Vaishnava priest, a patron of local arts, the head of a cultural institution located in Vrindaban, and a dear friend. My plan was to complete the entire circuit with members of the Gaudiya denomination and then spend additional time in a pilgrimage party composed of Vallabhacharyas, or Pushti Margis.

Shrivatsa made arrangements for me to join a group of pilgrims who would follow closely the traditional schedule established in the sixteenth century by the Gaudiya Vaishnava leader Narayan Bhatt, perhaps the most influential figure in the development of the Ban-Yatra. According to Narayan Bhatt, it is most auspicious to begin this pilgrimage at Janmashtami, the celebration of Krishna's birth, and finish with the full moon at the end of Bhadon.[8]

One night at about ten o'clock, eight days before my walk began, Shrivatsa and I climbed into his Jeep, inched out of the huge gateway of his garden compound, and began winding our way through the dark, narrow streets of Vrindaban. The going was slow as we waited for the many cows, pilgrims, and bicycle rickshaws to move aside. The air was warm and humid, giving the sensation of a gentle steam bath. The Jeep's headlights cut a path through the darkness, illuminating the aged, elaborately carved, drab yellow and red sandstone buildings that were stained and eroded by the yearly cycle of raging monsoons and intense heat. I felt a thrill in response to the sheer alienness of it all. We drove to the edge of town and eventually stopped in front of a large courtyard wall, where we were met by a pleasant voice coming from a dark sandstone archway. With the aid of a candle, a slender figure in a shimmering sari led us up a steep flight of stone stairs to an upper chamber. A cushioned wooden platform stood in the middle of a light blue stucco room; an electric fan steadily churned the sultry air. As we settled onto the platform we were served sweets and hot tea with milk and delicious spices by yet another beautiful daughter of the house.

Shri Maganlal Sharma soon appeared at the door. He was a distinguished-looking man: a tall, slender, graying gentleman of some sixty-four years. He was well known in Vrindaban and had been mayor of the town for many years until the central government dismissed all mayors of the Uttar Pradesh state sixteen years earlier, in 1972. A traditional panda, or pilgrimage guide, Maganlal was to be my pilgrimage guru, taking charge of all necessary arrangements for my journey. Although he himself was affiliated with a local Braj Vaishnava denomination known as the Radhavallabhis, most of his clients were Gaudiya Vaishnavas from Bengal. I was to be his first foreign client. After introductions, he immediately began to instruct me in the preparations required to perform the Ban-Yatra. He also informed me that I would be eating and sleeping with a group of twelve farmers and shopkeepers from rural Bengal, close to Calcutta. I struggled to understand his Hindi, a language I had heard little of for seven years. Feelings of strangeness and uncertainty gripped me. We parted with wide smiles and a searching look into each other's eyes.

Two days later I returned alone. On this visit I was to perform the ritual vow whereby I accepted Maganlal as my pilgrimage guru. I have always been somewhat nervous about affairs with gurus—perhaps I have taken them too seriously—but this one was easy to enter into, as it implied no obligations once the pilgrimage was complete. I reentered the room on the second floor, where the cushioned platform now functioned as a dais for the guru. I sat cross-legged on the cool marble floor at the feet of Maganlal, who was dressed casually in a white T-shirt with a faded brown cloth *lungi* wrapped around his waist. My soon-to-be guru had a pot of water drawn from the Yamuna River awaiting the occasion. Following his instructions I began washing my hands with this water. Next I ritually cleansed my body by taking Yamuna water in my left hand, and with my right hand lifted the water to my mouth three times while repeating Sanskrit mantras: "May the waters of holy Yamuna Ma bless me and wash away my impurities." As I recited additional mantras, I sprinkled water over my entire face three times. I was now ready to intone the vow. I poured more water from the pot into the palm of my right hand and then placed a small red rose on the water. While the rose floated in my hand, I recited the Sanskrit vow accepting Maganlal as my pilgrimage guru. When I had finished I offered him five rupees and a coconut and was now bound to him for the duration of my journey.

Seven years before I had arrived at a small market in the heart of the old section of Vrindaban, known as Loi Bazaar. As I wandered about aimlessly, dazed by an impressive case of culture shock, I heard a kind voice address me in polite Hindi: "Please come! Sit and drink some tea." The voice belonged to Mahesh Kumar, a merchant who, along with his father and two younger brothers, sold cloth from three stores. We were close in age, and over the following months I became good friends with Mahesh and his family. He assisted me through the numerous material difficulties one encounters while living in a foreign land; I teasingly called him my *bazar panda*, my guide to the market. It was to Mahesh that I now turned for help in acquiring the list of items Maganlal and Shrivatsa had determined I would need on my journey. In addition to those items I already had with me—backpack, cameras, film, batteries, snakebite kit, writing materials, water filter, plastic bottles, Swiss army knife, flashlight, toiletries, canvas shoes, and Dr. Bronner's soap—it was recommended that I purchase a *lota* (a small metal pot used for carrying water), a canvas bucket and rope for raising water from deep wells, a plastic bucket for bathing and washing clothes, a ground cloth, a cot and blanket for sleeping, mosquito repellent, two *gamcha*s (towellike cloths used for many purposes, including shading the head, wiping sweat from the face, drying the body after baths, and wrapping around the waist to make a short skirt), two pairs of white cotton pants, two light shirts, a pair of rubber sandals, a black cloth umbrella, and a metal trunk to contain many of these items, which would be transported by bullock cart. The combined cost of my purchases was around seven hundred rupees, or about fifty dollars. As I struggled to carry the items from various shops in the market, I encountered a holy wanderer with dark skin and long black hair who wore a small white cloth around his waist and carried only a lota and a walking stick. The contrast made me feel a bit ridiculous; a discernible smile and glint in the wanderer's eyes suggested amusement.

Janmashtami, the celebration of Krishna's birthday on the eighth lunar day of the month of Bhadon, marks the beginning of activities in Braj for the Ban-Yatra pilgrims. In 1988 Janmashtami fell on the third day of September. Bhadon is the second month of the monsoon season, which follows a period of sizzling heat. The rains bring a welcome greenness to the parched earth, but the weather during this time of year is very hot and humid. Those who intend to perform this pilgrimage arrive in Vrindaban days before Janmashtami. During this time the lanes of Vrindaban are choked with pilgrims from all parts of India, wandering about, visiting the temples that make this town famous. This is also a popular time for *rasa-lilas*, dramatic performances depicting the exploits of Krishna and his intimate associates in Braj.[9] These plays are enacted by young boys who delight their enthralled audiences for hours with the mischievous love of Krishna. Participation in these dramas helps prepare the pilgrims for the mood of the Ban-Yatra. One member of the audience who planned to go on the pilgrimage told me, "Today we see the lilas performed onstage; soon we will see where they actually occurred."

On the day of Janmashtami some of the pilgrims visit Mathura, the birthplace of Krishna; others choose to remain in Vrindaban. The focus of the Janmashtami celebrations for the Gaudiya Vaishnavas in Vrindaban is the temple of Radharaman. Radharaman, the "Pleaser of Radha," is a form of Krishna said to have manifest directly from a sacred black *shalagram* stone due to the devotional power of the six-teenth-century saint Gopal Bhatt Goswami. After entering the temple compound through a massive and elaborately carved sandstone gate-way, and following the lane which passes between the homes of the temple priests, the pilgrims are welcomed at the temple by the music of a drum and *shehnai,* and by the inviting shade of a multicolored patchwork awning. All participants fast for the morning of Janmash-tami. During that time Radharaman is bathed with gallons of Yamuna water and a liquid comprising five substances: milk, honey, yogurt, butter, and sugar. Throughout the bathing, Sanskrit mantras are in-toned amid the clanging of temple bells. When the birthday bathing is finished, this liquid mixture is distributed to all as *prasad*, grace in an edible form, and the fast is broken with food prepared from this sacred substance. The birth of the enemy of Kansa, the son of Vasudeva and Devaki and the foster son of Nanda and Yashoda, is thus celebrated in Vrindaban.

The day after Janmashtami is a festival called Nandotsav, a celebra-tion of Nanda's joy at the birth of his son. It is a joyous, raucous affair in which yogurt dyed with turmeric powder is thrown about and sweets are distributed liberally. It was on this day that my family left Vrinda-ban to begin their journey to Katmandu, Nepal, where they would be staying for the duration of my pilgrimage. Henry David Thoreau once wrote: "If you are ready to leave father and mother, and brother and sister, and wife and child and friends, and never see them again . . . then you are ready for a walk."[10] Thoreau has a point, but personally I found this aspect of walking somewhat difficult. I was to miss my wife and daughters profoundly throughout much of my journey. I said good-bye to them, suppressing tears amid the boisterous celebrations of Krishna's birth.

I could not indulge in melancholy emotions for long, however, since I had been instructed by my pilgrimage guru to prepare for another ritual. I was to perform the worship of Yamuna and Vrinda, the two presiding goddesses of Vrindaban, as preliminary preparations for the pilgrimage. I was told to begin with at least a symbolic bath in the Yamuna River. With lota in hand, I walked to Vrindaban's bathing *ghats*, the section of town which lines the riverbank. After working my way through a labyrinth of medieval buildings, I descended the sandstone steps which provide access to the river, bathed my head and heart with the slow-moving waters, and filled my lota to the brim. Although it was only nine o'clock, the sun was already hot. I boarded one of the many bicycle rickshaws that ply the streets of Vrindaban and rode to the house of Maganlal Sharma, carefully balancing the pot of Yamuna water as we careened around cows and bounced over bumps. There I met the twelve Bengali pilgrims with whom I would be camping. Three were men, brown and weatherworn from work in the fields; the other nine were women: three widows dressed in white, and the remaining six wrapped in colorful saris and sporting the red and white bangles of married women. This ratio seemed a little unusual, but I was soon to learn that there was a preponderance of women on the pilgrimage. We greeted each other—"Jai Shri Radhe!" (Glory to Radha, the Beloved of Krishna)—and then proceeded to a small temple located within the compound of Maganlal's residence to begin our worship.

The temple housed beautifully decorated images of Radha and Krishna. When we arrived the temple was crowded with small children playfully engaged in their own worship of the divine couple. They were promptly chased out of the temple, and we were instructed to sit in a circle on the black-and-white marble floor before the deities. Our guru, Maganlal, then made a swastika—an auspicious symbol of well-being—with red powder on the floor in front of each of us. To the right of the red swastika, his assistant—a young girl named Saraswati—placed a green pan leaf. Next she laid a small brown betel nut on each leaf. Everyone was then given a miniature pink sari, a garland of red and white flowers, a silver rupee coin, some fruit, and a few small roses.

We then waited. I was not sure why we were waiting and looked around for some clue. The world outside the temple was washed white by the brilliant rays of the morning sun, its heat intensifying by the minute. Inside, flies buzzed loudly as they pounced on everything. We pilgrims sat quietly, waiting.

At last a bicycle rickshaw arrived at the entrance of the temple. A very old, heavyset man with a bushy white beard and orange marks smeared across his forehead struggled to get down. With the aid of young Saraswati and two wooden canes, he hobbled slowly into the temple. Fearing he would topple over at any moment, I tensed, ready to spring to his aid. It took him a long time to reach his place in our circle. After easing himself onto his seat, he gazed sternly at us for some time through his frizzy gray hair. Then he suddenly burst into loud chant, surprising me with the tremendous energy with which he sang. His forceful voice boomed throughout the temple; I felt its vibrations in my stomach. He seemed to be encapsulating the temple in sound, pushing the outside world far away. Time passed, the Sanskrit chants ceased, and he stared silently at each of us. A smile suddenly creased his face, and Maganlal introduced him as the priest who would be conducting our worship.

We were instructed to place our pots of Yamuna water directly in front of us. A Tulsi plant growing in a yellow tin can which previously had contained cooking oil was brought into the center of the circle. The frizzy-haired priest lit incense and inserted it into the soil of the Tulsi plant. The pot of water and the Tulsi plant are the natural forms of, respectively, the goddesses Yamuna and Vrinda. The Yamuna, the most sacred of all rivers for Vaishnavas, is considered a natural form of Krishna, and its waters are said to grant all spiritual powers. The pilgrimage guides of Vrindaban insist that the worship of Yamuna is an essential preliminary ritual for the Ban-Yatra, and we will see how the Yamuna River can function as a barrier, refusing entrance to those unprepared for a sojourn in the forests of Braj.

Vrinda is considered the foremost goddess of the various forests of Braj. Tulsi, the natural form of Vrinda, thus represents all the forests of Braj; moreover, Tulsi is viewed as a seminal form of the entire world of nature. A story is told in Braj in connection with the worship of Tulsi: One day all the gods were arguing among themselves as to who should be worshiped first. It was decided that they would run a race around the entire world and that whoever completed the circuit first would win. The gods took off in a great roar—all except Ganesh, the elephant-headed son of Shiva and Parvati. Ganesh casually sat where he was, watching the receding swarm of gods. When they were out of sight he got up, circumambulated a nearby Tulsi plant, and then returned to his seat. The gods soon came rushing back and found Ganesh sitting where they had left him. "I have won," declared Ganesh. "But that is impossible," complained the gods. "You never left this spot. How can you have won the race around the entire world?" Ganesh explained that he had walked around a Tulsi plant, and since the Tulsi plant is the seminal form of the entire world, his act was tantamount to a journey around the manifest world. All of the gods had to agree, and that is why Ganesh is worshiped first among the gods.

The Ban-Yatra pilgrims, then, must worship Tulsi, the natural representation of all the forests of Braj, to honor the environs they are about to enter. Worshiping the Tulsi plant and circumambulating it are in a sense equivalent to performing the Ban-Yatra; but it is said that circumambulation of the seminal plant does not bring the joy that comes from circumambulation of the fully manifest Braj.

The priest commanded us to take the pan leaf in our left hand, dip it into our pots of Yamuna water, and transfer drops of water into our right palm. In this fashion we never directly touched the water in the pots. With the first drops of water we sprinkled our mouths and faces while repeating Sanskrit mantras intoned by the energetic priest. We then slowly and systematically proceeded to offer the flowers, fruit, betel nut, rupee coin, and cloth sari to the goddess Yamuna residing in the water pot. As each item was offered, the priest led us through the appropriate Sanskrit mantra. From time to time he spontaneously burst into joyous songs. The contagious nature of these songs frequently moved the pilgrims to join him. After completing these procedures we repeated all offerings to the goddess Vrinda in the form of the Tulsi plant. We rose upon finishing and circumambulated the Tulsi plant. Concluding the ritual, we paid our respects to the priest with a bow and a five-rupee note.

After the preliminary rituals were finished, we walked to the house of Maganlal and shared a delicious meal consisting of rice, lentil gravy, yogurt, and a variety of spiced vegetables. I had foolishly come with no water, thinking that the ritual would be short. Over four hours had now passed, and it was hot. For health reasons I had decided to drink only filtered water, so I was growing quite thirsty. The spicy food had made my face red and my thirst intolerable. My hosts looked greatly puzzled, as I refused all kind offers of cool unfiltered water. My throat was on fire; never before had I experienced thirst like this. I swore to myself that I would never again be separated from my water bottle. By two o'clock I had finished all business at Maganlal's house and was on my way back to Shrivatsa's compound. The sun was blistering. I drank five bottles of soda along the dusty road, but nothing seemed to help—a taste of what was to come.

I was told by my guru, Maganlal, that the Ban-Yatra would be most beneficial if I were first to perform the *parikrama,* or circumambulation, of Vrindaban. This was considered an expansion of the circumambulation of the Tulsi plant we had just performed. I decided it would help prepare me for the coming long walk and allow me to see parts of Vrindaban I had not seen in a while.

That evening I went to the bazaar to talk with my friend Mahesh. He agreed to do the sacred circumambulation with me. Mahesh suggested that because of the heat we begin in the morning at the time of the first temple services—around four-thirty—and insisted that we wear no shoes. We made arrangements to meet at Keshi Ghat, the most prominent bathing place on the river in Vrindaban and a popular starting place for the residents of Vrindaban who regularly perform its circumambulation. Here, where Krishna smashed the horse demon

Keshi, sent to Vrindaban by Kansa as part of his scheme to destroy Krishna, there is a small shrine commemorating the event. The shrine is connected to a temple dedicated to the goddess of the Yamuna River, perched at the top of the ghat's large sandstone stairs. The Yamuna is worshiped here every day at sunrise and sunset.

I awoke early, dressed quietly, and started down a stone-paved alley that leads to Keshi Ghat. The way was lined with people sleeping on cots—wooden frames woven with rope—set outside to catch the cool night breeze. Several cows had found a position for themselves in the line of beds and appeared to be sleeping soundly. The final approach to Keshi Ghat passes through an alley walled by massive stone buildings and dark archways. Walking here before dawn gives one the feeling of moving within another time. The end of the alley opens into the wide expanse of the Yamuna River.

I waited for Mahesh on an octagonal sandstone structure built out over the river near the temple dedicated to the goddess Yamuna. During May and June the Yamuna River can easily be crossed by wading, but during this monsoon season, when it rains heavily in the mountains, the Yamuna is full and flows swiftly between its banks, stretching for about a mile from shore to shore. The water gently slapped the base of the platform on which I rested. Stars splashed brilliantly across a black sky which showed little sign that this was the "rainy season." Distant temple bells filled the air, announcing *mangal-arati*, the auspicious first viewing of the deities for the day. I soon made out the figure of Mahesh making his way toward me.

Mahesh bent down, took some dust from the ground and put it to his head three times, and pronounced, "Jai Shri Radhe!" We were on our way. The clockwise circuit around Vrindaban is about eight miles in length and would take us nearly three hours to complete. We first followed a path that wove its way through dark buildings that lined the banks of the Yamuna. A few candles could be seen illuminating small chambers in which people were singing morning prayers and preparing for the day's activities. We broke through to a more rural open terrain as a pink glow began to appear on the eastern horizon. Crows squawked loudly. We passed through a grove of trees in which a small ashram had been established. A group of men in thin loincloths were gathered around a well. They were pouring buckets of water over one another's bodies as the first light of morning came streaming through the trees. The dirt beneath our bare feet was soft and cool, a nice change from the hard bricks crossed during the beginning of our walk.

Peacocks called out continually from the surrounding lush vegetation. We passed a wrestling camp, where young men gathered to lift dumb-bells made from old temple parts and test each other's strength in a pit filled with soft dirt. The Yamuna suddenly took a sharp turn, and we followed the bend for a short distance as the day began to warm.

Many perform the circumambulation very quickly. We encou itered a group of men "jogging" around the route in T-shirts and gamchas. Colorful saris flashed by us; these are the apparel of the modern *gopis*, the cowgirl lovers of Krishna. A cloth merchant Mahesh knew stopped to talk with us. He began each day by walking the perimeter of Vrinda-ban. Mahesh told me that he was considering doing the same. We were next overtaken by a gray-haired old man wrapped in a worn-out cloth. He had his arms raised high in the air and was singing softly, "Radhe! Radhe!" He seemed very content.

As the path veered sharply away from the river we entered settle-ments that have sprung up outside the old section of Vrindaban. It was beginning to get hot. We passed several mud houses with cow-dung patties plastered to their walls. The smell of pungent cow-dung fires, lit to prepare the morning meal, filled the air. Children could be heard boisterously performing their morning tasks. A small boy dressed in shorts and a T-shirt drove six frisky calves past us. We came upon the road leading to Mathura; the black asphalt burned our feet as we hurried across it. After stepping over the narrow-gauge tracks of the Radharani Express, which link Vrindaban to Mathura, we followed a path of rough bricks. Sharp stones jabbed our feet before we came to the soft sand and dirt lining the Yamuna on the other side of Vrindaban. We continued back toward our starting place, passing a long series of temples and ghats that line the river. During much of the year the ghats of these temples lead down to a plain of sunbaked dirt, but during the monsoon period they return to their rightful place on the river.

The most prominent feature of the skyline along the river is the tall red temple spire of Madan Mohan, Krishna as "He Who Enchants the God of Love." Madan Mohan, one of the first temples to be built in Vrindaban, was established by Sanatana Goswami, one of the leading Gaudiya Vaishnava figures responsible for the development of Braj. The current structure was constructed during the glory of the Mughal empire, but much of it has since been destroyed. We walked past an impressive string of ornate sandstone temples and guest houses built by kings and queens of Rajasthan, the desert regions to the west, to house pilgrims visiting the sacred sites of Vrindaban. My feet were growing quite tender from the journey, and I was happy when we reached Keshi Ghat to complete the circle.

Mahesh suggested that we end our tour around Vrindaban with a trip to Seva Kunj, a grove of small trees that has been preserved inside the town of Vrindaban. The poet-saint Hit Harivansh installed an image here in the sixteenth century of Krishna as Radhavallabha, the "Lover of Radha." This image is now housed in the nearby Radhavallabha temple, the center of a small sect and one of the most active temples of the town. Mahesh's family had recently purchased a house adjacent to the gardens of Seva Kunj, and he wanted to show me the results of their remodeling; thus we could combine devotional activity with more mundane affairs. Seva Kunj holds great devotional value for the residents of Vrindaban; it is believed that Radha and Krishna meet in a love bower, or *kunj*, in this grove every night. Enclosed within a high stone wall, the grove is open during the day but its gates are locked at night. The residents of Vrindaban say that anyone who might try to spend the night in these groves would by morning be either insane or dead from the excessive ecstasy caused by what they had witnessed. Only the monkeys of Vrindaban are able to withstand the sight of what goes on here at night, and they are present in this grove in large numbers. Some say this is because they were great saints in their previous lives.

The Seva Kunj grounds are a tangle of vines and interlaced trees. Inside the thick green growth is a small gem of a temple, beautifully constructed out of light marble. In front of it is a fountain whose cool waters attract the monkeys. The temple is called Rang Mahal, the "Pavilion of Colors"; delightfully colorful paintings of the gopis and the divine couple adorn its interior walls. "Rang Mahal" is also a common name for a stage or place of a dramatic event, and this, too, is appropriate, for an unusual lila was enacted here. It is portrayed in a special painting kept in the inner sanctum of this temple, which is the focus of the pilgrim's attention. The painting depicts Krishna lovingly massaging Radha's feet. A man massaging the feet of a woman, a god massaging the feet of a lover; this represents a remarkable reversal and an exceptional act of gracious service. It is for this reason that this grove is called Seva Kunj, the "Bower of Service." The painting revealed in the inner sanctuary of this grove indicates the supremacy of Radha among the Vaishnavas of Vrindaban. A contrast is sometimes made between Radha and the heavenly Lakshmi, consort of the majestic Vishnu, who is typically portrayed sitting at her lord's feet, submissively massaging his legs. A Vrindaban devotee once asked me: "Who would you rather have representing you? Lakshmi talks to the Lord while massaging his feet. There is a certain amount of influence here. But Radha talks to the Lord while he is massaging her feet!"

On the day we were to begin our pilgrimage I rose before dawn and started toward the bank of the Yamuna. I had been instructed by my guru, Maganlal, to rise with the sun and bathe thoroughly in the river. So, lota in hand and gamcha around my waist, I ventured through the twisting lanes that lead to Chir Ghat, a place on the riverbank in Vrindaban which celebrates the Krishna who stole the clothes of the bathing gopis and forced them to stand naked before him. An image of the amorous prankster rests on a limb of a tree at Chir Ghat, and cloths have been tied to the tree's branches. As Krishna smiled mischievously from atop his huge Kadamba tree, I surveyed the slimy brown water entering the Yamuna from the sewer gutters of Vrindaban and quickly made the decision to go to the opposite shore. A young boy clad only in tattered shorts was eager to take me in his boat. He rowed his weathered wooden craft with a strength unusual for that hour of the morning. Turtles, the sacred vehicles of the goddess Yamuna, bobbed unhurriedly about us in the murky waters.

Arriving at the sandy white bank of the far shore, I stripped down to my underwear. I entered the warm waters of Mother Yamuna and was engulfed in darkness. The force of the current surprised me; it pulled me down and turned me over gently. Emerging from the water, I felt renewed, like I was looking at the world for the first time. It was a gorgeous morning. The sun was streaming golden through misty gray clouds hovering on the horizon. A breeze blew ripples across the surface of the water. The kaleidoscopic miracle of life seemed to be reflected on this dancing surface. Bathed in the soft morning light, the red sandstone temple towers of Vrindaban looked magnificent.

A group of farmers had come while I was bathing, bringing shiny green squash and succulent papayas to be ferried to the busy markets on the other shore. They observed me for a while with apparent curiosity and then coaxed me back on the boat. Soon we were on our way back to the town of Vrindaban. As I relaxed in the morning sunshine on the gently rocking boat, I was filled with a sense of ease. This was surely an auspicious beginning.

By midmorning I had finished packing my metal trunk, which would be carried by bullock cart, and began waiting for Govinda. I was apprehensive. Govinda was a dark, roundish man of about thirty-five years of age. He was to be my personal guide on the pilgrimage, a role arranged by Maganlal to accommodate my special needs as an outside researcher. Govinda had failed to show up for two previous appointments, and I seriously doubted whether he would show up for this one. I had met Govinda only once before, but he had not made a good impression. I would have to trust him completely once we were out in the field, and so far he had done much to undermine my confidence in him.

By ten o'clock it was already extremely hot, the temperature approaching a hundred degrees. Finally, Govinda appeared at the door of my room and said that he had been instructed by Maganlal to take me to two temples. My pilgrimage was to begin with a visit to the temples of Gopishwar and Govindadev.

We wound our way through the narrow lanes of Vrindaban and walked up the few steps that lead into the temple of Gopishwar, a small temple located in the heart of the old section of Vrindaban near the Yamuna River. This temple houses a massive and ancient lingam, the phallic shaped, aniconic form of the god Shiva. Like many, I assumed that the Ban-Yatra was concerned exclusively with Krishna and his close associates. I was therefore quite surprised to learn that the Ban-Yatra begins, at least for the Gaudiya, Radhavallabhi, and Nimbarki Vaishnavas, in Vrindaban—the very heart of the intimate realm of Krishna—at a temple which houses a Shiva lingam.

Neither the priests of the temple nor the literature available on the history of Braj could provide any information regarding the history of the current temple building. Local legend—told to me by Shri Ram Gopal Goswami, the chief priest of the temple, and repeated in the popular guidebooks produced for pilgrims visiting the temples of Vrindaban—has it that the temple was originally established by Krishna himself as a boon to Shiva. It was later rebuilt by Krishna's great-grandson Vajranabh, who inherited the kingdom of Braj after the disastrous events of the Mahabharata war. The temple fell under neglect as Jains and Buddhists later came to power in this area; neglect turned to ruin as Muslims came to rule and destroyed many of the temples of the region. The Gopishwar temple was restored in the early sixteenth century by Rupa and Sanatana Goswami, two brothers sent to Braj by the Bengali saint Chaitanya to develop its sites. The two Goswamis assigned the worship of the Gopishwar lingam to a local priest. The Nimbarki Goswamis who maintain control of the temple today claim to be the descendants of this priest.

Gopishwar is an intimate temple. In the lane outside of its arched entrance is a row of tea stalls; wooden benches are set out invitingly, beckoning customers to relax awhile. Flower vendors, sitting on the steps leading to the temple, sell garlands of roses, marigolds, and *bilva* leaves, a plant sacred to Shiva. Inside is a circumambulatory pathway, paved with black-and-white marble squares, that leads the worshiper through eight scalloped archways. Eight brass bells of differing shapes and sizes are suspended at measured intervals around this pathway, which encircles the central chamber, a cubical structure measuring about fifteen feet across. Green tiles with white floral patterns and a red rose in the middle cover its outer walls. Three doors lead down into the central square of the temple, a site usually submerged beneath a thin layer of milky water and covered with trampled flowers. At the center of all this is the dark brownish red stone lingam.

Shiva is one of the main gods of Hindu culture. Though he displays powers associated with eroticism, he is commonly envisioned as a mountain-dwelling ascetic who is engaged in intense meditation and acts of severe austerity.[11] He is typically pictured sitting in transcendental contemplation on a tiger-skin mat in some isolated place on Mount Kailash, far removed from all civilization. His hair is long and matted; a look of aloof detachment is discernible in his half-closed eyes; he wears a snake as a necklace; and he is surrounded by fierce animals. In this form he serves as a model for many of the serious practitioners of yoga. For many Hindus, Shiva is the supreme principle of the universe; in Braj, however, Shiva is subordinate to Krishna. I was to learn a great deal about the religion of Braj by giving attention to the stories and rituals associated with Shiva in this area.

A stone lingam is found in the center of the inner sanctuary of almost every Shiva temple. In this regard Gopishwar is no different. Devotees come to this temple in great numbers in the early morning hours to worship the Shiva lingam, interacting with it in intimate ways: they rub and caress it while bathing it with milk and water, and they place offerings of flowers and bilva leaves directly on it. There is a casualness about the activities of the morning worship; one or two priests are usually present but are not directly involved in the morning offerings.

The evening worship of the Gopishwar lingam, however, is a different matter. The priests are now crucially involved in a ritual that takes a form which is, to my knowledge, absolutely unique in all of India. After washing the lingam in water, milk, and yogurt, the priests produce several decorative items from a metal trunk and begin preparing Gopishwar for worship. First a colorful hood is placed over the lingam. Then the priests tie a large silver mask to the lingam; the face of the mask is that of a beautiful woman. The lingam is given a silver crown, and the face is decorated with eyeliner, a bejeweled nose-to-ear ring, and bright red lipstick. An attractive petticoat and silk sari are next wrapped around the lingam. Once this ornamentation is finished, worship is conducted with the waving of the oil *arati* lamps, and Gopishwar, now a woman, is ready for the evening viewing. Gopishwar is the most important Shaivite temple in Vrindaban; it is crowded with worshipers every day. On the night of the festival of Shivaratri, when the ornate clothing of the lingam is changed every two hours throughout the night, the temple is jam-packed with visitors, a clear indication of the vitality of this temple in the overall religious life of Vrindaban.

What could all of this possibly mean? Why would the foremost representation of masculine asceticism be effaced with the decorative trappings of a beautiful woman? To begin the search for an answer one must focus on another peculiar feature of this temple. Almost all Shaivite temples face east; Gopishwar, however, faces north. Why? The temple priests explain that Gopishwar faces a tree standing just north of the temple, and in fact, the Gopishwar temple should be viewed as part of a larger complex that includes the temple compound of Bansi Bat.

When my guide realized I had never been to this site, he took me down an alley to the whitewashed gateway of the Bansi Bat temple. Passing through the gate, we stood before a large banyan tree which grows in the center of the temple courtyard. This is the tree called Bansi Bat, the "Flute Tree." Visitors are told that this is the very tree from which Krishna sounded his flute to summon the gopis to his secret love dance in the forest under the full autumn moon. To satisfy each gopi, Krishna multiplied himself to equal the number of gopis who had come to dance and make love with him. The temple compound of Bansi Bat draws one visually into Krishna's circular dance of love. Bright relief paintings of blue, pink, yellow, red, and green cover the walls encircling the entire courtyard. The paintings portray alternating Krishnas and gopis, each dressed differently and looking longingly into the eyes of the other. Behind them is a grassy scene with dark green palm trees; the blue waters of the Yamuna flow past their feet. In the northeastern corner of the courtyard of Bansi Bat stands a small shrine housing a white marble image of Shiva. A snake still adorns his neck, but now his hair is beautifully arranged, and his eyes are wide open, intent on what is happening in the center of the compound. He is dressed in a lovely sari, wears ornate earrings, and holds a lotus blossom in the palms of his hands, which are joined in supplication at his breast. Here Shiva has assumed the form of an alluring gopi.

When Krishna sounded his flute to summon the gopis to the love forest of Vrindaban, the mighty ascetic Shiva was sitting in meditation atop Mount Kailash, his Himalayan retreat. Shiva is the prototypical hardened ascetic; he has turned his back on the world of desire. He is the patron deity of many ash-smeared ascetics who are striving to achieve moksha, a liberation or mystical union. In Braj, however, Shiva is known as an ardent devotee of Krishna.[12] Hearing the irresistible notes from Krishna's flute, Shiva experienced an overwhelming desire to join in the love dance. He hurried to Braj, but no matter how hard he tried he was unable to cross the Yamuna River and enter the forest of Vrindaban. Eventually he sought the aid of the goddess Yamuna by performing her worship. Yamuna appeared to Shiva and informed him that he could not enter Vrindaban in the form of a male ascetic. She instructed him to bathe in her waters. Shiva did so and emerged from the water as a beautiful gopi. Shiva, however, had never before applied makeup; he knew only how to smear ashes on his body. Graciously, the goddess Yamuna did this for him. Shiva, now a gorgeous gopi, entered Vrindaban and leapt enthusiastically into Krishna's love play. Krishna was so pleased with Shiva's unusually powerful devotion and ability to dance—Shiva is, after all, Nataraj, or "Lord of Dance"—that he named him Gopishwar, meaning "Lord of the Gopis," or "Lord Who Is a Gopi," and granted him a boon: Shiva would be allowed to reside in Vrindaban near Bansi Bat, where he would be honored first by all who wished to enter into the love play of the forest. The nearby Gopishwar lingam which faces Bansi Bat attests to the continuing power of this boon.

My guide narrated the story of Gopishwar as we stood before the sari-draped marble figure of Shiva. He then explained that this was the reason I had worshiped the goddesses Yamuna and Vrinda, and had bathed that morning in the waters of the Yamuna. Inadvertently, I had transformed myself into a gopi.

This, I now learned, was the manner in which a Gaudiya Vaishnava pilgrim spiritually begins the Ban-Yatra, an exercise in stepping into the story of Krishna's play. At Gopishwar the pilgrims honor he who demonstrates how to obtain the gopi form which allows access to the forests of love. I was to discover many ways in which Shiva plays an important exemplary role in this pilgrimage. I was told on several occasions that since Shiva has already traversed the path, one can proceed on a successful pilgrimage only after one understands his path. Many of the pilgrimage guides insisted that one cannot be a true Vaishnava without worshiping Shiva. This was to provide me with much food for thought throughout my own pilgrimage. Charlotte Vaudeville has argued that prior to the Vaishnava buildup of Braj in the sixteenth century this area was important for the worship of Shiva.[13] In typical Hindu fashion, Shiva was not ousted when the Vaishnavas gained control of Braj but was encompassed by the Krishna cult and thereby transformed. An examination of Shiva in Braj is a productive avenue to understanding something essential about the religion of Braj.

How are we to "read" the activities that take place in the temple of Gopishwar? What do they tell us about the religion of Braj? The described activities, I think, can best be understood as a manipulation of the symbolism of the lingam. In order to understand what the manipulations mean, one must first have some idea of what the lingam means.

The lingam stands at the center of a Shaivite temple, contrasting dramatically with the explosion of images frequently found on the outside of Shaivite temples, such as those at Khajuraho, where the walls burst with an excessive display of life forms. The lingam represents moksha, liberation from the tumultuous realm of experience, or union with the undifferentiated Absolute Reality wherein all individuality is dissolved.[14] It is opposed to *kama*, or desire, that force which propels one into differentiated experience, defined as *samsara* in Hindu traditions. The lingam announces the unmanifest as opposed to the manifest. It is identified with Niskala Shiva or Nirguna Brahman, that is, ultimate reality which is completely without qualities. It is most literally a "sign" of that which has no sign; a "mark" of that which cannot be marked. It is, therefore, a representation of the formless. The lingam as center is empty, void; it is nothingness. It is also called *dhruva* or *acala*, meaning "fixed," "immovable," or "motionless." The lingam is the still point at the center of the dance, the calm at the heart of the storm; but at this center no dance is possible, no experience is possible, no life is possible, and certainly no love is possible.

In many ways the lingam can be seen as the goal of the ascetic in Hindu traditions. It represents the destination of those who aim to negate the chaotic surface of life, to rip away the veil of the world in search of pure presence or the absolute ground of Being. As Sudhir Kakar has argued, the lingam is the symbol of control or mastery.[15] The target of the ascetic's effort is the stable zero point of desire, known as *samadhi*, or *kaivalya*. Hindu ontology has it that the world of forms was produced out of an explosion of desire: In the beginning was a single point—*atman, brahman, purusha, bindu*—entirely alone. Looking around, it saw nothing other than itself. It had no delight. It desired a second. From this desire arose a male and a female, and from the interaction of these two came all of creation.[16] Consequently, the ascetic in search of the inert absolute, the undifferentiated void, must extinguish desire. The way of the ascetic is *pratilomika*, that is, it goes against the natural grain of desire. The ascetic turns his back on life and seeks to avoid the tumultuous emotions and tensions inherent in the world. Therefore one strategy for coping with human life, which is marked by dissatisfaction, is to extinguish desire, the very root of participation in the dissatisfactory world which seems to be beyond our control.

Moksha, however, is not the goal of Braj religion. The *bhakti*, or conscious "participation," of Braj Vaishnavism involves a very different kind of strategy; the lingam of Gopishwar is given the form of a beautiful gopi. The founding theologians of Braj insist that even if moksha is offered, the devotee of Krishna will not accept it.[17] The Braj theoretician Rupa Goswami is fond of quoting the following verse from the *Padma Purana*: "The supreme fruit in other sacred sites is only moksha, but in Braj, Krishna bhakti, which is desired even by those who have obtained moksha, is attained."[18] The devotee, one is frequently told in Braj, desires to taste sugar, not become sugar. This is not possible in an undifferentiated state; in order to taste, to experience, to love, form is essential. The lingam, the center point, is empty, void, and ananda, or "enjoyment," does not take place at the empty center. For the sake of enjoyment the zero point must explode outward into the ever-expanding kaleidoscopic multiplicity of forms—and in doing so, become pointless.

The very land of Braj is considered to be divine by the inhabitants of Braj. One of the major sixteenth-century developers of Braj, Narayan Bhatt, writes in his *Vraja Bhakti Vilasa* that "Braj is the very form of Krishna."[19] A Braj version of the creation of that form explains that the single point, dividing itself, became the blue Krishna and the golden Radha, and the intermingling love play of the two produced the green land of Braj.[20] The center point spreads ever outward, losing itself in the expanding (and pointless) circle of Braj *through* the play of Radha and Krishna and *for* the play of Radha and Krishna. Thus the world itself is divine. With Vaishnava bhakti we have entered a realm where matter matters, and the senses make sense.[21]

The activities of pilgrims in Braj certainly bear this out. The religion of Braj is one that features a proliferation of forms. Mountains are worshiped, stones touched, trees embraced, dirt ingested, dust rolled in, water sipped, and ponds bathed in. Instead of seeking to penetrate appearances to come to some underlying essence, as does the ascetic, the Braj devotee worships forms and caresses surfaces. Here manifest differentiation is celebrated. The religion of Braj does not deny the chaotic world of diversity for the sake of finding an undifferentiated, unmanifest, colorless core; rather, it involves an acceptance and enjoyment of the whole show, in whatever form it takes.

A central tenet of the religion of Braj is that all life is lila, or purposeless play. Strictly speaking, then, there is no goal to Braj religion; all goals are surrendered in the acceptance of lila. The point is not that there is something to accomplish, somewhere to go, but rather that there is no point, no goal. From the viewpoint of lila everything is fine just the way it is; here the emphasis is on perspective, not accomplishments. The object, then, is not to achieve some end point but to learn to experience ananda, that pointless "enjoyment" which transcends the dualistic distinction of happiness and unhappiness. In fact, from this perspective, it is goal-oriented activity—striving for some other condition—that causes unhappiness and takes us away from enjoying the form that the lila assumes right here, right now. The promise of a more perfect goal creates a sense of imperfection in that which is. But in Braj all natural forms are accepted as lila, with all their apparent limitations and imperfections—which are now perceived otherwise since the point of perfection has been abandoned. The symbolism of the lingam is associated with the quest for mastery, whereas Braj Vaishnavism involves a surrender to unpredictable play. The symbolism of the lingam involves the will for nothingness, whereas the religion of Braj involves the nothingness of will. Will without desire is opposed to desire without will. Here the certitude of the center must be given up; infinite play is possible only when one is cut loose from a fixed and stable center. The aloof security of the lingam is abandoned for the insecurity that is Krishna's play. Asceticism is a resistance to what appears. Accepting the play of life—lila—implies enjoyment of whatever appears in that life.

To better understand the frame of mind that the pilgrims must enter as they begin the Ban-Yatra, it will be helpful to explore a bit further this contrast between the symbolism of the lingam and the religion of Braj. The former is associated with the attempt to master dissatisfaction by aiming for a stable point beyond the tumultuous play of the world, by aiming for the zero point of desire. The religion of Braj, on the other hand, aims to enter fully the realm of desire where moving emotions come into play. The highest cultural expression of this movement is the gopi, the crafty cowgirl who is beside herself with love.

Thus, in Vrindaban the central lingam must be given distinct form—a moving form, a beautiful form, a form appropriate for the dance of love, a form capable of enjoying the play of Krishna; it must be transformed into a gopi who quivers with desire. Far from aiming for a stable zero point of desire, Shiva as Gopishwar puts on lipstick and swings into the play of desire. This brings us to the heart of the matter—the strategy with which the religion of Braj deals with dissatisfaction and the attitude it takes toward desire.

Discontent, dissatisfaction, unhappiness—these are problems central to the religious struggle with human existence. The goal of most human activity is the satisfaction or fulfillment of desire. Ordinary desire operates within the realm of happiness and sorrow. When the object of desire is present, one is happy; when the object of desire is absent, one is unhappy, dissatisfied. The common response in this situation is to try to control and hold onto those objects which cause pleasure. In a world marked by impermanence, this, of course, is impossible. The quest for satisfaction, however, is also doomed because of the very nature of ordinary desire. The dynamics of this fruitless search for satisfaction have been explored by the psychologist Jacques Lacan. Every object of desire, he tells us, will reveal itself to be necessarily ephemeral and is destined to be supplanted by another because it is incapable of stopping up the radical sense of lack caused by the loss of the "original object."[22] The original object for Lacan is the lost object, that which is missing, the mythical object of lack which engenders the incessant flight from one demand to another. It is the unnamed object, the aim of all quests for completion. It is the point of perfection, the object of primal satisfaction; it is the point of undifferentiation. It is symbolically expressed, for Lacan, as the phallus. The phallus, as a symbol of the lack of desire, must be understood in two ways: "The lack *of* desire is, in the first place, the lack that constitutes or creates desire. I desire because I lack. In the second place, the lack *of* desire designates the satisfaction of desire. To be totally satisfied is to lack desire."[23] The two are interrelated because the perfection that this object promises makes all that is seem imperfect. This original object of desire, Lacan reminds us, is always missing, ever out of reach, unreal; thus, in search of it, we are destined to be dissatisfied in desire.

The ascetic strives to cope with this situation by renouncing all other objects, by giving up all desire except desire for the original object, a stable center beyond the uncontrollable play of appearances. The original object becomes a point of fixation—the sole aim—but is tracked at the expense of all else. In pursuit of the object that will fulfill all desires (the phallus), the ascetic turns his back on the world and loses life.

Within the world of Braj religion, however, ultimate pleasure is not sought through the negation of desire, the rejection of this human quality that seems to be an inseparable part of life. One way to understand the particular nature of this perspective may be to introduce for comparative purposes the point of view of Sigmund Freud, whose basic economic understanding of psychological tensions is widely accepted in the modern world. Freud identified an instinctual tendency which he defined as the "death instincts."[24] The death instincts strive toward the reduction of tensions to a zero point; their goal is to bring the living being back to the inorganic state of complete repose. The death instincts are best viewed in the context of two other cornerstones of Freud's economic theory: the principle of constancy and the pleasure principle, which are closely associated with one another in that displeasure is understood as the experience of an increase in tension and pleasure as a decrease in tension. The death instincts ultimately aim for a state wherein all excitations have been reduced to the zero point; Freud called this state Nirvana. This is what Freud means when he says, "The pleasure principle seems actually to serve the death instincts."[25]

Shiva smears his body with ashes and withdraws to Mount Kailash to sit fixed in stable samadhi. What he values is *vishranti*, or "repose." Kakar reads Kailash as a remote, isolated, secure hideout that one flees to because of disappointment with the external world.[26] This Shiva, however, is unable to cross the Yamuna River and enter into the love play of the forests of Braj. To participate in Krishna's unpredictable lila, Shiva must give up the stable center and return to the wavering realm of desire. The religion of Braj involves the cultivation of desire. As Lee Siegel writes, "The entire life of the Vaishnava bhakta was to consist of a 'holy yearning,' the intense desire caused by separation."[27] The holy yearning of the gopis is the subject of many of the stories and much of the literature of Braj.

Opposite to the death instincts, Freud posited another psychological tendency he called the "life instincts." Whereas the death instincts tend toward dissolution and nondifferentiation, the life instincts tend toward greater differentiation and creation of a vitality which presupposes a high level of tension. Freud had difficulty fitting the life instincts and the closely related force of Eros into his economic theory of energy; he was unable to show how these obeyed what he described as the conservative character of instincts. There is something excessive about Eros. Eros, in fact, caused Freud to ponder the possibility that tension might sometimes be pleasurable, and this moved him to consider a distinction between the pleasure principle and the Nirvana principle.

The pleasure of the gopis is not conceived in the psychoanalytic way—the immediacy of gratification, the release of tension, and the resolution of excitation—for it points to the possibility that excitation itself is pleasurable. Freud argues that the deferment of immediate gratification, what he calls sublimation, is frustrating and leads to discontentment. The excitement of the gopis, however, is maintained without the kind of frustration that causes the ascetic to withdraw. It is desire as love in separation—*viraha*—that is celebrated in the religion of Braj. Separation prolongs desire, whereas gratification ends it. Reflecting on the passion of Radha, the foremost gopi, Kakar writes:

> The augmentation of passion or, more specifically, heightening of sexual excitement is then the "great feeling," the *mahabhava*, that pervades the Radha-Krishna legend. Radha incarnates a state of permanent amorous tension, a here-and-now of desire that carries within itself a future expectation of pleasurable release but . . . oh, not yet! Her concern is not with the "lineaments of gratified desire" but with their anticipation. Radha personifies an enduring arousal that does not seek orgasmic resolution. Hers is an effort to reach the very essence of eroticism.[28]

Here desire itself is relished; sexual satisfaction is equal to death. In the gopis we encounter an eroticism wherein disappointment does not lead to withdrawal, a desire wherein absence does not lead to dissatisfaction. This is not a satisfaction *of* desire but a satisfaction *in* desire. It is this kind of desire which Shiva must embrace to participate in the love play of Braj. And it is into this kind of desire that the pilgrim must enter; the Ban-Yatra begins, according to the Radhavallabhi, Nimbarki, and Gaudiya Vaishnava guides of Vrindaban, with a bath in the Yamuna and a "glimpse" of Gopishwar at Bansi Bat, the one who shows the way.

We were now ready to proceed to the most historically important temple of Vrindaban, the temple of Govindadev, which houses the amorous couple Radha-Krishna. We had no trouble finding Govindadev, a place of many beginnings; it stands on a small hill rising above the surrounding plain and is the physical and spiritual center of Vrindaban.

The temple of Govindadev is an impressive building. Frederick S.

Growse, the district magistrate of Mathura from 1870 to 1877, was moved to say in his district memoir of 1882 that Govindadev "is the most impressive religious edifice that Hindu art has ever produced, at least in Upper India."[29] It is certainly by far the largest temple built in northern India since the beginning of Muslim rule in the early thirteenth century. What remains is nearly eighty yards long and thirty yards wide. Walls ten feet thick rise high into the air, making Govindadev the most noticeable structure on the Vrindaban skyline. Constructed during the height of the Mughal empire, this massive structure was built out of a fine red sandstone—a material usually reserved for Mughal imperial buildings. The design is a mixture of Muslim and Hindu architecture, Muslim design sandwiched between layers of Hindu design. Although the outside of the temple is ornate, it is covered with none of the beautiful images one sees on earlier temples, such as those built centuries before at Khajuraho. To resist idolatry, Muslims prohibit the use of living forms in religious architecture. Govindadev's architecture thus represents a "dialog in stone"[30] and shows Hindu sensitivity to the Muslim rulers of the time. One can learn a great deal about the development of Braj from the history of this temple.

It has always struck me as remarkable that Braj, located directly between the imperial cities of Delhi and Agra, blossomed under Muslim rule. Many of its early temples and shrines are the products of the sixteenth century, the height of the Mughal period. Muslims had established a presence in north-central India in the early eleventh century with the raids of Mahmud of Ghazni, a strong ruler from a town in Afghanistan near Kabul. But it was not until 1192 that a later ruler of Ghazni, Muhammad Ghuri, penetrated the plains of north-central India and defeated the forces of Prithvi Raj, the famous Rajput who ruled from Ajmer and Delhi. Mahmud of Ghazni's eyes were on the rich plunder of India's temples, but Muhammad Ghuri's aim was political control of northern India. Muhammad returned to Ghazni and left behind his able slave, Qutb-ud-Din Aibak, to rule the kingdom of Delhi. When Muhammad was assassinated in 1206, Aibak became the first sultan of Delhi, thus founding what was to become known as the Delhi Sultanate. The Delhi Sultanate was to continue for over three centuries, ruled by a number of families, until stronger forces overpowered it.

In 1525 a Turk named Babur, who claimed to be a descendant of Genghis Khan and had ruled over Afghanistan from Kabul for over twenty years, rode over the Khyber Pass and invaded India. Within a year he had defeated the Lodis, who had ruled much of northern India under the Delhi Sultanate since 1451, and established himself as the first Mughal emperor. After his death in 1530, Babur was succeeded by his eldest son, Humayun, who later was driven from power by Afghans led by Sher Shah. Humayun retreated to Kabul, where he ruled for ten years while Sher Shah ascended the throne of Delhi and established a government known for its efficient system of administration and concern for the welfare of its subjects. It was he who built the road between Delhi and Agra, now the main artery of Braj. Sher Shah ruled for only five years, and when he died he was succeeded by his son, Islam Shah; the latter reigned for nearly ten years but eventually lost power to warring factions of Afghans who created an atmosphere of anarchy and confusion. Humayun, who had been closely following events in Delhi, decided the time was ripe to strike, and he recovered his lost throne in Delhi in 1556. He had ruled for barely six months, however, when he fell from the steps in his library and died. He was succeeded by his eldest son, Akbar the Great. Akbar was only fourteen at the time of his father's death, but he soon proved himself to be brilliant in military campaigns and government administration. Since the Afghans were now perceived to be the enemies of the Mughals, Akbar sought an alliance with the Hindu Rajputs, who ruled the desert regions to the west and were known for their military skill and valor. This alliance was to have a major impact on developments in Braj.

Meanwhile, an independent Muslim kingdom extending over much of what is now Bengal was ruled by one Husain Shah from his court at Gaud during the years 1493–1518. Among Husain Shah's ministers were two brothers from a Karnataka brahman family that had left southern India because of family problems.[31] Though these two worked for a Muslim king, they kept close ties with Hindu Vaishnava communities. Sometime in the early years of the sixteenth century the two brothers, known in the Muslim court as Dabir Khas and Saker Malik, met the charismatic saint Chaitanya; this meeting transformed their lives.

Chaitanya was a brahman born in Navadvip, Bengal, in 1486. He had married and was pursuing a traditional education when, sometime in his early twenties, his life radically changed. He went to Gaya to perform rites for his deceased father; when he returned he was mad with love for Krishna. He soon became the inspirational leader of an enthusiastic group of Krishna devotees. Chaitanya spread his devotional passion by traveling throughout Bengal and other parts of India;

his travels in Braj will be discussed in chapter 2. Upon meeting Chaitanya, the two brothers quit the service of Husain Shah and entered into the service of Chaitanya, who renamed them Rupa and Sanatana. Chaitanya sent them to Braj, where they were to establish sites for Krishna's worship and a literary foundation for the budding movement that came to be known as Gaudiya Vaishnavism. They were soon joined by four others, all of whom became distinguished as the Six Goswamis of Vrindaban.

Rupa Goswami arrived in Braj in 1517.[32] Chaitanya had already visited Braj by this time and had sent a previous disciple, Lokanath, to work on discovering the sites associated with Krishna's lilas. This was, of course, in the last years of the Delhi Sultanate, and it was during the reign of Sikandar Lodi that the physical "re-discovery"[33] and cultural construction of Braj began. Sikandar Lodi is almost always characterized as a religious bigot who was very destructive to Hindu culture. Alan Entwistle remarks, "Ironically, it was during the reign of Sikandar Lodi, a staunch oppressor of Hinduism, that propagators of the emotional variety of devotion to Krishna came in search of the sacred places of Braj."[34] Any number of Hindi histories of Braj claim that Sikandar destroyed the temples of Mathura and gave the temple images to butchers to weigh meat.[35] But our sources for the Lodis come from the Mughal period, and the Mughals had much at stake in portraying the Afghan Lodis as unjust rulers. We may never know what kind of ruler Sikandar Lodi really was, but the fact that it was during his reign that the early founders of Braj culture arrived in Braj should at least cause us to wonder whether something more complex was going on at this time. "In spite of Sikandar's reputation for bigotry," S. M. Ikram comments, "it seems fair to surmise that in the cultural sphere his period was one of active mutual interest among Hindus and Muslims for each other's learning, thus conducing to a reapproachment."[36] The picture we get of these times is certainly one of a fluid society with increasingly improved networks of transportation and communication extending throughout the subcontinent.

At the time of Rupa's arrival in Braj, Vrindaban was nothing more than a dense jungle, sparsely inhabited. Rupa lived first in the city of Mathura but later settled in the forest identified as Vrindaban, intent upon discovering its famous sites. It is reported that one day he was sitting at the foot of a tree on the bank of the Yamuna River, weeping because he had failed to discover anything in Vrindaban, as Chaitanya had directed him to do.[37] Suddenly, a beautiful young boy appeared before him and asked why he was crying. Rupa explained his sorrow;

in response, the boy led him to a place called Goma Tila (Mother Cow's Mound) and said, "A marvelous cow comes to this place and sheds its milk. Think about what this means." Listening to the boy's melodious voice and gazing at his beautiful form, Rupa fainted and fell to the ground. When he regained consciousness, he realized what had happened, called the villagers together, and told them that Krishna as Govindadev—the one praised in the scriptures as the presiding deity of Vrindaban[38]—was at this very place. They dug in the ground at the spot indicated by Rupa and found the black stone image of Govindadev. Rupa had a temple built on this site—a predecessor to the temple that now stands here—to house the newly found image. Gaudiya sources usually date this event in 1533.[39] A golden image of Radha was later sent from Orissa to be placed at the left side of Govindadev.

Vrindaban tradition has it that the spot revealed to Rupa is the Vrindaban *yoga-pitha*, literally a "place of union." There are several yoga-pithas in Braj, but this one is special because it is the place where Krishna and his favorite lover, Radha, come together for their nightly tryst. Radha is married to another but is foremost among those who risk all for an encounter with Krishna in the forest. It is on this spot that she makes love to Krishna, attended by eight close girlfriends, or *sakhi*s; thus, the octagonal shape of the central domed chamber of the present temple. Each side contains a prominent niche, the station of an attending girlfriend.

A stone inscription on the exterior of the northwestern side of the temple reads as follows:

In the 34th year of the era inaugurated by the reign of the emperor Shri Akbar, Shri Maharaj Man Singh, son of Shri Maharaj Bhagavan Das of the "turtle" family of Shri Prithviraj, established the temple of Govindadev on the *yoga-pitha* of Vrindaban. The superintendent of the work was Shri Kalayandas; his assistant was Manikchand Chopad; and the architect was Govindadas of Delhi. Signed by the chief mason Gorakhadas. Blessings to all![40]

Akbar's reign began in 1556; thus, the Govindadev temple was completed in the year 1590. Man Singh, the man responsible for the construction of the temple, was quite remarkable; the way he accomplished this tells us much about early Mughal patronage of Braj culture.

In January 1562 Akbar, not yet quite twenty, set out from Agra with his royal entourage for a pilgrimage to the tomb of the famous Sufi mystic Muin-ud-din Chishti (d. 1236) in the Rajasthani town of Ajmer.

On the way he received a message from Raja Bharmal Kachhwaha of Amber (a fortified town located on a protected hill just north of modern Jaipur) requesting an audience. When the two leaders met, Bharmal offered his eldest daughter in marriage to Akbar. Akbar accepted and told Bharmal to make preparations; on his way back to the court in Agra they were married. This marriage was an event of great significance in medieval Indian history, for it led to the alliance between the Rajputs and the Mughals which was to form the political backbone of the Mughal empire. It was also at this time that Bharmal's eldest son and grandson entered into the service of Akbar, the first Rajputs to do so. Bhagwant Das and his son Man Singh, then a boy of only twelve, returned with the emperor to his capital in Agra. Man Singh and Akbar were to become close associates for life; Man Singh would rise to the highest rank ever achieved by a Hindu under Muslim rule. He led successful military campaigns against the recalcitrant Rajputs to the east and was appointed by Akbar governor of Kabul in 1585, governor of Bihar in 1587, and governor of Bengal in 1588. For the next twenty years Man Singh remained in charge of the eastern provinces, where he most likely came under the influence of the growing movement of Gaudiya Vaishnavas.[41]

The year 1562 seems to have been a pivotal one for Akbar. The historian Ashirbadi Srivatsava notes: "Sometime about the middle of 1562 there was a remarkable change in Akbar's outlook on life. . . . Although there is no recorded evidence to show as to what factors were responsible for this revolutionary change, it is very likely that it was wrought by his association with yogis, sannyasis and other saintly persons and his close contact with the Kachhwaha ruling family of Amber, whose bravery, loyalty and unflinching devotion made a deep impression on his discerning, impressionable, and receptive mind."[42] The first political expression of this change took place in the same year, when Akbar issued a decree forbidding the enslavement of prisoners of war and their forced conversion to Islam.[43] The next year, Akbar was on a tiger-hunting expedition near Mathura when it was brought to his attention that, following the custom of previous Muslim rulers, his government was levying a pilgrimage tax on Hindus visiting sacred places. Deciding that this was an unjust tax, Akbar abolished it.[44] He continued a liberal policy toward Hindus by abolishing the customary tax imposed on non-Muslims in the year 1564.[45] These were all signs of a changing policy that created a political atmosphere which was favorable to the development of Braj.

As early as 1565 Akbar was involved with the temples of Braj. Rupa

Goswami had died in 1563, and the Govindadev temple became the responsibility of his nephew, Jiva Goswami. In an imperial document dated 1565,[46] Akbar conferred a revenue land grant to one Gopaldas, the priest of Govindadev (and Madan Mohan, the temple founded by Rupa's brother Sanatana), who was a subordinate of Jiva Goswami. An imperial grant of this nature allowed the named person to collect all taxes from a certain quantity of land as steady income. This—the earliest surviving revenue grant made by Akbar to a Hindu priest for the support of a temple—was made on behalf of Raja Bharmal of Amber. Three years later, an imperial farman dated 1568 and represented in the court by Akbar's famous Hindu minister, Todar Mal, recognized Jiva as the rightful manager of the temple and granted him all claims to the temple offerings.[47] Thus, the patronage extended by the Amber court to the Gaudiya Vaishnavas in Vrindaban preceded Man Singh's construction of the colossal Govindadev temple and indicates something of Akbar's new outlook toward the temples and holy men in Braj.

The story is told in Braj that Akbar himself, having heard of Jiva Goswami and other famous saints of Vrindaban, visited Vrindaban in the year 1573. It is said that he was taken blindfold into one of the sacred groves and there experienced some kind of divine vision which convinced him this was indeed holy ground and led him to support the projects being conceived in Braj.[48] By 1580 at least seven temples in the region of Braj had received imperial land grants.[49] Akbar's famous brahman counselor, Birbal, seems to have been involved in the extension of royal patronage to the followers of Vallabha, who were expanding the temple on top of the sacred Govardhan mountain of Braj. In 1593 Akbar issued an imperial order prohibiting in the districts of Braj the killing of peacocks, birds sacred to Krishna, and the harassment of cows.[50] The order was obviously issued with a sensitivity toward the growing religious view of the sanctity of the area. A few years later Akbar extended even further support for the temples of Braj; Govindadev seems to have been the crown jewel in his project.

The opening dedication of Man Singh's Govindadev temple took place in the year 1590. Man Singh provided funds for the daily payment of the priests and ongoing maintenance of the temple. Shortly afterward Akbar ordered his close counselor and historian, Abul Fazl, to draw up a list of the existing temples of Braj to determine what kind of land grant would be appropriate for each. The resulting list has survived and is one of the most fascinating religious documents to come out of Akbar's reign.[51] It names thirty-five temples that had gained some importance in Braj by this time. The grants were now made to the temples instead of to named persons, a practice very rare in the Mughal system of revenue grants, since this in effect made the grants perpetual.[52] The list of temples will be explored further in chapter 2, but what is important for our present concern is that whereas grants made to other temples carried only the details of their particular group, the grant made to Govindadev included details of the entire scheme of imperial grants made to the temples of Braj. Clearly, Govindadev, the largest Hindu building to be constructed during the reign of Akbar, was considered the centerpiece in the royal patronage of Braj.

The development of Braj seems to have been a project with widespread implications; it involved the creation of a substantial center of Hindu culture at a time when Hindu morale was low in northern India. The land of Braj gave physical expression to a form of Hindu devotion that had century-old roots in the cult of the *Bhagavata Purana* and provided a new means by which one could enter into and participate in the world of Krishna's lila. The development of Braj was clearly inspired by charismatic Vaishnava leaders such as Chaitanya, Vallabha, and others,[53] and was carried out by their diligent followers; but much of the early success in the physical development of Braj was insured by imperial patronage resulting from the political compromise which recognized the vital service important Hindu officers were rendering the Mughal emperor Akbar.

Akbar's son, Jahangir, who reigned from 1605 to 1627, continued the temple grants established in 1598 and added two more temples to the list. Jahangir visited the Govindadev temple in 1620; he did not seem to be terribly impressed with its architectural style but noted instead the bad odor produced by the many bats inside.[54] Man Singh increased the payment made to the Govindadev temple in the year 1608, and the ruling family of Amber remained closely involved in the management of Govindadev throughout the reign of Jahangir. In 1627 Jahangir was succeeded by his son, Shah Jahan, the builder of the Taj Mahal. Under Shah Jahan the management of the Govindadev temple was formally insured by a royal farman transferring the land grants made to Govindadev to the Amber family of Rajputs, then under the rule of Raja Jai Singh. Another document has been discovered which sheds light on the imperial attitude toward the temples of Braj during the reigns of Akbar, Jahangir, and Shah Jahan.[55] It appears that some minor officials had prohibited the ringing of temple bells for worship services in Vrindaban. Shah Jahan issued a farman stating that no one should restrict the use of temple bells in Vrindaban, and temple bells resound throughout Vrindaban yet today.

Much was to change within the reign of the next Mughal emperor. In the year 1658 Shah Jahan fell seriously ill, and there was rumor of his impending death. Impatient to assume the throne, his third son, Aurangzeb, imprisoned him in the Agra fort in a room from which he could gaze at his beloved Taj Mahal. As soon as he had secured the throne—by killing his three brothers—Aurangzeb introduced reforms that were designed to make the empire a more genuinely Muslim state. His reign signaled a departure from the political philosophy his ancestors had followed in governing the Mughal empire; he reinstated many of the earlier Muslim policies designed to discriminate against Hindus, such as the tax on non-Muslims, reimposed in 1679. What actually happened under Aurangzeb's rule is often unclear, but it was during his reign that the mighty Mughal empire began to crumble and active Mughal patronage of Braj came to a close.

Aurangzeb's actions in Braj seem to have been influenced by two major events. First, Dara Shukoh, Aurangzeb's older brother, had been in charge of the area of Braj and had been popular with his Hindu subjects. Following his murder and the flight of his troops, the Jats— militant farmers inhabiting the region of Braj—rebelled. Harsh actions were taken against them; a large imperial army was sent in to crush the rebellion, and the leader of the Jats was publicly executed.[56] Second, a brilliant military leader named Shivaji had risen to power among the Marathas, challenging Mughal power in the southwestern part of the empire. Raja Jai Singh, the ruling Rajput of Amber, was put in charge of subduing Shivaji. After failing to defeat Shivaji in military action, Jai Singh eventually persuaded him to come to the court in Agra and meet with Aurangzeb.[57] Jai Singh personally guaranteed Shivaji's safety. In 1666 Shivaji attended the court at Agra, but for some reason he was placed among a number of minor officers. Greatly insulted, Shivaji publicly displayed his displeasure by noisily storming out of the court. He was immediately placed under arrest, but Jai Singh, who had assured Shivaji's safety, managed to have him transferred to the house of his own son Ram Singh. Shivaji was too clever to be contained. He feigned serious illness and began distributing large baskets of sweets in apparent preparation for death. One day he hid in one of the baskets leaving the house of Ram Singh and escaped. Aurangzeb was furious and suspected Jai Singh and other members of the house of Amber, particularly Ram Singh, of complicity. Because of this Jai

Singh fell out of royal favor; after his death in 1667 the house of Amber lost its strong influence over the emperor's actions in Braj. The patronage sponsored through the cooperative efforts of the Amber Rajputs and the Mughals, which had helped nurture the culture of Braj, came to an end.[58] Developers of Braj would now have to look to different sources of power to support their cultural projects. In 1669 imperial forces destroyed the Krishna temple of Keshav in Mathura. The images of the temple were taken to Agra and buried under the steps of the Jahanara mosque.[59]

The temples of Vrindaban, including Govindadev, did not escape destruction. It was during this time that the inner sanctum of the Govindadev temple was razed.[60] The priests of the temple managed to escape with the image of Govindadev before the destructive forces arrived, and they sought the protection of their long-standing patrons, the Rajput rulers of Amber. Govindadev was first taken to Kamban in the Bharatpur district of Rajasthan, which was under the control of Kirat Singh, a son of Jai Singh. A temple was built for Govindadev in Kamban, but in 1714 Govindadev was moved to the "Vrindaban" gardens near the Amber palace. Eventually, in 1735, King Jai Singh II, a devotee of Govindadev who had assumed the role of guardian for the Gaudiya Vaishnava sect of Braj, built a temple of Govindadev at the center of the royal palace in his newly built capital of Jaipur. This is where Govindadev currently resides. Today Govindadev is the most popular temple of Jaipur; there one can witness large gatherings of enthusiastic devotees who have come to participate in the daily showings of the deity discovered by Rupa Goswami many years ago.

It was, however, at the Govindadev temple in Vrindaban that my pilgrimage was to begin. After we had walked around the old temple of Govindadev, admiring its imposing form, my guide, Govinda, took me to another temple built just behind the old temple. A wealthy Bengali devotee by the name of Nanda Kumar Basu had visited the old Govindadev temple in 1820 and, saddened by its dilapidated condition, decided to restore the glory of Govindadev in Vrindaban by building a new temple.[61] The priests of the Govindadev temple in Jaipur are also in charge of maintaining this temple. Govinda purchased a leaf basket filled with milk sweets and a small blue cloth for us to offer to a replica of Govindadev and his beloved Radha. We entered the temple, had sight of the divine couple united at this central spot in the love forest of Vrindaban, and thereby began our tour of Braj.

Govinda and I reached the house of Maganlal Sharma at two o'clock.

The twelve pilgrims from my group assembled, and we performed the Ban-Yatra *sankalpa,* a solemn vow to finish the pilgrimage. At around four in the afternoon we went out to the road leading to Mathura, where we joined a growing crowd of pilgrims with whom we would be walking. We waited for others to come before beginning. I sat down on a fallen tree near a tea stall and took out my notebook. Several people were looking at me with apparent curiosity but refrained from speaking. I felt apprehensive and strangely alone. An old woman with short white hair, wearing the white sari of a widow, sat next to me on the log. She fanned herself with the end of her sari. One of the men from my group, dressed in a crisp white shirt, his hair oiled and combed neatly over his dark, shiny skin, came and stood beside me. He smiled but said nothing. My friend Mahesh unexpectedly pulled up on his motorcycle; he had come to see me off. By now hundreds had gathered and were stirring about restlessly, raising a cloud of dust in the still air.

Between five and six hundred people had joined this particular pilgrimage, which had been organized by the Brajbasi Panda Society of Vrindaban. Most were from northeastern India. Approximately 75 percent were from Bengal, mostly in and around Calcutta and Navadvip; 15 percent were from the small mountain state of Manipur; 5 percent were from Assam; and the remaining 5 percent were from Rajasthan and Braj. More than half were women: small Bengalis who favored red and white saris, and broad-faced Manipuris who wore lavender-pink and peach colored sarongs and were fond of smoking bidis. Excited voices could be heard in every direction. A small band of men arrived playing drums and cymbals. One of them carried a tall bamboo pole with a golden flag attached to the tip. Soon there was a call to action, and the crowd began moving. Several of those around me bent down, took dust from the road, and put it to their heads three times. I lifted my pack to my shoulders and said good-bye to Mahesh as we set out for the city of Mathura, the official starting place of the pilgrimage.

Vrindaban and Mathura are separated by a distance of about ten miles. The connecting road passes through a meager forest, a great contrast to what it must have been in the days when Akbar came to these woods to hunt tiger. We stopped at two prominent temples along the way. One is a very recent temple started by a "crazy" saint named Pagal Baba. This temple consists of a series of seven white marble shrines which are stacked on top of each other, making it the tallest temple in the Vrindaban area. The second temple, an imposing stone

structure which has been painted red, was built by wealthy industrial-
ists, the Birla family. As we walked along the paved road in the late
afternoon sun, I was amazed at how hot it was for this time of day.
My feet were swelling, and already I was dripping with perspiration.

Although our major destination for the day was to be the place of
Krishna's birth in Mathura, along the way we also visited a site called
Akrura Ghat, located on the western bank of the Yamuna River, halfway between Vrindaban and Mathura. It is a quiet, peaceful place on
a wide stretch of the river that is rarely visited these days since it is
far from the new road which now carries the traffic between Vrindaban
and Mathura. An old temple stands on a small hill a short distance
from the river. Now abandoned except on special festival days, it was
previously an important site, perhaps best known as the place where
the Bengali saint Chaitanya spent much time during his visit to Braj
in 1514. The importance of Akrura Ghat, however, has to do with its
identification as the site where Krishna's charioteer received a dual
vision.

Krishna's wicked uncle Kansa schemed to lure Krishna to Mathura
and there destroy him. To accomplish this end, he sent his chariot
driver, Akrura to fetch Krishna from Vrindaban. While he was driving
Krishna and his elder brother, Balarama, to Mathura, Akrura stopped
to bathe in the Yamuna. As he plunged his head into the water, his
eyes were filled with the sight of Krishna. He quickly looked back out
of the water expecting to find an empty chariot, but there sat Krishna
exactly where he had left him. Akrura again turned his gaze into the
water and saw that there, too, Krishna remained. Gaudiya Vaishnavas,
who are preoccupied with the play of Vrindaban, make much of this
story, for while they agree that Krishna leaves Braj forever via Mathura, they maintain that in another sense he remains in Vrindaban,
forever engaged in his delightful play.[62] Although Krishna's story in
Braj begins in Mathura, and although the Ban-Yatra officially begins
in Mathura, Gaudiya Vaishnavas begin their pilgrimage in Vrindaban,
the place where the story has no beginning or ending, the place of
Krishna's endless and unpredictable love play.

NOTES

    1. The epigraph is from Rasakhan, *Rasakhan-Granthavali,* ed. with intro-
duction by Desharajasingh Bhati (Delhi: Ashok Prakashan, 1987), 154. This
poem by Rasakhan, a sixteenth-century Muslim convert, is extremely popular

in Braj; many living in the area have memorized it. It is usually placed at the beginning of the collections of his poetry. The translation is mine.

2. Although it is commonly understood that Krishna, the resulting manifestation, is an incarnation, or avatar, of the supreme Vishnu, the Vaishnavas of Braj contend that Krishna was unique in that he was the complete manifestation of the true nature of Vishnu *(svarupa)*, or the very source of all manifestations *(avatarin)*.

3. For more, see Ramkrishna Gopal Bhandarkar, *Vaisnavism, Saivism and Other Religious Systems* (Varanasi: Indological Book House, 1965), Part I, for a fairly standard account of this history.

4. This is the argument of Charlotte Vaudeville in "The Cowherd God in Ancient India," in *Pastoralists and Nomads in South Asia*, ed. L. S. Leshnik and G. D. Sontheimer (Wiesbaden: Otto Harrassowitz, 1975), 92–116.

5. Ibid., 116.

6. For a history of the use of the term *Braj* see Alan Entwistle, "From Vraja to Braj," *Re-discovering Braj, International Association of the Vrindaban Research Institute Bulletin* 14 (1988): 14–18.

7. See my "Vraja: A Place in the Heart," *Re-discovering Braj, International Association of the Vrindaban Research Institute Bulletin* 14 (1988): 19–25.

8. See Narayan Bhatt, *Vraja Bhakti Vilasa* (Kusum Sarovar: Krishnadas Baba, 1951), 177–80. This book is a virtual compendium of the Ban-Yatra and represents the first textual outline of the elaborate structure that emerged in the sixteenth century.

9. See John Stratton Hawley, *At Play with Krishna: Pilgrimage Dramas from Brindaban* (Princeton, N.J.: Princeton University Press, 1981); and Norvin Hein, *Miracle Plays of Mathura* (New Haven, Conn.: Yale University Press, 1972).

10. Henry David Thoreau, "Walking," in *The Writings of Henry David Thoreau*, col. 9 (New York: Houghton, 1896), 252–53.

11. The ambiguous nature of Shiva is aptly explored by Wendy Doniger O'Flaherty in *Asceticism and Eroticism in the Mythology of Shiva* (London: Oxford University Press, 1973).

12. *Bhagavata Purana* 12.13.16 declares that Shiva (Shambhu) is the best of the Vaishnava devotees.

13. Charlotte Vaudeville, "Braj, Lost and Found," *Indo-Iranian Journal* 18 (1976): 195–213.

14. Here I am for the most part following Stella Kramrisch, *The Presence of Siva* (Princeton, N.J.: Princeton University Press, 1981), 162–78.

15. Sudhir Kakar, *The Inner World: A Psycho-analytic Study of Childhood and Society in India* (Delhi: Oxford University Press, 1981), 156.

16. See, for example, *Brihadaranyaka Upanishad* 1.4.

17. See, for example, Rupa Goswami, *Bhaktirasamritasindh*; 1.1.14.

18. Ibid., 1.2.235. As elsewhere, I have translated the word *Mathura* as *Braj* to fit the extended meaning in such contexts, for here Mathura-mandala means Braj.

19. *Vraja Bhakti Vilasa* 1.93, p. 14.

20. For a contemporary expression of this see Shrivatsa Goswami, "Charai-veti! Charaiveti!, in *Shri Ban Yatra* (Vrindaban: Shri Chaitanya Prem Sans-than, 1986), 8.

21. Lee Siegel, *Sacred and Profane Dimensions of Love in Indian Traditions as Exemplified in the Gitagovinda of Jayadeva* (Delhi: Oxford University Press, 1978), 12.

22. Jacques Lacan calls this the *object (a)*. See Anika Lemaire, *Jacques Lacan* (New York: Routledge & Kegan Paul, 1979), 173–75.

23. Mark C. Taylor, *Altarity* (Chicago: University of Chicago Press, 1987), 105.

24. Sigmund Freud, "Beyond the Pleasure Principle," in *The Essentials of Psychoanalysis* (Middlesex: Penguin Books, 1986), 218–68.

25. Ibid., 268.

26. Kakar, *The Inner World*, 156.

27. Siegel, *Sacred and Profane Dimensions of Love*, 139.

28. Kakar, "Erotic Fantasy," 83.

29. Frederick S. Growse, *Mathura: A District Memoir* (New Delhi: Asian Educational Services, 1882), 241.

30. This phrase is from Shrivatsa Goswami of Vrindaban.

31. From Jiva Goswami's *Laghu-tosani;* see S. K. De, *Early History of the Vaishnava Faith and Movement in Bengal* (Calcutta: Firma K. L. Mukhopa-dhyay, 1961), 146–47.

32. Prabhudayal Mital, *Braj ke Dharm-Sampradayo ka Itihas* (Delhi: National Publishing House, 1968), 313.

33. Charlotte Vaudeville argues that prior to the sixteenth century there were no Krishna shrines in the forests surrounding Mathura; see her "Braj, Lost and Found."

34. Alan Entwistle, *Braj: Center of Krishna Pilgrimage* (Groningen: Egbert Forsten, 1987), 136.

35. See, for example, Krishna Datta Vajpeyi, *Braj ka Itihas* (Mathura: Akhil Bharatiya Braj Sahitya Mandal, 1955), 140–41.

36. S.M. Ikram, *Muslim Civilization in India* (New York: Columbia University Press, 1964), 78.

37. The following account is taken from Pulinbihari Datta, *Vrindaban Katha* (Calcutta: Manasi Press, 1920), 29–33.

38. The Mathura Mahatmya of the *Varaha Purana* identifies Vrindaban as the site of Govindadev and claims, "Those who see Govinda in Vrindaban do not go to the city of death, but go to the region of the auspicious" (151.49).

39. See Naresh Chandra Jana, *Vrindabaner Choe Goswami* (Calcutta: Calcutta University, 1970), 85. Naresh Chandra Bansal and others record the date as 1535; see his *Chaitanya Sampradaya: Siddhant aur Sahitya* (Agra: Vinod Pustak Mandir, 1980), 66.

40. The Devanagari text is recorded in Growse, *Mathura*, 243–44.

41. Rajiva Nain Prasad, *Raja Man Singh of Amber* (Calcutta: The World Press, 1966), 135–37.

42. Ashirbadi Lal Srivastava, *Akbar the Great*, vol. 1 (Agra: Shiva Lal Agarwala, 1972), 58–59.

43. Ibid., 59–60.

44. Abu-L-Fazl, *The Akbar Nama*, vol. 2, trans. H. Beveridge (Delhi: Rare Books, 1972), 294–95.

45. Ibid., 316–17.

46. This document, and several others discussed below, are in the manuscript collection of the Vrindaban Research Institute. They have recently been analyzed and translated by Tarapada Mukherjee and Irfan Habib in a paper entitled "Akbar and the Temples of Mathura and Its Environs," which was presented to the annual meeting of the Indian History Congress, Goa, November 5–9, 1987. This article was published in *Proceedings of the Indian History Congress* 48 (1987): 234–50. Unfortunately, however, translations of the discussed documents were omitted from the published article. The document mentioned here appears on pages 91–92 of the presented paper and is discussed on pages 235–37 of the published article.

47. Ibid., 93–94; discussed page 236 in the published article.

48. Vajpeyi, *Braj ka Itihas*, 153.

49. Mukherjee and Habib, "Akbar and the Temples of Mathura," 238.

50. See Krishnalal Mohanlal Jhaveri, *Imperial Farmans (A.D. 1577 to A.D. 1805) Granted to the Ancestors of His Holiness the Tikayat Maharaj* (Bombay: The News Printing Press, 1928), document IVA.

51. This is among the documents analyzed and translated by Mukherjee and Habib, "Akbar and the Temples of Mathura."

52. Ibid., 240 of the published article.

53. The others include Hit Harivansh, the poet-saint who founded the movement known as the Radhavallabha Sampradaya, and Swami Haridas, the great musician who inspired a following in Vrindaban and is reputed to have been the teacher of Tansen, the legendary singer of Akbar's court. Members of the Nimbarki Sampradaya had been present in this area for over a century, but the devotional style that is now associated with them in Braj seems to have developed in the climate of rich activity and mutual influence of those who settled in Braj in the sixteenth century.

54. Jahangir, *Tuzuk-i Jahangiri*, ed. Sayyid Ahmad (Ghazipur and Aligarh: 1863–64), 279; quoted by Tarapada Mukherjee and Irfan Habib, "The Mughal Administration and the Temples of Vrindavan During the Reigns of Jahangir

and Shah Jahan," *Proceedings of the Indian History Congress* 49 (1988): 289.

55. Mukherjee and Habib, "The Mughal Administration and the Temples of Vrindavan," 299.

56. The story of the rebellious Jats and their rise to power is told in detail in chapter 4.

57. Jadunath Sarkar, *History of Aurangzib*, vol. 4 (Calcutta: M. C. Sarkar, 1912–24), 51–83.

58. P. D. Mital claims that the Ban-Yatra ceased to be performed on a large scale during the reign of Aurangzeb and had to be revived at a later date; see his *Braj ka Sanskritik Itihas* (Mathura: Sahitya Sansthan, 1966), 91.

59. Ram Sharma, *The Religious Policy of the Mughal Emperors* (Bombay: Asia Publishing House, 1972), 172.

60. There is some debate about this. Some claim that the destruction of the Vrindaban temples was the result of the military invasions of Afghan troops in the mid-eighteenth century.

61. Ashim Kumar Roy, *History of the Jaipur City* (New Delhi: Manohar Publications, 1978), 163–64.

62. I have heard this point from many residing in Braj. The story is usually told to demonstrate how Krishna is even more present in his seeming absence. It was told to me again by Shri Dipak Bhatt, the living representative of the tradition of Narayan Bhatt in Unchagoan, while making the point that the very land of Braj is Krishna, thus arguing that Braj could not exist if Krishna left it.

2

The Twelve Forests

Deliverance is not for me in renunciation.
  I feel the embrace of freedom in a thousand bonds of delight.
Thou ever pourest for me the fresh draught of thy wine of various
  colors and fragrance, filling this earthen vessel to the brim.
My world will light its hundred different lamps before the
  altar of my temple.
No, I will never shut the doors of my senses.
  The delights of sight and hearing and touch will bear thy delight.
Yes, all my illusions will burn into illumination of joy, and all my
  desires ripen into fruits of love.

RABINDRANATH TAGORE,
Gitanjali

Eight miles southwest of Mathura is a small forest of palm trees called
Talban, meaning "Palm Forest." At one time palm trees laden with
delicious fruit were plentiful here. Krishna's childhood friends, the
young cowherds of Braj, were once playing nearby. With shouts of
glee, they spotted the ripe fruit and, mouths watering, greedily ran into
the forest, scrambling up the trees and tossing down the ripe coconuts.
The sweet taste of the fruit was almost theirs when suddenly a huge
ass-demon named Dhenuka appeared, kicking at them threateningly.
The boys fled the forest in great terror.

But the forbidden fruit was much too tempting to forget. The boys
approached Krishna and Balarama and requested their assistance; together they all eagerly returned to Talban. Entering the forest, Balarama began to exercise his unusual strength, shaking the palm trees
so that ripe fruit started raining from the trees. Hearing the sound of
the falling fruit, the demon Dhenuka charged the boys at full speed,

making the earth tremble. He leapt into the air and aimed a ferocious kick at the chest of Balarama. Balarama caught hold of the demon's hind legs, swung him around, and hurled him into the air. His body crashed to earth, lifeless. The jubilant young cowherds then safely enjoyed the succulent fruit.

One common Western understanding of Indian religions is that they foster asceticism, self-denial, and a rejection of the world. Though this is true of some Indian religious traditions, it is not true of the religion of Braj. The Talban story emphasizes the enjoyment of physical forms. Whereas some religious moves in South Asia devalue the world of forms and suppress desire, that force which connects us to forms, this particular move seeks to enjoy the world of forms by using desire.[1] Krishna's cowherd friends do not deny their natural passions, as does the ascetic who is in search of the One beneath the play of life's surfaces, but rather they are involved in a passionate enjoyment of all the delicious curves the surface has to offer. The demon Dhenuka restricts their roaming enjoyment, their free wandering and uninhibited play. A word for the senses in Indian languages—go—also means cow. Braj itself means a pastureland for cows, a place where cows can roam freely. It can also mean a land in which the senses can roam freely, since here the land itself is understood as Krishna and all forms are to be enjoyed. Balarama subdues the restraining demon, allowing the cows to wander freely and enjoy the forests, allowing the cowherds to wander freely and enjoy the luscious fruits the land has to offer.

In many ways Krishna and Balarama are heroes for the Brajbasis, or residents of Braj; they are particularly the heroes of the guides who lead the pilgrimage. Krishna and Balarama are fine wrestlers—they never use anything but their own bodies to kill demons—and they have a mighty appetite for food and other good things the world has to offer. The anthropologist Owen Lynch has written an insightful article on the pilgrimage guides of Mathura, who are known as Chaubes; most of what he writes applies also to the Brajbasi pilgrimage guides of Vrindaban. "Chaubes," he observes, "epitomize the quintessence of Braj character, the *mastram*. . . . The *mastram* is a person who is *mast* (happy, lusty, proud, carefree, intoxicated); he enjoys a carefree lifestyle with a sense of physical and emotional well-being. A Chaube who knew some English said, 'Eat drink and be merry; that is how we live, we have no worries here.'"[2] The ideal of mast is central to the religion of Braj: "Being *mast* is in the nature, soil, streets, air, atmosphere, blood, and culture of the Brajbasi."[3] A person who is in the state of mast is "laid-back"; this quality is more profound than it may sound at first. A person is mast—radiant with joy—because that person is not entangled in the confusion brought about by ordinary attachments, since all egoistic designs have been surrendered to Krishna's play. The mast person is one who is free from the pangs of loss, worry, and anxiety, and is thus free to experience "the utmost possible joy from life," the "touch of divine bliss"—ananda. That person knows how to enjoy the world fully, without becoming ensnared by the restrictive nets of confused attachment.

Four things help contribute to the feeling of mast: good food (*bhojan*), physical exercise (*kasrat*), singing about and meditating on the Lord (*bhajan*), and an intoxicating plant related to marijuana (*bhang*). The Chaubes of Mathura (and other pilgrimage guides of Braj) are famous for their ability to consume huge amounts of food. Their food is ideally *sattvic*, that is, food which promotes a peaceful, insightful, and compassionate state. Milk and milk sweets are prominent in their diet. Chaubes are fond of wrestling and are respected for their courage and strength. They maintain gardens that serve as gathering places for wrestling and other forms of spiritual exercise. By reciting prayers and singing songs, the Chaubes claim, one becomes absorbed in Krishna and experiences great enjoyment. The last of these things conducive to a feeling of mast, and perhaps the most important, is bhang, which aids in the accomplishment of the three previous activities. It is categorized as a sattvic intoxicant and is distinguished sharply from other types of intoxicants, particularly alcohol. Drinking or eating bhang prepared in one of a number of delectable forms is said to enhance one's moral qualities and allow deeper emotional experiences. The state it induces is considered religiously valuable, producing a condition of tranquil yogic insight. Many of the pilgrimage guides I accompanied took bhang daily. I was to learn toward the end of my journey that Balarama himself is a great fan of bhang.

The Ban-Yatra pilgrims, like the young cowherds, also eagerly enter the forests of Braj to enjoy various fruits. The Mathura Mahatmya of the *Varaha Purana*, a section of the text probably compiled during the early sixteenth century,[4] extols the benefits of visiting Braj and declares that by wandering through the twelve forests of Braj one becomes fully gratified and achieves liberation.[5] The twelve forests, then, are crucially instrumental for entering into the world of Krishna.

Talban is one of the twelve forests. We arrived there after leaving Mathura and passing through the forest of Madhuban. Today Sankarshan Kund (Balarama's Pond), a beautiful large pond seasonally dotted with blue lotus flowers, dominates the site. I was told by a resident of a nearby village that the pond was formed by the force of the ass-demon Dhenuka smashing into the earth. Beside the pond stands a small whitewashed temple compound housing the images of Krishna, Balarama, and Balarama's consort, Revati. The only palm trees that remain cluster around the temple of this compound.

Krishna and Balarama made this forest safe so the cowherds could wander freely here with their cows. As we approached the temple of Balarama, we passed through a large herd of white cattle with soft, droopy ears and liquid brown eyes, and black water buffalo with tough, wrinkled skin and long, twisted horns, grazing lazily on the shores of Sankarshan Kund. These not only provide the nearby villagers with fresh milk but also yield the by-product of thousands of cow-dung patties. The villagers collect the patties, dry them in neatly ordered rows, and then stack them into towers—the skyline of a small city of cow-dung structures. Some of the towers were walled in with more cow dung and covered with a thatched roof to protect them, as a later source of cooking fuel and fertilizer for the many fields that surround Talban.

A red flag flew from the tall white spire of the temple. The pilgrims took turns going inside. The images of Balarama, who stood in the center, and Krishna were made of black stone; Revati was white. All three were dressed with bright clothing, jeweled crowns, and garlands of flowers. Some of the pilgrims simply looked at the images and left;[6] others deposited coins on a metal tray in which a stick of incense had been lit, before rejoining those outside resting under the trees of the compound.

Ban-Yatra means "journey through the forests." The theme of the forest is at the heart of this pilgrimage. Regardless of what has actually survived in this age of deforestation, Braj is conceived of as a forest. Bengalis preparing to go on the Ban-Yatra do not usually say, "I am going to perform the Ban-Yatra." Rather, they frequently say, "*Ami bone jabo*"; simply: "I am going to the forest."

The forest, the essential setting for the play of Krishna, is contrasted with the city.[7] Any city will do—several of the pilgrims from Calcutta told me that one of the reasons they had come to Braj was to escape the hustle and bustle of that city—but in the Krishna story the forest is contrasted specifically with Mathura, the seat of political power, and Dvaraka, the city in which Krishna later settled and married. The city is a center—of government power, of commerce, of work, of purposeful activity in general. Diana Eck writes: "The earliest hieroglyphic symbol of a city was a circle with a cross in it, for the city is a crossroads of commerce and culture."[8] It is the destination of a business trip, a place where things are to be accomplished. The city is also a domestic center, a home, where life is structured and controlled by social conventions. It is a place of moral order where passions are channeled by the institutions of marriage. Bright lights illuminate its streets at night.

The forest, on the other hand, is not a center. It is unmarked territory. There are no office buildings or permanent homes there; rather, one passes through the forest, sneaks into the forest, frolics within the forest. The darkness and density of the trackless forest shields one from the judgmental gaze of society. Life in the forest is characterized by aimless wandering and spontaneous play. It is also, and perhaps foremost, the site of the illicit love affair.[9] Whereas the structured love of the city is funneled into the production of children, the unbound love of the forest aims at ongoing excitement.

Although the older idea of the forest as a site conducive to the practice of asceticism is never left completely behind, for the most part it is not applied to the forests of Braj. One does not go to Braj to withdraw from passionate life and sit still in meditation. One goes for *ban-bihar*. *Bihar* is a word rich in meaning; it means both "enjoyment," especially "sexual enjoyment," and "wandering" or "roaming." Similarly, one of the meanings of the word *Braj* is "moving," "going forth," or "wandering." Thus one does not enjoy the forests of Braj in a static state but only in motion. According to the religion of Braj, pleasure is not the result of some state of constancy;[10] rather, there is a special pleasure in moving. In the forest, as we have just seen in the story associated with Talban, the natural passions are given free rein to roam and enjoy whatever might come their way.

Braj is conceived of as a forest; more precisely, it comprises twelve forests. It is frequently represented as a twelve-petaled lotus, with each petal denoting a forest (see the map on page xxiv). The city of Mathura is located at the center of the lotus; the path of the Ban-Yatra follows its circular periphery. The scheme of the twelve forests constitutes the essential basis of any journey through Braj. Though the twelvefold scheme appears to predate the sixteenth century, the detailed itinerary of the journey through the twelve forests is the product of that time. It was first systematized by a figure of immense importance for the development of Braj, namely, the great *Acharya*— "Teacher" or "Founder"—of Braj, Narayan Bhatt.

Descriptions of the places of pilgrimage in Braj are found in five major Vaishnava Puranas;[11] although these scriptures cover a wide range of time periods, none of the sections pertaining to Braj appear to have been written before the sixteenth century. The scheme of the twelve forests is mapped out in a number of these texts in a section entitled the Mathura Mahatmya. (A Mahatmya is a text that extols the greatness of a particular place and the benefits derived from visiting it.) The oldest and most detailed description of the pilgrimage sites in Braj is found in the Mathura Mahatmya of the *Varaha Purana*, an independent section of the text consisting of twenty-nine chapters. Scholarly research suggests that this section is a revised version of an earlier Mahatmya composed around the beginning of the sixteenth century by a pilgrimage priest of Mathura not yet influenced by the Vrindaban Goswamis.[12] It consists of a haphazard conflation of old materials compiled before the concept of the pilgrimage circuit of the numerous places associated with Krishna's activities in Braj had been fully formulated. It therefore gives a sense of how pilgrimage in the area of Mathura was conceived on the eve of the extraordinary developments that transformed the culture of Braj in the middle decades of the sixteenth century. Pilgrimage in this text is viewed primarily as a technique for cleansing oneself and achieving merit, in contrast to the later insistence that the Ban-Yatra is a purposeless journey.

The Mathura Mahatmya of the *Varaha Purana* is in the form of a conversation between Mother Earth and Varaha, the boar manifestation of Vishnu who rescued Earth by raising her on his tusks from the bottom of the ocean. Varaha tells Earth much of what is to come, including the wonderful city of Mathura, where he is to take birth in the future, and its beautiful surrounding forests in which he is to play.

This text describes the area around Mathura as a circle—a mandala—having the shape of a lotus and a circumference of twenty *yojanas* (a yojana is a little more than eight miles). Varaha announces that this circular area, which later came to be known as Braj,[13] is the place on earth most dear to Vishnu because it is associated with the activities of Krishna, the full manifestation of the supreme form of ultimate reality according to Vaishnava theology in Braj. He declares: "Braj is the most excellent of all the holy places, O Goddess, because Krishna played there; all of it has been made pure by the touch of his feet."[14] Again and again the Mathura Mahatmya praises the land of Braj and the benefits of performing pilgrimage there. It claims that the worst of sins fall away in Braj and one's highest aims are achieved by circumambulating its mandala. A visit to Braj is compared with a visit to Banaras (Varanasi): "The benefit of being in Varanasi for a full thousand years, O Goddess, is obtained by being in Braj for only a moment."[15]

Pilgrimage to holy places is declared in the Mathura Mahatmya to be the most beneficial type of religious activity that one can perform. Knowing that it is not possible to visit all pilgrimage sites in a single lifetime, Mother Earth asks Vishnu if there is any way to gain the benefit of all pilgrimages. Varaha replies: "The one who wanders through Braj attains greater benefit than by visiting all other holy places in the entire world. The one who arrives in Braj and circumambulates it has circumambulated the entire world."[16]

The Mathura Mahatmya of the *Varaha Purana* describes the circumambulation of Braj, or the Mathura-mandala, by means of the scheme of the twelve forests, which is presented in the context of a story about a wicked hunter who accidentally drowned in the Yamuna River at Mathura and was thereby reborn a king by the name of Kshatradhanu.[17] King Kshatradhanu had a favorite wife with whom he liked to play in beautiful forests and gardens. After passing many years in such enjoyment he had a dream in which he suddenly remembered Mathura, the glorious place where he had died. He felt a strong desire to see Mathura before he died again, and so he turned over the kingdom to his eldest son and went on pilgrimage there, accompanied by his favorite wife and four divisions of the army. After arriving in the city of Mathura, he set out to see the twelve holy forests which surround it. (The reader may find it useful to refer to the map on page xxv in conjunction with much of the following discussion.) He visited, in order, Madhuban, Talban, Kundban (Kumudban), Kamyakban (Kamaban), Bahulaban, Bhadraban, Khadiraban, Mahaban, Lohajanghaban (Lohaban), Bilvaban (Belban), Bhandiraban, and Vrindaban. The Mahatmya lists the benefits derived from each forest; all desires are fulfilled, for example, for the one who sees Madhuban, the first of the twelve forests. After completing the circuit of Braj, the king surrendered his life in the waters of the Yamuna and attained the realm of Vishnu.

This same twelve-forest scheme is repeated in the Mathura Mahatmya of the *Narada Purana*[18] and the Mathura Mahatmya attributed to Rupa Goswami.[19] Whatever it indicates about actual pilgrimage activity in the area of Braj prior to the work of Narayan Bhatt in the sixteenth century, this list of twelve forests indicates the heart of an ideal itinerary which provided a framework for later developments.

The history of the journey through the forests of Braj, the Ban-Yatra, can be told in a variety of ways. Though the first textual description of a detailed itinerary for the journey through the twelve forests is found in the *Vraja Bhakti Vilasa* of Narayan Bhatt, many of those living in Braj trace precedents of the Ban-Yatra back to the very time of Krishna. One is usually told that this was some five thousand years ago. The Vaishnava Puranas, textual accounts of the mythology and history of Indian culture, are the primary source of such claims. Three well-known stories, which have their basis in Vaishnava scripture, are typically cited as precedents for the journey through the twelve forests.[20]

According to the first story, told in the *Bhagavata Purana*, Krishna eventually left the forests of Braj for the city of Mathura, creating great sorrow in those he left behind, particularly in his cowherd lovers, the gopis. In order to console them in his absence, Krishna sent his close friend and courtly adviser, Uddhava, to the encampment of his adoptive father and mother, Nanda and Yashoda. There Uddhava spent many months with the residents of Braj, trying to relieve them of their sorrow with lessons of asceticism and renunciation. However, he who came to convert the gopis was soon converted by them; Uddhava was so deeply moved by the intense passion of the gopis that he became convinced of the superiority of their position. Soon after his arrival, Uddhava asked to see the places associated with Krishna's activities in Braj since the gopis had told him that the very rocks and forests of Braj were what kept Krishna in their minds. The residents took him on a tour of the forests, recounting the particular episode from Krishna's youth that had occurred at each site. Uddhava passed many days in Braj, wandering through the forests and enjoying the memory of Krishna. Hindi scholars writing in Braj maintain that Uddhava's visit to the sites of Krishna's youth was a seminal form of the Ban-Yatra that was developed in detail later in the sixteenth century.[21]

The journey of an exemplary Vaishnava figure is also frequently used to illustrate the conviction that the seeds of the Ban-Yatra were sown during the time of Krishna. The travels of the celestial sage and model devotee Narada are recounted in the *Narada Purana* and the *Padma Purana*.[22] During his wanderings over the world, Narada heard that Krishna had been born in Braj. The sage immediately proceeded to Braj and wandered about looking for signs of Krishna. He was particularly interested in the forest sites of Krishna's secret love play. He was unsuccessful in discovering these until he encountered the goddess Vrinda, who instructed him to bathe in a lake called Kusum Sarovar.[23] Narada emerged from the waters of this pond as Naradi, a beautiful, ornamented woman, and was then able to see with new eyes and participate in the love play that takes place in the secret groves of Braj. Here, it is often pointed out, is precedent not only for wandering in Braj in search of Krishna but also for the necessity of the pilgrim to be transformed into a gopi to gain access to the intimate lila grounds.

Another Puranic story typically cited as precedent for early peripatetic activities in Braj can be found in a late section of the *Skanda Purana*. This text recounts how after Krishna's clan had been destroyed in the great war referred to in the *Mahabharata*, the heroic warrior Arjuna took Krishna's great-grandson Vajranabh from the capital city of Dvaraka to Braj and there established him as king.[24] When King Parikshit later visited Vajranabh in Braj, Vajranabh told Parikshit that his own kingdom was nothing but an uninhabited jungle. He complained that the circumstances of the war had rendered his kingdom worthless and that all signs of Krishna had been wiped out. Parikshit sent for Shandilya, the former priest of the cowherds, who took Vajranabh on a tour of Braj, marking each site of Krishna's activities and telling him the lila associated with it. The remembrance of Krishna then became possible. Because these sacred sites were without guardians, Shandilya advised Vajranabh to establish villages to care for them. Many of the important settlements of Braj are mentioned. In addition, Vajranabh is said to have established images of Krishna and important shrines for Shiva. In particular, he established the four important temples of Govindadev in Vrindaban, Keshavadev in Mathura, Haridev in Govardhan, and Baladev in Dauji, and the four important Shiva shrines of Gopishwar in Vrindaban, Bhuteshwar in Mathura, Chakreshwar in Govardhan, and Kameshwar in Kamaban.

A common feature of all these stories is the need for physical forms to gain access to the world of Krishna. Uddhava experienced powerful and new emotions wandering through the forests marked by Krishna's lila; Narada sought entrance into Krishna's lila by searching for perceptible signs; and Vajranabh's kingdom was an empty world before Shandilya revealed its tangible sites. The world of Braj is inaccessible without concrete vehicles for conception. The concrete forms provide a language by means of which a previously inaccessible world is evoked and realized. These stories seem to be telling us—among other things—about a process of externalization.[25]

Vajranabh's "reclamation" of the important sites of Braj is said to have occurred about one hundred years after Krishna had left Braj. It has been called the first search for Braj, and Vajranabh's tour a seminal form of the Ban-Yatra.[26] According to these accounts, however, Vajranabh's reclamation did not last. Buddhists and Jains later came to power in this region and made Mathura their center. During this period the sites associated with Krishna fell into neglect. Neglect turned to ruin, Vaishnava historians claim, as Muslims came to power and completely destroyed whatever remained of the earlier sites. From fear of the foreign invaders, the temple priests hid the images in ponds or buried them in the forests and fled.[27] By the close of the fifteenth century, nothing remained of the glory of Braj; its forms had been covered and it had returned to dense jungle in which nothing could be distinguished, just as Vajranabh had found it many years before.

Time was ripe for another reclamation, which came at the beginning of the sixteenth century, primarily through the influence of the two Vaishnava saints Chaitanya and Vallabha, and the diligent work of their followers. For Vaishnava historians, their activities were divinely inspired and amounted to the second search for Braj, the second "reclamation."

The French scholar Charlotte Vaudeville, however, questions the Vaishnava portrayal of Braj history. She observes that all Vaishnava sectarian literature from the sixteenth century on has it that Krishna's lila sites had become "lost" or "invisible." After examining the evidence she argues: "The fantastic story of the disappearance of the ancient Krishnaite shrines and *lila-sthala*s of Braj and their miraculous rescuing from oblivion in the first part of the sixteenth century points to the unescapable conclusion that, prior to the arrival of the Vaisnava reformers in Braj, there was hardly any Krishnaite shrine in the whole rural area. The only great Vaisnava temple which was surely anterior to that time was the famous Keshava temple at Mathura, which was to be destroyed by Aurangzeb."[28]

Whether the developments of the sixteenth century were a "reclamation" or amounted to a new creation, vast amounts of work went into the cultural construction of Braj. These developments can be viewed as a process of externalization; that is, in the sixteenth century a world that had existed primarily as an interior world, described in Vaishnava scriptures and realized in meditation, blossomed into an exterior world of material forms, and this culture was expressed physically. The sixteenth century was the time of a great "coming-out" party in which the material forms of Braj culture were "uncovered" and "revealed." In this regard the activities of Braj in the sixteenth century provide us with a rare glimpse into a process whereby myth directly influences history.

Maura Corcoran has done a study of the concept of Vrindaban, and by extension all of Braj, in which she tracks in literature the historical development of the concept of Braj from a mythical space, defined as the fictional setting of a primordial story, to a symbolic space, defined as a meditative map used as an aid to visualization, to a geographical space, defined as a place of pilgrimage activity.[29] In the second stage, Braj is conceived as a mandala, an indication of the Tantric elements present in the meditative techniques associated with this literature. The historical development culminates in the sixteenth century, when the gap between the three concepts is closed, resulting in the "concept of identity between the transcendent and the immanent, the symbolic and the geographical." With this identification "there is no divine and terrestrial Vrndavana—the terrestrial is the divine."[30] Corcoran suggests that this development has something to do with the concept of lila—that the inaccessible is the utterly accessible.

What this means specifically is that the symbolic or meditative mandala becomes identified with a certain physical space. The metaphysical is now viewed as nondifferent from the physical. Corcoran views this as a homologous move to the identification of symbolic forms, *yantra*s, with geographical places, *pitha*s, in Shakta Tantrism.[31] A similar development took place in Japan under the influence of Tantric Buddhism, where "the site of practice became a natural mandala, a large geographical area endowed with all the qualities of a metaphysical space."[32] Allan Grapard calls this the "mandalization of space," which he defines as "a vast historical process which aimed at making all Japan a sacred site: that of the manifestation of the divine in its many forms and the site of practices leading to the realization of Buddhahood."[33] Similarly, in the sixteenth century, Braj became not only a spiritual realm wherein the divine manifests itself (*lila-dham*) but also a site for physical practice (of the Ban-Yatra). Perhaps no figure contributed more to this process of myth mapping or mandalization than Narayan Bhatt, remembered by his followers as the Braj-Acharya, the Great Founder of Braj.

Narayan Bhatt, the first to work out a detailed itinerary of the Ban-Yatra, was more active than any other historical figure in establishing the physical sites of Braj. The sources for the life story of Narayan Bhatt are twofold: he himself makes occasional comments about his own life in a Sanskrit text he composed, entitled the *Vrajotsava Chandrika*; and a biography, entitled the *Narayana Bhatta Charitamrita*, was written in Sanskrit around the end of the seventeenth century by a descendant of Narayan Bhatt, six generations removed, by the name of Janaki Prasad Bhatt.[34] Manuscripts of the *Vrajotsava Chandrika* and of Janaki Prasad's biography were preserved by the descendants of Narayan Bhatt who live in the village he established in Braj called

Unchagaon; these two texts were published by the Braj scholar Krish-nadas Baba in 1960 and 1957, respectively. Krishnadas Baba informs us that Janaki Prasad was born in 1665. After thoroughly studying the works of Narayan Bhatt, he had a dream in which his ancestor commanded him to write the biography. Since the biography agrees with all statements in the *Vrajotsava Chandrika* and provides much more detail, I draw upon it for the following account of the life of Narayan Bhatt.

Narayan Bhatt's life story is instructive; it is in such stories that we see the fascinating conflation of myth and history referred to in the preface. His story begins with an incident in the life of the sage Narada.

Once upon a time Narada, the celestial sage and model devotee, was wandering the earth absorbed in thoughts of Krishna. He began vis-iting all the pilgrimage sites on earth, searching for the best among them. After touring all the famous pilgrimage sites, with no resulting satisfaction, he arrived in Braj. There he saw that the entire region was permeated with signs of the lilas of the playboy Krishna. Narada was ecstatic; he knew his search for the best place of pilgrimage had come to an end. He went to the Yamuna River in Mathura and bathed in its nectarlike water. Meditating on Krishna, he circumambulated the birthplace of the mischievous child again and again. He then set out to visit the forests, and there noticed that the earth and mountains were marked with the footprints of Krishna. As a result of seeing these physical forms, an awareness of Krishna became firmly established in his heart. Touring all of Braj in this manner, the celestial sage was overwhelmed with joy.

All the ponds and lila sites of Braj, however, had disappeared at this time and were unknown even to the people who lived in the area. Braj had become an undifferentiated jungle, overgrown with trees and creepers. Reflecting on this, Narada sat down, engaged in yoga, and began concentrating on Krishna. Krishna, occupied in love play with Radha, suddenly appeared before his eyes. Narada praised the couple in a voice choked with emotion. Greatly pleased with Narada's devo-tion, Krishna spoke:

You have seen all of Braj. You have seen Mathura and my Vrindaban. You have seen Yamuna, the best of rivers, and Govardhan, the best of mountains; you have seen the hills marked with my footprints and all my groves and forests. There is no pilgrimage site on earth known to surpass Braj, *the highest form of my own body*, which steals the mind of the devotee. I dwell here eternally, never leaving Braj; but Braj is not always visible to souls caught in the wheel of time. You are my dearest devotee; thus I have shown it to you. What wish do you have in mind, great sage?[35]

Thus addressed, Narada expressed his wish. Recognizing that the physical sites of Braj would establish devotion in the hearts of those who saw them, Narada requested that Krishna make them visible once again. Krishna told him that people were now living in a decadent age and were generally without merit; therefore, they could not perceive his lilas. However, since Narada had made such a request, Krishna promised to reveal again the land and lilas of Braj. Narada would be the primary agent of this revelation; he was to become the great Acharya of Braj and disclose its ponds, mountains, love bowers, groves, and forests, thus giving the people concrete forms for realizing Krishna's lila.

Meanwhile, in the southern Indian town of Madurai there lived a learned brahman named Raghunath Bhatt. The Bhatt family of Madurai were followers of the great Vaishnava Acharya Madhva. Raghunath Bhatt had a son named Bhaskar who married Yashomati; in the year 1531 Narada was incarnated as their son. Bhaskar Bhatt celebrated the birth of his son with great ceremony, naming the child Narayan. Narayan Bhatt grew up studying Vedic philosophy and the important Vaishnava scriptures with his uncle Shankar, and was initiated into the practices of Vaishnavism by his father. He completed his formal education at the age of twelve; soon after, he began to develop a keen interest in Braj.

One day the young Narayan Bhatt journeyed to the Godavari River, which runs some distance to the north of his birthplace. After bathing in the river he sat down on the bank and began to meditate on Krishna. Suddenly, he had a glorious vision of Radha and Krishna in a bower of love. Krishna reminded him that he was really Narada, the chief of the sages, who had taken birth in the family of Raghunath Bhatt in order to restore Braj. Krishna commanded him to go immediately to Braj and begin his work of revealing the lila sites. His mission was to uncover and make external that which was hidden and existing only in an unmanifest form. Krishna gave Narayan Bhatt a stone image of himself as a small boy and informed him that this image, being a true form of himself, would help locate the hidden sites of Braj. Krishna directed him to take the image and go first to Radha's sacred pond in Braj, where he promised to reveal himself once again, this time as Madanmohan, the one who enchants even the god of love.

Narayan Bhatt took the image and set out for Braj, about eight hundred miles to the north. When they were all alone in the forest, the image of Krishna as a boy would spring to life and run mischievously through the trees; when he tired, he would climb affectionately into Narayan Bhatt's lap. But when they met anyone on the road, the boy would resume the form of a stone image. Moving in this manner, they arrived at Radhakund, Radha's pond situated at the foot of Mount Govardhan, in the year 1545. A temple to Krishna in the form of Madanmohan had been established at Radhakund by Sanatana Goswami, who had turned the service of the temple over to one Krishnadas Brahmachari. When Narayan Bhatt arrived at Radhakund, the doors of the temple were closed. He was puzzled; Krishna had told him in the vision on the bank of the Godavari River that he would have a view of Madanmohan upon his arrival. He sat down and began to meditate. The doors of the temple suddenly burst open and Madanmohan stood at the door, accompanied by Radha. Narayan Bhatt fell at their feet, but Krishna raised him up and once again reminded him that he was Narada come to earth to reveal Braj in physical form. Krishna also informed him that he was incarnated with the emotional nature of the gopi Rangadevi and instructed him in the secrets of Braj.

Hearing voices, Sanatana and Krishnadas came to the door and were astonished by the sight of Radha and Krishna engaged in conversation with the new arrival. Krishna then addressed Krishnadas, explaining to him that the man standing before him was an incarnation of Narada come to restore Braj. Krishna requested Krishnadas to befriend Narayan Bhatt and introduce him to the highest teachings of Gaudiya Vaishnavism. Krishnadas accepted Narayan Bhatt as his disciple and initiated him into the Gaudiya tradition. They soon became fast friends.

Narayan Bhatt then began the work he had set out to do. His biographer tells us that he reestablished all the lost temple sites established by Krishna's great-grandson Vajranabh but went on to identify the location of much, much more. He disclosed the full extent of the Radhakund pond complex and then revealed four more important ponds around Mount Govardhan: Manasi Ganga, Kusum Sarovar, Govindakund, and Chandra Sarovar. He proceeded to Mathura and identified the location of the birthplace of Krishna, the palace and prison of the wicked Kansa, and many other sites, including the Shiva shrine of Bhuteshwar. From Mathura he crossed the river to Gokul and there restored the dwelling place of Nanda and Yashoda and all the important sites of Krishna's childhood lilas in Mahaban. He went next to Vrindaban and established the sites of the love games, including the flute tree Bansi Bat, and the scenes of many other well-known activities, such as the place where Krishna subdued the monstrous serpent Kaliya and killed the horse-demon Keshi.

Narayan Bhatt revealed the location of Radha's town of Barsana, along with all the important surrounding sites such as Unchagaon, the village of Radha's closest girlfriend, Lalita. He identified Radha and Krishna's secret rendezvous spot in the forest of Sanketban and there established the temple of Radharaman, the Pleaser of Radha. He went on to Kamaban and disclosed many sites, including the sacred pond Vimala Kund, the eating place Bhojan Thali, the foot-marked mountain Charan Pahari, and the Shiva shrine Kameshwar.

Narayan Bhatt mapped out the location of the major mountains in Braj, the ponds, pleasure groves, and other sites of love play; he identified the villages where Krishna's various cowgirl lovers and cowboy companions were born. Perhaps most importantly, he mapped out the position of the twelve forests as they are conceived of yet today. He laid out the entire mandala of Braj and determined its circumference to be twenty-one yojanas (84 *kos*, or about 168 miles).

Narayan Bhatt lived at Radhakund for five years and there composed seven books. The titles of these make clear his interests: *Vraja Bhakti Vilasa* (The Play of Braj Devotion), *Vraja Pradipika* (Light on Braj), *Vrajotsava Chandrika* (Moonlight on the Celebrations of Braj), *Vraja Mahodadhi* (The Ocean of Braj), *Vrajotsava Alhadini* (The Joy of the Celebrations of Braj), *Brihat Vraja Gunotsava* (The Great Celebration of the Qualities of Braj), and *Vraja Prakasha* (The Manifestation of Braj). After leaving Radhakund, Narayan Bhatt established the village of Unchagaon, where his descendants still live today. There, his biographer tells us, he wrote fifty-two more books on Braj and its religious culture.

Janaki Prasad reports many miraculous episodes in the life of Narayan Bhatt. Two among these give further expression to the theme of "uncovering" and tell how he came to establish the two most important temple complexes with which he is associated; a third suggests how he was able to finance the various projects he initiated in Braj.

Narayan Bhatt was once sitting in the forest south of the village of Unchagaon when he noticed a group of cows lying in the shade of a tree. The sun was hot and tigers were about, but he nonetheless observed that one of the cows got up and, displaying no fear of the tigers, went into a dense stand of trees. His curiosity piqued, Narayan Bhatt rose and followed the cow. The cow walked through the woods until it came to a spot where a beautiful golden boy was seated. Milk began to flow from the cow's udder, and the boy drank it. The golden boy then vanished, and the cow returned to the others under the shade tree. Narayan Bhatt suddenly realized that he had just seen Balarama. He began to feel drowsy and fell asleep. Balarama appeared to him in a dream and told him that he should dig on the very spot where he had witnessed the cow giving milk. There, buried under the earth, he would find an image of Balarama. With the help of the local villagers Narayan Bhatt unearthed the image, constructed a temple for it in Unchagaon, and installed the image of Balarama along with his consort, Revati. This is one of the major temples of Narayan Bhatt's family. Still in the hands of his descendants, it also houses the image of Krishna as a small boy that had accompanied Narayan Bhatt on his travels.

The second story is about the establishment of the famous Radha temple in the town of Barsana. One day Narayan Bhatt was out wandering, absorbed in the mood of a gopi. He climbed the mountain of Brahma situated to the south of Unchagaon. There he encountered a beautiful young girl whom he immediately recognized as Radha. She told him that there were images of herself and her lover hidden on top of this mountain. Requesting that he return in the middle of the night, she promised to reveal their location. Radha then disappeared. Narayan Bhatt followed her instructions and uncovered the images of the divine couple. He installed them in a temple he had constructed on top of the hill and began worshiping them under the names Larili and Lal meaning "Darling" and her "Beloved." This temple was to become one of the most important in Braj.

During the period in which Narayan Bhatt was busily uncovering the sites of Braj, the Mughal emperor Akbar came to Mathura and heard the miraculous stories associated with him. Akbar sent a royal messenger to fetch Narayan Bhatt to Mathura. Though the messenger rode a horse and Narayan Bhatt was on foot, the saint somehow managed to stay far ahead of the messenger. Amazed, the messenger requested Narayan Bhatt to sit and wait while he went ahead for further instructions from the emperor. Akbar, upon hearing this strange news, ordered the messenger to escort Narayan Bhatt back home. The emperor then sent his famous Hindu treasurer, Todar Mal, to meet with Narayan Bhatt. Todar Mal was so impressed with Narayan Bhatt that he asked what service he could provide. The enterprising saint responded by requesting Todar Mal to finance the excavation of ponds and the construction of temples in Braj.

Narayan Bhatt attracted a large following while residing at Unchagaon and came to be known as the Great Founder of Braj. He married and had a son named Damodar Bhatt to whom, after a time, he slowly began to transfer authority over his following and responsibility for the temples in Unchagaon and Barsana. When his death drew near, Narayan Bhatt called his following together and addressed them. His final words were: "Devotion to Braj should be performed. The land of Braj is worthy of worship. This very Braj is the highest place. Braj is the body of Shri Krishna. Krishna, the son of Nanda, never leaves Braj."[36] He then turned his seat over to his son, bowed to his favorite deity, Balarama, and disappeared into the Triveni River while meditating on Krishna.

Since there are few sources for the life of Narayan Bhatt, it is difficult to assess the historical references in Janaki Prasad's biography. The dates all seem plausible, and surviving documents that record the involvement of Akbar's finance minister, Todar Mal, in the development of Braj make it seem likely that he did support the construction of the Unchagaon temple and other projects initiated by Narayan Bhatt. Other sources are extremely brief, but all agree that Narayan Bhatt was responsible for establishing much of the elaborate network of sites and shrines located in Braj.[37] Janaki Prasad claims that no one was more dedicated to the restoration of Braj than Narayan Bhatt, and this is certainly difficult to dispute. In terms of the sheer number of sites he established, Narayan Bhatt contributed more than any other leading figure to correlating an imaginary mythical realm with the physical topography of Braj. He was crucially involved in the historical process whereby an interior world became expressed in external forms.

After he had determined the location and "uncovered" all sites referred to in scripture and oral tradition, Narayan Bhatt set about establishing the Ban-Yatra. It was from his time on, Janaki Prasad tells us, that people began performing the Ban-Yatra in increasing numbers. The Ban-Yatra was to be the preeminent way for people to realize the world of Krishna's lila; it is the ritual form par excellence for encountering the tangible forms of Braj and experiencing the world they evoke. In the Ban-Yatra pilgrimage people could see (*darshan*, literally "seeing," is one of the most essential activities of the Ban-Yatra pilgrims) the physical forms of the land of Braj and read the language of the text that had been uncovered. The very forms that serve as vehicles for expressing the world of Krishna's lila are also the very vehicles for experiencing that world.

There is certainly reason to believe that Narayan Bhatt was the first to establish the Ban-Yatra roughly as it is practiced today.[38] A book he completed at Radhakund in 1552 entitled the *Vraja Bhakti Vilasa* contains the most extensive description of the places of Braj ever written, identifying hundreds of sites. It describes the twelve major forests as well as some 113 minor groves, and determines the length of the circumambulation of each, names the presiding deity, and gives the mantra for participating in its power. Within this text is the oldest formulation of the Ban-Yatra itinerary.

Narayan Bhatt distinguishes what he calls the Braj-yatra and the Ban-Yatra. The Braj-yatra is primarily concerned with the villages of Braj, lasts for four months, and follows a 336-kos (about 662-mile) path in the shape of an eight-petaled lotus flower. The Ban-Yatra is primarily concerned with the forests and proceeds along a circular path of 84 kos (about 168 miles, not including all the circumambulations of the various sites and forests). The Braj-yatra is to be performed for the removal of sins; the Ban-Yatra is to be performed for no purpose other than the "realization of the ultimate meaning of everything."[39] My own observations have indicated that this distinction does not hold today; the Ban-Yatra format seems to dominate the pilgrimages through Braj today, even when they are called "Braj-yatra."

Narayan Bhatt states that the Ban-Yatra is to be performed in twenty-three days. It is to begin on the eighth day of the waning moon in the month of Bhadon; this is Janmashtami, Krishna's birthday.[40] Narayan Bhatt declares that performance of the pilgrimage at this time is most effective; performed at any other time, the results will be significantly less. Those persons intending to perform the Ban-Yatra are to proceed to Mathura and there celebrate the birth of Krishna. The next day, the pilgrims are to remain in Mathura and participate in the festival of Nanda, the observance of Nanda's joy at the birth of his son. The pilgrims stay that night in Mathura and on the morning of the third day begin walking by doing the nine-kos (eighteen-mile) circumambulation of Mathura. The pilgrims are to rise early on the morning of the fourth day and hike to see Madhuban, Talban, and Kumudban, performing the circumambulation of each before returning to Madhuban for the night. During the fifth and sixth days the pilgrims visit Bahulaban and Radhakund. The seven-kos (fourteen-mile) circumambulation of Mount Govardhan is performed on the seventh day. After spending the night in Govardhan, the pilgrims walk to Paramandirban, a village just north of Dig, travel the next day to Kamaban, and pass the following day touring its sites.

On the eleventh day the pilgrims arrive in Barsana, climb Brahma's hill, and worship Radha. The next day they circle Khadiraban and then walk to Nandagaon, where they will sleep for the night. The pilgrims rise the next morning and continue by circumambulating Bhadraban. Sheshashayi and Chatraban are visited on the fourteenth and fifteenth days of the journey, and on the sixteenth day the pilgrims arrive in Vrindaban, where they "spend the night in happiness."

The next day the pilgrims cross the Yamuna River and walk to Mahaban. They then proceed to Baladev (Dauji), where they are to pass the night and "realize all desires," and then on to Lohajanghaban (Lohaban). The twentieth day involves a circumambulation of Bhandiraban and a night's stop at Bilvaban (Belban). The pilgrims return to Mathura on the following day, feed brahmans, and rest for the night. The next day the pilgrims are to go to Kamaban and perform a special vow before going on to Gadhaban to watch a performance of Krishna's love play with the gopis. The next day is the full moon; that night the pilgrims watch a performance of Krishna's love play illuminated by the autumn moon, and the pilgrimage is complete.

Thus ends the ideal textual itinerary of Narayan Bhatt.[41] For most Gaudiya and Pushti Margi Vaishnavas, however, the itinerary of the journey through the twelve forests of Braj has a more immediate and personal model. The saints Chaitanya and Vallabha both journeyed around Braj, and today the followers of both claim that their sect was most responsible for the profound changes that took place in Braj during the early years of the sixteenth century, including the establishment of the Ban-Yatra. On the whole, the competitive attitude of the two sects seems to have been absent during the early decades of the sixteenth century, and developments seem to have taken place in an atmosphere of mutual influence. But by the end of the sixteenth century, rivalry began to develop as sectarian temples became seats of power and their priests began to bid for followers and patrons. Both sects maintain and celebrate stories of the visit of their founding saints to the forests of Braj; these function significantly in the pilgrims' experience.

For the Gaudiya Vaishnavas the most popular and authoritative account of Chaitanya's life is the *Chaitanya Charitamrita*, written in 1615 by Krishnadas Kaviraj, a star pupil of the Vrindaban Goswamis. The *Chaitanya Charitamrita* contains a detailed account of Chaitanya's own journey to Braj, which is the most accessible and well-known paradigm of the Ban-Yatra for Gaudiya Vaishnavas. Most of the pilgrims with whom I traveled were familiar with it and referred to it often. It is almost certain that the description of Chaitanya's travels in Braj which appears in the *Chaitanya Charitamrita* is a retrospective account influenced by the pilgrimage circuit established by Narayan Bhatt later in the sixteenth century, rather than a record of Chaitanya's actual journey. But no matter; it serves as a significant framework for modern-day Gaudiya pilgrims.

Chaitanya set out for Braj from his residence in the eastern seaside town of Puri sometime around 1512, but Rupa and Sanatana Goswami advised him to turn back because he was accompanied by such a large crowd of followers that they feared he would attract unfriendly attention from the Muslim rulers of the territory he had to pass through on his way to Braj. In 1514 Chaitanya tried again. Taking permission to leave from Lord Jagannath, the main temple deity of Puri, he left unnoticed, this time accompanied by only one brahman attendant named Balabhadra Bhattacharya. After traveling for some time, Chaitanya approached Mathura; beholding the city from afar, he fell to the ground and offered obeisance with great love. When Chaitanya arrived in Mathura he met a local Sanodiya brahman who was a disciple of Madhavendra Puri, a mysterious and influential figure from southern India who was involved in the establishment of Krishna worship at Mount Govardhan.[42] This brahman guided Chaitanya around the sacred sites of Mathura. They bathed in the Yamuna and then visited the birthplace of Krishna and the Keshav temple built there; they also went to Shiva's place of Bhuteshwar. But Chaitanya wanted particularly to see the forests of Braj, and so arranged to tour the twelve forests with the aid of this local guide. The *Chaitanya Charitamrita* states: "His love increased a thousand times at the sight of Mathura, but it increased a hundred thousand times wandering through the forests."[43] It is in the forests that one truly comes to know something of Krishna.

Chaitanya traveled first to the forests closest to Mathura: Madhuban, Talban, Kumudban, and Bahulaban. He was overwhelmed in these forests, diving into ponds, hugging the trees, and marveling over the deer and peacocks. He then headed toward Mount Govardhan. When he arrived at the village of Arit, he inquired into the location of Radha's pond, but no one knew its location, not even his brahman guide. Realizing that the pond had been lost, Chaitanya entered a meditative state and identified a small pond lying in the middle of a paddy field as Radhakund. He bathed there in a state of ecstatic love.

When Chaitanya arrived at Govardhan, he threw himself to the ground, hugged a rock from the mountain, and became delirious. He next visited the temple of Haridev in the village of Govardhan, bathed in the pond of Manasi Ganga, and performed the circumambulation of Mount Govardhan. He had heard that the saint Madhavendra Puri had established a temple to Krishna Gopal on top of the mountain, but since he considered the mountain too sacred to set foot on, he wondered how he would attain sight of the image. Out of love for Chaitanya, Krishna Gopal came down off the mountain to a small grove so that Chaitanya could see him.

Chaitanya continued on to the forest of Kamaban and then to Nanda's village of Nandagaon, where he discovered in a cave atop the mountain the images of the child Krishna and his adoptive parents, Nanda and Yashoda. Then, visiting the forests of Khadiraban, Bhandiraban (via Sheshashayi and Khelaban), Bhadraban, Shriban (Belban), Lohaban, and Mahaban, Chaitanya wandered through the sites of Krishna's childhood activities. He finally arrived in Vrindaban and toured the site of Krishna's love play. There he lost consciousness of all else. He stayed between Mathura and Vrindaban at Akrura Ghat for several days, making short trips to the bank of the Yamuna in Vrindaban at such famous sites as Keshi Ghat, Kaliya's pool, and Chir Ghat. While resting near the riverbank, Chaitanya heard the sound of a flute, which caused him to lose all control. He had entered such an ecstatic state by wandering through the forests of Braj that his brahman attendant became extremely worried about his condition and begged him to return to Puri.

Contemporary Gaudiya Vaishnavas, who assume Chaitanya was the main agent in the recovery of Braj, make much of his journey through the twelve forests. According to Gaudiya Vaishnava theology, at least since the time of Krishnadas Kaviraj's popular biography, Chaitanya was a very special incarnation. It is believed that outwardly he was a model devotee; inwardly he was a dual incarnation of Radha and Krishna in the same body. Here is another example of the conflation of "history" and "myth." Accordingly, Chaitanya's journey through Braj had several dimensions. Through the saint's peripatetic activity, the divine couple once again enjoyed together the lilas in the forests of Braj; moreover, in so doing, they reidentified the sites of their lilas. Thus, Chaitanya's journey through Braj is sometimes called a *Braj-prakash-lila*, or a "play which reveals Braj."[44] Braj as a place had been lost to memory, and Chaitanya's journey restored it to memory. His journey, therefore, has also been called a "theatre of memory."[45] His activities *remembered*—that is, gave tangible form to—that which was previously inaccessible. Finally, as model devotee, Chaitanya revealed the way to enter and participate in the lila of Radha and Krishna. He wandered through the forests of Braj, experiencing the concrete forms of the land directly with all senses. Here is a vivid model for the ritual of the Ban-Yatra.

The founder of the Pushti Marg, the saint Vallabha, was a southern Indian brahman born in 1479.[46] Pushti Margi sources relate that Vallabha received an orthodox education and at an early age had mastered all the major Hindu scriptures to the degree that he was able to defeat learned scholars in philosophical debate. While on pilgrimage throughout India in 1493 he saw Krishna in a dream. Krishna instructed him to go immediately to Braj and reveal the true identity of a divine form that had emerged from the top of Mount Govardhan. While staying at the site of Gokul, Krishna's childhood home across the Yamuna River from Mathura, Vallabha received a vision of how souls were to be saved in the present decadent age. Krishna revealed to him that the way of realizing a connection with ultimate reality, or *Brahma-sambandh*, was by completely surrendering all one's actions and possessions to Krishna before enjoying them.[47] It was at this point that Vallabha began initiating disciples into the Pushti Marg, the "Way of Grace." The tradition dates Vallabha's visit to Gokul in either 1492 or 1494, but some scholars contend that this date may be nearly twenty years too early.[48] Sometime around 1502 Vallabha married, an act that had significant consequences, since it established a hereditary lineage of religious authorities and steered the sect away from ascetic values.

The most well-known and detailed account of Vallabha's tour of Braj is contained within a work called the *Chaurasi Baithak Charitra*, which is attributed to Vallabha's grandson Gokulnath. This text, written in the language of Braj-bhasha in either the seventeenth or eighteenth century, describes events associated with each site visited by Vallabha during his wanderings throughout India. A *baithak* is a shrine built to commemorate some significant act performed by a saint on a certain spot. Eighty-four such baithaks of Vallabha are included in the *Chaurasi Baithak Charitra*; twenty-two of these are in Braj. Vallabha's baithaks in Braj structure and focus pilgrimage activity for the Pushti Margis. The *Chaurasi Baithak Charitra* presents Vallabha's baithaks in Braj in a narrative of a year-long pilgrimage through the twelve forests and other important sites. Vallabha's tour of Braj follows what seems to have become a fairly standard route by the seventeenth century, suggesting that the description of his circuit is also most likely a retrospective reworking influenced by developments of the mid-sixteenth century, decades after the death of Vallabha. Pushti Margis know the life story of Vallabha well, and his own journey through Braj, mapped out by the baithak shrines, serves as an inspirational paradigm for contemporary Pushti Margi pilgrims. Vallabha, too, is viewed as an important character in the story of Braj—Pushti Margi sources make it clear that he is believed to have been an incarnation of Krishna—so his journey around Braj takes on the double meaning that we have seen in the other saints of Braj.

Vallabha began his tour of Braj in Gokul. In fact, three of his twenty-two baithaks in Braj are in Gokul, indicating the importance of this site of Krishna's childhood activities for Vallabha and his followers. It was here, under a *chonkar* tree on the bank of the Yamuna, that Krishna revealed to Vallabha how souls were to be saved in the present age. From Gokul, Vallabha went to Vrindaban, where he encountered the disciples of Chaitanya. After this he proceeded to Mathura, contracted a local brahman guide,[49] bathed at Vishram Ghat, and commenced circumambulation of Braj.

Vallabha began his journey through the twelve forests with a visit to Madhuban, Talban, Kumudban, and Bahulaban. He then went on to Radhakund and stayed there a month, having visions of Radha and Krishna before passing on to Govardhan. After a halt at the pond of Manasi Ganga in the village of Govardhan, he began wandering through the sites located around the base of the mountain. All Pushti Margi sources give much attention to Mount Govardhan. It is their spiritual center and is considered to be the setting of the nightly love play of Radha and Krishna, which Gaudiyas typically associate with Vrindaban. Vallabha went next to Parasoli, where he bathed in the pond of Chandra Sarovar and had a vision of Krishna and the gopis in the circular dance of love. He continued circling the mountain and came to the sites of Govindakund, Anyor, and the Mukharvind, "lotus mouth," of the mountain at Jatipura. His circumambulation of Mount Govardhan culminated in a visit to the temple built on top of the mountain.

Vallabha continued on around the circuit, coming next to the forest of Kamaban. From there he proceeded to the important sites of Barsana, Sanketban, and Nandagaon. He spent six months at Nandagaon, another important place in the life of the baby Krishna, exploring the surrounding lila sites. He then went to the forest of Kokilaban and on to the sites of Bathain, Sheshashayi, Ram Ghat, Nanda Ghat, and Chir Ghat. The forests of Bhandiraban, Bhadraban, and Belban formed the next stations; Vallabha then stayed at the pond of Mansarovar, his last baithak in Braj, and there witnessed a reunion of the divine couple.

He returned to Mathura by way of the forests of Lohaban and Maha-ban, visiting the nearby sites of Raval, Dauji, Brahmanda Ghat, and Gokul. Upon ending his tour of Braj in Mathura, Vallabha paid his brahman guide a sum of one hundred rupees.

Although no two Ban-Yatras are alike and itineraries vary from pe-riod to period and from sect to sect, since the sixteenth century the circular scheme of the twelve forests has served as a skeletal frame for the pilgrim's route, which is then fleshed out according to the de-signs of the officiating guides. Comparing the account of Chaitanya's tour of Braj found in Krishnadas Kaviraj's *Chaitanya Charitamrita* with Gokulnath's account of Vallabha's pilgrimage recorded in the *Chaurasi Baithak Charitra,* we find much agreement. They differ only in that instead of visiting Khadiraban, Vallabha visited the forest of Kokilaban. These also agree in name, although not in order, with the list of the twelve forests found in the Mathura Mahatmya of the *Varaha Purana*, the *Narada Purana*, and the *Mathura Mahatmya* of Rupa Goswami.

Regardless of the exact itinerary, all Ban-Yatras are circular journeys. The twelve forests of Braj could conceivably have been arranged in a line, like the stations of the cross, or some other formation leading to a climactic goal, with a fixed point of destination. Braj, however, is conceived as a circle, a mandala, and the path of the journey through the twelve forests is importantly circular. Circumambulation, or pari-krama as it is called in northern Indian languages, is perhaps the single most important religious activity that the Ban-Yatra pilgrims perform. In fact, several Gujarati pilgrims told me that they refer to the Ban-Yatra as "doing parikrama"; they made a distinction between yatra, which they used to denote other pilgrimages, and parikrama, a term they reserved specifically for the circular pilgrimage of Braj. The Ban-Yatra is often called the Chaurasi Kos Parikrama, the "Circumambula-tion of Eighty-Four Kos." Ban-Yatra pilgrims are to circle the edge of a natural phenomenon and thereby honor, see, and enjoy it, not pene-trate its surface to achieve a central core. The pilgrims do not move to arrive at some final destination but instead circle around the outer limit of Braj. All of Braj is to be viewed and enjoyed by circling its periphery. It is this that makes the Ban-Yatra distinct from most other types of pilgrimage.

What, then, is the point of all this circling? There is no point. What is in a point, anyway? Absolutely nothing. A circle is a point that has expanded outward, losing itself in the process. The center is empty, void; living things are all on edge. Life on edge is full of tension, but that is where life is fullest. As we saw in chapter 1, the creation of the world is accounted for in the Upanishads, that group of early texts which sets the foundation for much philosophical thought in India, as an expansion of a single point. In the beginning was atman—a single point—alone. Looking around, it saw nothing other than itself and therefore had no delight, was bored. It desired another. It then caused itself to split in two, and therefrom arose a male and female. From the interaction of these two came all of creation.[50] The center of the expansion is the zero point of nothingness out of which everything came; but at this center no life is possible, and certainly no enjoyment is possible. For the sake of joy—ananda—the zero point exploded outward into the ever-expanding kaleidoscopic multiplicity of forms and became pointless—became a circle.

The land of Braj is understood to be the result of such an expansion, spreading through the love play of Radha and Krishna and for the love play of Radha and Krishna.[51] In one sense there is no difference between the center and the periphery of the circle; they share in the same ontological nature. Form is emptiness and emptiness is form; periphery is point and point is periphery.[52] But in another sense, there is all the difference in the world. The ultimate experience of ananda is possible only in touch with the edge, where the point has been lost in its expansion into all delectable forms. Hence, the Ban-Yatra is not a direct assault on the climactic center; it does not aim for the orgasmic reduction of tensions but follows a path of unending curves and plays around with things on edge, enjoying the ongoing foreplay of the universe.

In the end this journey goes nowhere. It has no clear destination. Ban-Yatra pilgrims walk over two hundred miles to end up where they began. In a world understood as Krishna's playground, there is no point in going anywhere. Remember, from the perspective of Braj Vaishnavism, it is goal-oriented activity—striving to be somewhere else—that takes us away from enjoying what appears right here, right now. The Ban-Yatra is not, therefore, a journey to a center.

The only academic theory developed to analyze the phenomenon of pilgrimage cross-culturally has been put forth by the anthropologist Victor Turner. First in a seminal article entitled "The Center Out There: Pilgrim's Goal" and then in later works, Turner outlined the main features of his theory.[53] For Turner, pilgrimage is a process of "beginning in a Familiar Place, going to a Far Place, and returning ideally 'changed' to a Familiar Place."[54] He observes that pilgrims follow a route that is increasingly charged with sacrality as they approach a final point of destination, the "center out there." After encountering this center through symbolic activity, the pilgrims return home, which is defined as profane, in contrast with the sacred center. Noting the linear nature of this sequence, Turner saw the usefulness of employing Arnold van Gennep's tripartite diachronic model of transitional rites, or "rites of passage," to analyze pilgrimage.[55] Van Gennep identified three phases of a ritual process: the *preliminal*, wherein a person is detached from a previous position in the social structure; the *liminal*, wherein the person enters an ambiguous transitional stage; and the *postliminal*, wherein the person is reincorporated into the social structure. Turner built his career exploring the marginality of the middle phase of this process. Liminal entities, he maintains, are necessarily obscure. They slip into the cracks betwixt and between ordinary categories of classification and are ground down to a uniform condition to be fashioned anew.[56] Social relationships are characterized in this middle phase by what Turner calls *communitas:* "a direct, immediate confrontation or 'encounter' between free, equal, levelled, and total human beings, no longer segmented into structurally defined roles. . . . It means freedom, too, from class or caste affiliation, of family and lineage membership."[57] Communitas, which is associated with the sacred for Turner, is "central to religion";[58] it is certainly central to his understanding of pilgrimage. In fact, for Turner, the liminal or "antistructural" quality of the pilgrimage place is the occasion for communitas, which Turner asserts is the common and essential feature of all pilgrimages. The occasional antistructural experience of communitas in an environment set off and protected by a ritual frame "removes the sting" and reduces tensions caused by hierarchical social structures and allows those involved to continue life within these structures. Pilgrimages, as all rituals for Turner, are controlled undoings of social structure, so that the doings may continue. This is the central function of pilgrimage. The pilgrim's goal, then, is the sacred "center out there" which serves as a symbol of the ideal and provides relief from the burdens of ordinary existence.

Turner's theory has fastened a rather tyrannical grip on pilgrimage studies; it is difficult to find a recent study of pilgrimage that does not make use of it. And yet this theory strikes me as inadequate for our present considerations for several reasons. First, it is reductive. Even if it is true, much more can be said about pilgrimage. Social scientists, moreover, have not tended to confirm Turner's assertion that communitas is the universal feature of pilgrimage, and many have argued against this claim.[59] It may also be the case that instead of satisfying by reducing tension, "anti-structural" activities actually increase desire by giving one a taste for the forbidden. More importantly, however, Turner's theory tends to obscure the specificity of particular pilgrimages. His model is essentially linear and does little justice to the circular journey of the Ban-Yatra. I respond to Turner's claim that all pilgrimages are directed toward the goal of the "center out there" by suggesting a simple typology of pilgrimages, which compares pilgrimages that value a center with those that devalue a center.[60] The first type involves a linear journey and has a clear destination, the center; the second type involves a circular journey that resists the center and has no clear destination. The implications of the differences between these two types of journeys are significant.

A sensitive study of the fascinating pilgrimage of the Huichol Indians of central Mexico by the anthropologist Barbara Myerhoff—who considers herself a student of Turner—provides a vivid example of the first type of pilgrimage.[61] The central event in the religious calendar of the Huichol is a journey to a place called Wirikuta. This pilgrimage begins with preliminary rituals in the home village that cleanse and bind the group of pilgrims and prepare them for the long journey to Wirikuta, where they will collect peyote. Wirikuta, Myerhoff's informants told her, is the undifferentiated place of origins and therefore the center of the world: it is identified as the place of beginnings, the place of creation, the place where the First People lived. Wirikuta is paradise for the Huichol, an ideal place of original perfection. This symbolism of perfection and primordial undifferentiation makes Wirikuta comparable to the Hindu lingam as a point of destination.[62] Huichol religion, Myerhoff informs us, is preoccupied with a nostalgic desire for a return to the land of Wirikuta. She interprets the Huichol pilgrimage to Wirikuta as "a prototypical ritual—a return to Paradise, a journey back to human origins, a retrieval of man's beginnings before Creation, when all was oneness," a journey motivated by a "desire for total unity."[63] The Huichol cannot stay in Wirikuta, however, and soon go back to their homes. Periodic returns to Wirikuta, Myerhoff contends, function to assuage the intense longing for a lost paradise. Her praise of the effectiveness of this pilgrimage for soothing the "nostalgic desire" or "yearning for paradise" follows Mircea Eliade, who has identified this nostalgia and its concomitant concern with the center as the pivotal feature of religion in his influential work *The Myth of the Eternal Return*.[64]

The Ban-Yatra exemplifies a very different type of pilgrimage.[65] It does not begin at one's normal home, and there is no significant ritual content in the journey from home to Braj. How one arrives at Braj is irrelevant; the Ban-Yatra does not begin until certain preliminary rituals have been performed after the sacred zone has been entered. This pilgrimage is concerned only with the circling of Braj. Theories of pilgrimage that are dependent on a linear model of transition are not useful for exploring the richer meaning of this circular pilgrimage.

In the mind of those involved in this pilgrimage, the Ban-Yatra is to be distinguished from other types of journeys, especially journeys to definitive destinations. I once called the Ban-Yatra a *tirtha-yatra*, the common name for pilgrimage in Hindu tradition, in a conversation with Shuklaji, a man who was to become my guide. He responded with the following:

> The Ban-Yatra is not a *tirtha-yatra*, because Braj is not a *tirtha*; it is Krishna's *dham*. There is a story about this. Listen: Once all the *tirthas* had gathered in Prayag [modern Allahabad] to honor Prayag, King of All Tirthas. Braj, however, was absent. This greatly angered Prayag and the other *tirthas*, who decided to attack Braj. But when they arrived at the border of Braj, they saw Shri Krishna wearing a forest garland and attended by the cowherds. Prayag was first astonished but then began to complain: "You made me king of *tirthas*, but Braj does not obey me." Krishna replied: "It is true that I made you king of all *tirthas*, but Braj is my *dham* and I did not make you king of my *dham*.

The word *tirtha* in this context might best be translated as a pilgrimage center. More precisely, it is a place to "cross over," a passageway through which to reach another world.[66] Though it is not a goal itself, it is the doorway to the goal, and is thus closely tied to goal-oriented activity. *Tirtha-yatras* are for those trying to reach the other shore. The word *dham*, on the other hand, might best be translated as "abode," or simply "home." The distinction Shuklaji was trying to make is that in a *tirtha-yatra* one journeys in anticipation of crossing over to the highest reality; in the Ban-Yatra one wanders around in Krishna's *dham* of Braj, realizing that this is the highest reality. A sense of lack motivates many journeys; this one is an opportunity to enjoy what *is*. From within the dham-perspective there is no need for the doorway of a tirtha. Once one has reached Braj there is thus no reason to journey elsewhere, and no single point stands out as being more important than any other. Entwistle recognized this in his book on Braj: "Where Braj is concerned, the ideal is not one of entering into and then returning from an experience, but of remaining totally immersed in love for Krishna. . . . Pilgrimage to Braj, rather than being a process of transition from the profane to the sacred, is really one of realizing the sacred within the profane by cultivating the appropriate sensibility."[67] If Entwistle is correct, and I firmly believe that he is, then we must come to understand the function of this pilgrimage other than in the way Turner suggests.

Braj is a framed space—though the frame is by no means impermeable—which marks everything in it as special.[68] The boundary of Braj functions to focus the attention of the pilgrims on higher truths. Pilgrims come here accepting that they have arrived at Krishna's dham, in which everything that happens is Krishna's lila. Several told me that the Ban-Yatra is an exercise for seeing things as they really are, namely lila.[69] What Ban-Yatra pilgrims come to realize in Braj is that much of the lila looks like ordinary activities, or conversely, that ordinary activities are Krishna's lila. This opens the way for a perspectival awakening: that which is present in Braj in an intensified form is also available elsewhere. There is no need to search for a passageway out of this world, there is no need for radical change, for this very world is itself divine. Once this realization takes place, the frame suddenly appears artificial. The function of the geographical boundary of Braj parallels the limiting function of the *murti*, or image, used in Vaishnava worship. Several Vaishnavas in Braj have told me that from a philosophical perspective (*siddhant*) there is no difference between the image and any other thing in the material world; from this perspective all things are nondifferent, as everything is Krishna. However, the *realization* that everything is Krishna cannot take place at this level, and one cannot establish a relationship with Krishna. Analyzing the Vaishnava concept of lila, Edward Dimock writes: "It is, of course, our inability to see the totality of things, our being limited to seeing the single attribute rather than the true multiplicity, that is the major problem in the matter of revelation."[70] For the purpose of realization, or *bhavana*, limitations must be drawn. Therefore, the undifferentiated is differentiated into a specific form, a special image, and Braj is marked off as a special place. Both are concentrated forms which support concentration on divinity. But once the realization takes place, it extends beyond artificial boundaries. There is, then, ideally no return to a previous state; in a sense there is no end to the Ban-Yatra. The Ban-Yatra is a circle; the pilgrims walk a great distance only to end up where they began. "The return to the beginning is apt. For the

devout soul pilgrimage has no beginning, no end. It is constant circling. . . ."[71] Stated another way, there is no real difference between
the beginning and the end.

The Ban-Yatra is, in the end, an eccentric pilgrimage. The realization
generated in the pilgrim's experience is that all life is Krishna's lila.
There are no fixed centers anywhere. This realization tends to be
downplayed by the pilgrimage guides, who have much to gain by maintaining the view that Braj remains special, but it comes up frequently
in the discussions of the pilgrims. Chaitanya himself is their model;
after he "left" Braj he continued to see Braj everywhere.[72]

All this suggests another reading of pilgrimage activity besides the
sociological perspective suggested by Turner. Whether it does or does
not function as an occasion for communitas or as a release valve for
social tensions—and, frankly, I saw little indication of this among the
pilgrims with whom I walked[73]—the Ban-Yatra aims at a perspectival
opening. Life as it is is Krishna's lila. If one could truly come to see
this, one would give up the quest for a special "center out there" and
enjoy the form that life takes anywhere, anytime.[74]

Much is at stake over the differences between these two types of
pilgrimage. From the perspective of pilgrimages that ultimately value
the center, the absence of a center would be a tragedy. The center,
Eliade tells us, is the point of access to the transcendental paradise
which represents perfection and the sacred zone of absolute reality.[75]
Without the center, one would be cut off from the sacred and trapped
in an unbearable, meaningless, profane world. The loss of Wirikuta,
for example, would amount to the end of the temporary cure—a taste
of paradise—that the Huichol pilgrimage accomplishes. And yet, from
the perspective of pilgrimages that devalue the center, the absence of
a center can be viewed as the key to the possibility of freedom.

Although Myerhoff generally interprets positively the effectiveness
of the journey to Wirikuta in dealing with the Huichol's intense nostalgia, at times she hints at another possible reading of this kind of pilgrimage. She writes that with an awareness of the perfection of
Wirikuta always in mind, "the present is but a minor deviation from
'reality,' a human interlude, atypical and transitory, bracketed by a
beginning and final condition of Paradise."[76] The original perfection of
Wirikuta, experienced repeatedly in pilgrimage activity, highlights the
imperfection of the ordinary world all too clearly. Perhaps it is the
case that instead of being an effective cure for the unhappy nostalgia
Myerhoff speaks of, the idea of original perfection—the goal of the
pilgrim's journey—ironically is the very cause of this nostalgia. True

enjoyment is possible only in the "center out there" and "back then," not where one is now. Read in this light, such centers appear as the focus of an unhealthy fixation.

Myerhoff deviates explicitly only once from her positive assessment of the results of pilgrimages like the Huichol journey to Wirikuta. The Huichol pilgrimage guides warn of the danger of staying in Wirikuta; the pilgrims literally run out of Wirikuta once they have collected the peyote for which they have come. They recognize that life is not possible in the undifferentiated center. Myerhoff introduces a psychoanalytic reading of this process:

> The Freudian view would identify the dangers of remaining in Wirikuta as those of indulging in incest and failing to relinquish an infantile fantasy of the mother as mate. An orthodox psychoanalytic approach would call our attention to the overt biological and sexual symbolism of the journey to Wirikuta. The pilgrims enter a sacred region called "Where Our Mothers Dwell" through a place known as the "vagina"; they use in their rituals a knotted cord which can be seen as representing an umbilicus. In this reading Wirikuta is a symbol for the womb and the reentry is a fantasy of incest which indicates the failure to cope with or resolve the oedipal conflict.[77]

Though Myerhoff chose to do no more with this reading, it opens up a possible line of thought that may be pursued further. From this perspective, linear pilgrimage to "the center out there" appears as a fixation on the original object, the "mother" in psychoanalytic language, which arrests mobility and keeps the passionate energy of the libido from moving on to enjoy other objects that present themselves. If this center were given up, however, one would be free to appreciate a wider range of experiences.

While the affirmation of the perfect center entails the devaluation of everything that is, the devaluation of the perfect center opens the possibility of affirming that which previously seemed imperfect. Imperfection is dependent on the concept of perfection. Myerhoff presents the Huichol pilgrimage to the center Wirikuta as a way of temporarily realigning the "is" with the "ought,"[78] but from the perspective of the second type of pilgrimage, the center out there is what defines the gap and creates the tension between the is and the ought. The center out there steals away appreciation of what is here. Freed from the fixed center point, nostalgia is gone, the gap between the is and the ought disappears, and one can delight in whatever appears. Everything is Krishna's lila. Though the boundary around Braj is necessary for the perspectival shift which leads to the realization that all life is Krishna's lila, that realization is not bound to this geographical frame. The pilgrims are ideally to take this realization with them; the circle is to continue. Following the lead of Chaitanya, after performing the Ban-Yatra every place is ultimately viewed as Braj and all wanderings are Ban-Yatras.

Although we were to begin walking every other day well before sunrise, and so had arrived at the forest of Talban (described at the beginning of this chapter) on the morning of our first full day after spending the night just outside of Mathura, our party had left Vrindaban slightly after four o'clock the previous afternoon, allowing little time to explore the city of Mathura. Our pilgrimage was structured in such a way as to leave time only for a superficial view of Mathura, whereas other Vaishnava pilgrims—most notably the Pushti Margis—typically spend several days there. I later pointed this out to one of our guides. He replied, "What do we have to do with the city of Kansa?" Mathura, the point of the beginning and end of the story of Krishna's activities in Braj, holds little interest for the Gaudiya Vaishnavas. Being the center, many do not even regard it as part of Braj. Mathura may also be devalued by some Vaishnavas, since it has long been identified as one of the seven pilgrimage centers of moksha, the destination of those seeking liberation from the world of multiple forms.[79] We stopped in Mathura just long enough to see its most important site, the huge temple built near the site of Krishna's birth.

Mathura is an ancient city, with a continuous history stretching back for almost twenty-five hundred years. It developed as an influential urban center during the Mauryan period beginning in the fourth century B.C.E. and served as a principal home for Buddhism for some eight hundred years.[80] Archaeological excavations have produced evidence that the site of the great temple of Krishna was previously the location of a large Buddhist monastic complex.[81] Mathura later became a powerful political and commercial center of Kushana rule in the first century C.E. The great walled city was a center for the arts. Long famed for its dramatic performances, Mathura also nurtured artisans who developed the archetypal Asian Buddha and produced some of the finest early Buddhist sculpture as well as some outstanding Vaishnava iconographic art.

There is evidence to suggest that Krishna has been worshiped in this area in some form since the fourth century B.C.E.[82] Mathura thus "provided a base for a religious cult which was initially specific to the region, but was soon to attain a far wider geographical and social circumference."[83] It has been argued that during the early centuries of the first millennium, "Mathura was THE creator and disseminator of Vaisnava art modes as well as the probable center of Vaisnava *bhakti* cults."[84]

A magnificent temple stood on the site of Krishna's birth for centuries until it was burned to the ground and its wealth carried off by Mahmud of Ghazni when he invaded India from Afghanistan in 1017. His secretary Tarikh Yamini of Al Utbi records that Mahmud defeated a Hindu king established in a fort in Mahaban and then went on to sack Mathura, where he

> saw a building of exquisite structure, which the inhabitants declared to be the handiwork not of men but of Genii. The town wall was constructed of solid stone, and had opening on to the river two gates, raised on high and massive basements to protect them from the floods. On the two sides of the city were thousands of houses with idol temples attached, all of masonry and strengthened with bars of iron; and opposite them were other buildings supported on stout wooden pillars. In the middle of the city was a temple, larger and finer than the rest, to which neither painting nor description could do justice. . . . If anyone wished to construct a building equal to it, he would not be able to do so without expending a hundred million dinars, and the work would occupy two hundred years, even though the most able and experienced workmen were employed.[85]

Mahmud's secretary must have been referring to the grand temple of Mathura, which housed the presiding deity of Keshavadev.

The Keshavadev temple was rebuilt in 1150. Some version of the temple must have been the one seen by Chaitanya and Vallabha on their visits to Mathura. Mughal records from the reign of Jahangir indicate that the temple was destroyed again in the early sixteenth century, during the reign of Sikandar Lodi. Though one must always question the Mughal portrayal of the earlier Afghan rulers, these records say of Sikandar Lodi:

> He was so zealous a Musalman that he utterly destroyed many places of worship of the infidels, and left not a single vestige remaining of them. He entirely ruined the shrines of Mathura, that mine of heathenism, and turned their principal temples into *saraes* and colleges. Their stone images were given to the butchers to serve them as meat-weights, and all the Hindus of Mathura were strictly prohibited from shaving their heads

and beards and performing their ablutions. He thus put an end to all the
idolatrous rites of the infidels there; and no Hindu, if he wished to have
his head or beard shaved, could get a barber to do it.[86]

Another temple was built on the site around 1615 by Bir Singh Deo
of Orchha, a Hindu kingdom located to the south of Braj. Bir Singh's
elder brother, the king of Orchha, had been supported by the emperor
Akbar, and Bir Singh sought the aid of Akbar's recalcitrant son, Prince
Salim, in a civil war against him. The aid was reciprocated: Salim
suspected that his father's close friend and adviser, Abul Fazl, was
trying to block his succession to the throne, and in 1602 arranged for
Bir Singh to murder Abul Fazl. After Salim succeeded to the throne
three years later, taking the title Jahangir, he ousted Bir Singh's elder
brother and made Bir Singh king of Orchha. Bir Singh took an increasing interest in religious affairs as he grew older, some say to atone for
his earlier misdeeds. He conducted a pilgrimage to Braj in 1614, which
inspired him to contribute to the restoration and construction of many
sites and temples within the region, and to build the magnificent temple
of Keshavadev in Mathura.[87] The French traveler Jean-Baptiste Tav-
ernier visited Mathura in 1650 and called the Keshavadev temple "one
of the most sumptuous edifices in all of India." His description continues: "The temple is of such a vast size that, though in a hollow, one
can see it five or six *kos* off, the building being very lofty and very
magnificent."[88] This structure, too, was razed; in 1669 the Mughal emperor Aurangzeb ordered its destruction and had the images taken to
Agra to be buried under the steps of a mosque "so that people might
trample upon them forever."[89] He then had a mosque built on the site
where the Krishna temple once stood. The mosque remains in place
today and is a focus of growing tension between Muslims and Hindus
in northern India.

Mathura came under British rule in 1803 and became a military
station on the frontier. In 1832 it was made the capital of a new district.
A few British administrators, such as Frederick S. Growse, began to
take interest in the ancient Keshavadev temple and other monuments
in the area, and to "detest the bigotry of the barbarians who destroyed
it."[90] In this climate, dreams of renewing the site began to grow.

Construction of a new temple and pilgrimage complex finally began
in 1953, financed by a group of wealthy businessmen who had purchased the site in the early 1940s. The present structure, an impressive
building made with great amounts of white marble, stands beside the
mosque built by Aurangzeb. It features a central shrine for Radha and

Krishna but also houses a host of other deities. Beneath the nearby mosque is an older underground chamber that is said to be the prison cell in which Krishna was born. A small image of Krishna as a baby now rests there in a cradle. This room was the focus of our visit to Mathura. The pilgrims I was with eagerly jammed themselves into this dark, crowded chamber. Bodies pressed against sweaty bodies filled the room, come to see with their own eyes the place where baby Krishna came into this world.

We left the Janmabhumi complex around 10:30 p.m. and headed south through dark back streets toward our first camp. On the way our guides pointed out a large tank with an intricate design of steps leading down to shallow water. The tank is called Potarakund, the "Diaper Pond," since this is where Krishna's mother, Devaki, is said to have washed his first diaper. As we walked, one of the women from our group took my hand in hers. I looked at her, surprised. She was a Bengali woman in her early forties; her damp hair hung in a long braid down her back. I observed that she was dressed with the ornaments of a married woman. She avoided my eyes, looking at the road straight ahead. This all struck me as very unconventional, but I was too hot and tired to figure out or even care about her intentions. Human contact felt good.

Around eleven at night we arrived at our camp, which was set up in a large field behind the temple of Bhuteshwar, a site sacred to Shiva, who is understood to be the protector of Braj (Kshetrapal). Bhuteshwar, Shiva as "Lord of the Spirits," is specifically said to be the guardian of Mathura, and is a prominent form of Shiva in his protective role. This is one of the four Shiva shrines said to have been established by Krishna's great-grandson Vajranabh. An old temple, which had recently been whitewashed, stood within a small brick courtyard. Inside the temple, a single bare light bulb illuminated a four-foot-tall white lingam with a black-mustached face protruding from its side. The Mathura Mahatmya of the *Varaha Purana* recommends that here the pilgrim ask Shiva to bless his or her journey: "O Shiva, Promoter of All Auspiciousness, Accomplisher of All Aims, through your grace, may my pilgrimage be successful."[91] Near the temple a steep, dark stairway leads down into the underground chamber of Bhuteshwar's consort, Pataleshwari, the Goddess of the Underworld. The pressing crowds from the temple of Krishna's birth, however, were not present at this site; many had simply stumbled on to find their tents.

We would be living for the next twenty-one days in a traveling settlement of old green-and-white army tents held up with bamboo poles. A crew of about thirty bullock-cart drivers and workers from Vrindaban accompanied the pilgrimage and traveled ahead to pitch tents, unload our baggage, and secure drinking water. The tents, numbering between eighty and ninety, were arranged in a haphazard fashion, never the same from one camp to the next. This lack of order became especially noticeable to me after traveling later with a group of Vallabhacharya, or Pushti Margi, pilgrims. The Vaishnava sect of Pushti Margis recognizes the religious authority of the descendants of the founding saint Vallabha. One of his male descendants, called a maharaj, heads a Pushti Margi pilgrimage. The tents of the Pushti Margi group I traveled with were arranged in an orderly and hierarchical fashion around the central tent of the maharaj, Shri Mathuresh Goswami; those paying the most money were positioned closest to the maharaj. Not so with the Gaudiya Vaishnavas; they recognize no central authority. The arrangement of the tents in our camp reflected their chaotic democracy.

I was in for a surprise at our Bhuteshwar camp: I learned that my "personal guide," Govinda, had abandoned me and left me in the charge of his younger brother, Mohan, who would be cooking for me and twenty other people. The pandas (pilgrimage guides) of Braj do not enjoy a good reputation; I was beginning to learn why. Too tired to worry about it then, I gulped down a few *puris* (small, round puffed breads) and began getting ready for bed. It was after midnight. A tonga driver had parked his cart near my tent and was brushing the sweat from his horse. I sat down on my trunk, removed my shoes, and confirmed my worst fears. After walking only twelve of the more than two hundred miles we were to walk, my feet were already developing serious blisters. I had received permission from my guru, Maganlal, to wear canvas shoes, thinking I would be unable to complete the entire pilgrimage barefoot, as many were to do. But I made a classic mistake. Assuming that shoes of this type did not require much preparation, I failed to break them in properly. Moreover, my feet had softened and swelled terribly from the heat, causing my shoes to pinch. Our guides wisely wore rubber sandals, but once my soles were marked with open sores I was committed to the protective layer of canvas. The tonga driver walked by and noticed my feet; he assured me that they would be fine after a couple of days. Wanting to believe him, I returned to my task of getting ready for bed. Three Bengali women shared my tent; I knew nothing about them at this time. Even at this hour the air was hot and humid. I decided to move my cot outside to catch a breeze. I locked my valuables inside my trunk and lay down to listen to the gentle chirping of crickets and stare at the brilliant stars above.

All too soon a bullock driver was shaking my cot and shouting in Hindi, "Radhe! Radhe! It is time to get your things in the bullock cart." I grabbed my flashlight and looked at my watch. It was 2:45. I located my water pot and headed for the "jungle," a euphemism for the "toilet" of the open fields. Upon returning, I dressed, slung my pack on my back, and joined my group. By 3:45 we were walking sleepily in a southerly direction. The stars were still bright, making artificial light unnecessary. We walked along a hard road cut through the middle of farm fields. A warm breeze already made my skin sticky. The flames of a huge oil refinery, recently built with Soviet aid, were visible in the distance. A man walking beside me expressed apprehension about the impact this refinery would have on the environment of Braj and called it the modern Kansapuri, or city of the wicked Kansa. A small group of people marched past us singing Bengali songs to Radha and Krishna, the steady clacking of bamboo walking sticks marking their rhythm. After we had walked several miles the eastern horizon began to turn golden. As we came to Madhuban, the first of the twelve forests, a crimson sun duplicated itself in the glowing pond of Krishna Kund, creating a gorgeous sunrise. We hiked the remaining four miles to Talban, treading a soft dirt road lined with green grass that rose in graceful waves over our heads. Beautiful green fields appeared on both sides of the path as we neared Talban, the second of the twelve forests. White egrets stalked the edge of swamps that retained the monsoon water. Narayan Bhatt had stated that the Ban-Yatra should be performed during the four months of the rainy season to be most beneficial. Last year the monsoon had failed to come, causing severe drought and hardship. This year, however, the life-giving rains had arrived, yielding green countryside and ample ponds. Bathing in ponds is an essential aspect of the Ban-Yatra; perhaps one reason Narayan Bhatt insisted that the pilgrimage be performed during this season is that ponds which would be quite low during other times of the year were now full to the brim.

The pilgrims took on what was to become their characteristic formation: our party stretched out for miles, winding through the countryside and forming a long line of colorfully clad bodies walking in single file or in groups of two or three. This was the most pleasing and leisurely part of the day. Those walking alone frequently would be singing softly to themselves or silently enjoying the visual display around them. Those walking together usually engaged in conversation; most of my talks with fellow travelers took place during our early-morning walks. I walked some distance with an engineer from Calcutta, a slight

man in his late fifties. The tour of Braj had been a lifelong dream; he
was excited to have at last the chance of achieving it. He expressed
concern over being able to complete the circuit, but the spring in his
steps convinced me that he would make it.

After seeing the palm trees, temple, and pond of Talban, we retraced
our steps to find our camp near the village of Maholi in Madhuban.
This spot once served as the headquarters for a division of Akbar's
troops. Madhuban, the first forest one encounters after leaving
Mathura, has at least two stories associated with it, expressing the
two dimensions of the young Krishna's activities: he rids the earth of
demons and makes possible the experience of love. Textual sources
usually explain that this forest is called Madhuban because here
Krishna killed a demon named Madhu. Thus, one of Krishna's epithets
is Madhusudan, the "Slayer of Madhu." But I heard another story
while walking there. As I approached Madhuban, moving slowly on
painful feet, I was overtaken by a tall, dark, lean figure with curly hair
and a trim mustache. He was wearing a yellow shirt, a long green lungi
wrapped around his waist, and brown plastic sandals; he carried a
heavy, well-aged bamboo walking stick. He walked with a vivacious
bounce, and his eyes, yellowed by the sun, twinkled as he spoke. I
liked him immediately. He addressed me in broken English. His full
name was Krishna Gopal Shukla; I called him Shuklaji. Having been
abandoned by Govinda, I was to adopt Shuklaji as my personal panda,
though he was quick to inform me that he preferred the title Brajbasi—
meaning simply, a "resident of Braj"—because of the negative connota-
tions associated with the word *panda*. Shuklaji was to influence greatly
my view of this pilgrimage. As we entered Madhuban, he told me that
it is a forest where flowers are plentiful and bees produce honey in
abundance. This is the place where the gopis secretly come to collect
honey for Krishna; thus it is called Madhuban, the "Sweet Forest."

Shuklaji was thirty-six years old at the time I met him, the father of
two children and the eldest son of four brothers and three sisters. He
had studied literature and received a degree from the local college in
Vrindaban; he was also an accomplished astrologer. His father had
received a bullet wound in the leg during a battle for independence
from the British, and since it was now difficult for him to walk great
distances, much of the burden of supporting the family fell on Shuklaji's shoulders. He had already guided twelve Ban-Yatras and was
selected as one of five heads of the Brajbasi guides leading this pilgrimage. As far back as he knew, his forefathers had been Brajbasi pilgrim-

age guides. The family belonged to the Nimbarki Vaishnavas, a sect closely related to the Gaudiyas in Braj, and was involved in the worship of Shiva at the Gopishwar temple in Vrindaban.

Although Shuklaji's family belongs to the sect of Nimbarki Vaishnavas, its hereditary area of business is around Katoya, a commercial center in the north-central Barddhaman district of West Bengal, which is populated with many Gaudiya Vaishnavas. The key Vaishnava areas of India are divided up among the Brajbasi families of Vrindaban, who are organized into the Brajbasi Panda Society of Vrindaban. Each Brajbasi family has its own area of recruitment in which no other family is to conduct business. Shuklaji informed me that there are some two hundred Brajbasi panda families operating in the town of Vrindaban, though only about twenty are presently involved in guiding Ban-Yatra pilgrims through the entire region of Braj. The sons of many families are now forced to pursue other professions. Shuklaji travels to Bengal twice annually, where his family has maintained a temple for many years, to recruit what he calls "passengers." New contacts are made through previous clients. On this journey Shuklaji had twenty-five passengers, fifteen women and ten men. Among them were housewives, farmers, landowners, preachers, businessmen, and shopkeepers.

I had many opportunities to observe Shuklaji with his passengers over the next twenty days. He was a very responsible and concerned guide, carefully shepherding his flock as he moved up and down the marching line. He was also very playful. He insisted that everyone have a good time and would cheer on one person after another. His passengers were all fond of him and loved to illustrate his unusual bravery through a story of how he had once jumped into a deep well to save a baby. I asked Shuklaji why his passengers had come. "To have a view [darshan] of Lord Krishna's activities," he said. "They want to see with their own eyes what they have read or heard about in the *Bhagavata Purana*, to see the lila places for themselves. This increases their belief. Temples are made by men, but the things we see on Ban-Yatra, such as footprints in stone, are natural, so that anyone can believe in the things done in Braj. Seeing these signs in stone, anyone can believe in the supernatural things that happened in Braj and can begin to see Krishna here." Darshan, or "seeing," is a central act in the Ban-Yatra; the desire to see a sacred object or site is a common motive for pilgrimage.[92] The objects viewed become tangible vehicles for an intense emotional experience, which in turn affirms the beliefs that the objects express. Shuklaji added that his passengers come also to wander, free from domestic burdens and anxieties, and to experience the wild life of the forests with no set program.

I was to suffer intensely in the sweet forest of Madhuban. Very distressed, and having no close friend to talk with, I sought solace in writing. My writing was filled with that panicky despair you get when you realize that some distant and detached part of yourself has volunteered you for a difficult task you are now obliged to perform. I addressed my thoughts in my journal to my wife.

September 8, 1988—10 A.M.

What I would do to be with you in some cool room in Katmandu. I am so worried. I have just come back from taking a bath in a slimy green pond. What disease lurks there? How will I ever keep clean? I tried to wash my clothes but they came out brown. It is our second day out and the complete balls of both my feet are huge blisters. I have several blisters between my toes and my shoes are bloody from wearing into my heels. How will I ever be able to walk over two hundred miles? My trusty guide abandoned me the very first day and left me in the care of his younger brother and friends who are cooking for a group of Bengalis. I am to eat with them, but how I will survive their cooking is beyond me. They are in their tent smoking chillums of hash and cooking in the dust with water that looks like it came right out of the pond. Help! How did I ever get myself into this situation? This feels like the hardest thing I have ever done in my life. The heat is unbelievable. It is well above a hundred degrees; there is no place to get away from it. And it is only ten o'clock. Twelve to two will be the hottest. I have already given serious thought to packing up and calling it quits. Somehow I am going to have to find some inner strength.

I am sharing a tent with three Bengali women. I know that they too are suffering greatly, yet one of them takes time to apply religious marks to her body and meditate in the rear of our stifling tent. What makes people do this?

* * *

Things have gone from bad to worse. At 10:30 I got the nerve to try the boys' cooking. They store the rice in their gamchas which they were wearing around their waists a few minutes earlier and serve the food with their hands which have been who knows where. I choked down a few bites, smiled politely, and staggered out of their tent. At this point I felt that I definitely could not go on; I then discovered that my body was covered with prickly heat.

A man came up to me and suggested that I sit in the shade of a large tree near the steps of the pond. I am there now, and it is so tolerable that I was again beginning to think that I might make it. But I have just discovered another blister between my toes that is filled with blood and the doubt returns.

I just met a man from Calcutta. He agrees with me that this pilgrimage is very hard. "It is harder than climbing the highest mountain," he told me. "Then why are you doing it?" I asked with great curiosity. His reply: "To get enjoyment."

There is now quite a crowd under this huge green tree. Everyone is trying to escape the heat. I entertain myself with glimpses of bodies exposed in the endless changing of clothes due to the heat. Which brings me back to suffering. I am getting to know the man from Calcutta, who is now lying next to me. He is very friendly. His name is A. K. Nath. He is fifty-five years in age and is in charge of renewing driver's licenses in Calcutta. He told me that if I complete this pilgrimage, I will not be reborn anything less than a human. Such belief! But I do not share it. Why then am I out here suffering?

I am trying to take my mind off my misery by observing what is around me. Brown bodies and red, white, blue, green, and yellow clothes litter the ground. Voices blend into a continuous buzz. Crows squawk incessantly. Every time a breeze stirs the muggy air, tiny yellow and red flowers rain down on me from the tree towering above. Everyone waits, each in their own way, for the heat to subside. Children jump and splash noisily in the pond, seemingly oblivious to our suffering. They are playing, letting out a cacophony of laughter. I envy them. Their play seems a world apart from our suffering. How does one enter that world of play?

Many of my fellow travelers have crowded up against the shaded walls of a crumbling building. Though it was painted white long ago, broken chips reveal that it was constructed of red sandstone, indicating that it most likely goes back to the Mughal period. A large black square has been painted on its wall and is used as a blackboard, for this is also the location of the village school. About two dozen children were crowded around a lesson board set up under this tree when we arrived this morning. The teacher competed unsuccessfully with the pilgrims for the students' attention before giving up and going home.

People keep peeling off layers. It is amazing to see how modesty is cast aside in this heat. Most of the women have taken off their bodices; we men are in nothing but skimpy gamchas.

                                                                2 P.M.
I somehow managed to drift off into a dreamland where I thought everything was fine. But upon waking I am again in a panic. Writing seems to be the only thing which helps, so I continue. I was just lying here thinking how long it will be before I see you. I want to be with you. I am frightened. A cloud has come. I had better get up before I explode.

I have got to stop focusing on my own pain and try to figure out what is going on around me. There is a group of sannyasis [renunciants] sitting against a shaded wall of our compound. Their involvement amazes me. They have thick necklaces wrapped around their necks made of large Tulsi beads and alternating wooded petals on which the word "Radha" is written. They sit eagerly telling stories. Like the children, they are laughing. I feel such an outsider to their world. What enables them to laugh? And who is their "Radha"? I should go talk with them. I should go get my camera. But I hesitate. I don't move. What am I doing here? It is only 2:25. Time moves so slowly in this heat.

Hell with it! Either I am going to get into it or get out of it. I can't stay like this. I'm going for my camera and talk with people.

I found the people I met friendly and they were generally amused with me. I talked with many—about the heat, of course. The group of sannyasis proved too intense to penetrate. I looked on eagerly from the edge of their circle but was not invited in. When evening arrived and the sun finally became tolerable, I went out walking with Mr. Nath. I was feeling the acute need for companionship and enjoyed his company. I even found myself laughing with him once or twice at the absurdity of our situation. He explained that we experience what we need most, even if we cannot see its benefits at the time or appreciate the particular form in which it comes. For some reason, he believed, we both needed this exact experience.

We wandered about together, meeting other pilgrims. I asked them why they had come on this pilgrimage. Hearing my question, many women giggled embarrassingly, making me think the question was silly or strange. Very frequently I received only a curt reply. A shy young woman from rural Bengal told me simply: "To walk with Radha." A businessman from Calcutta said: "To see [darshan] the sites of Krishna's playful activities [lila-sthal]." This was a common response. An elderly Bengali woman answered: "I was seriously ill two years ago and thought about this pilgrimage. I thought it would help." A middle-aged man from Assam replied: "To make my life better." A second Calcutta businessman remarked: "To get away from the noise of the city and experience the peace of the forest." But by far the most frequent response I heard was the one first spoken to me by a seventy-two-year-old man who had retired from government service in the civil court at Calcutta and was performing the Ban-Yatra with his wife: "Although we are experiencing many difficulties, we are doing this pilgrimage to experience enjoyment." The Bengali word he used was "ananda."

Mr. Nath introduced me to three sannyasis he had met earlier. They had done the Ban-Yatra several times before and were obviously enjoying themselves. They, too, told me that they were performing this pilgrimage to get ananda. There was that word again, a word I would hear often in discussions about this pilgrimage during the next few weeks. How could such suffering lead to "enjoyment"?

Mr. Nath and I then went to a nearby well. Together we pulled on a long rope, bringing up buckets of water from deep within the earth. We splashed it about recklessly, taking turns pouring the cool liquid over each other's head. Returning with a bucket of drinking water to my tent, which was pitched on a dusty plain just below the pond, I learned that one of my tent mates was ill. She had a high fever and appreciated the cool water I offered her. This provided an opportunity to talk further with the women who shared my tent.

The name of the sick woman was Rajarani. Nearly seventy years old and now a widow, she was performing the pilgrimage by horse-drawn tonga. Some thirty to forty tongas accompanied our pilgrimage party, carrying those unable or unwilling to walk. According to the Mathura Mahatmya, journeys by carriage are not beneficial and should therefore be avoided.[93] But when pilgrims are as frail as Rajarani, perhaps exceptions are made. Rajarani was still quite beautiful; her soft brown skin glowed under white hair. She had always dreamed of coming to Braj to do this pilgrimage but had waited for the right opportunity. It had now come. She had traveled from Calcutta with her companion, Renu, a forty-year-old divorced nurse without any children. Renu had a sturdy build and a dark, broad face; her smile was firm but infectious. She had been on many pilgrimages—mostly to high mountain places—and declared this one to be the most difficult. There was a solid strength about Renu which I grew to count on during the following days. The third member of our tent was a widow from rural Bengal. The other two women did not even know her name. She was that type of Bengali widow who has in many ways been trained to remain invisible. I never did learn her name; I simply called her Didi, "older sister."

I went out again after talking with my tent mates. In the shade of a large tree growing on the other side of the pond, I encountered four members from my party who had come together from Bengal. They informed me that they were returning to Vrindaban the following day because one of their group was ill and the rest of them had concluded that the food was intolerable. These were poor farmers from outside Calcutta; if they thought the food was bad, imagine my thoughts. Again the question arose: What does all this suffering have to do with the journey through sweet forests, expressly in pursuit of enjoyment?

That evening many of us walked a short distance from our camp to a thickly wooded mound called Dhruv Tila. Shuklaji told me the story associated with the site.[94] Dhruv was a king's son who had left home at the age of five because he had been rejected by his father, then under the influence of a dominant queen. The favored queen told Dhruv that he could return to his father's throne only if he died and was reborn through her womb; his mother urged him to seek refuge with Lord Vishnu. After leaving the royal city, Dhruv met the sage Narada, who instructed him to proceed to Madhuban, a forest marked with the presence of Vishnu. There he was to bathe in the Yamuna River three times a day and engage in contemplation of Vishnu. After six months of austere practice, Dhruv had a vision of Vishnu, who as a boon gave him the promise of an eternal abode. Upon his death he assumed his place in the heavens as the polestar around which all other stars turn, located at the only spot in the universe that does not move. There is now a temple in this grove that houses an image of Vishnu appearing before Dhruv, who stands just to his left.

That night, as Dhruv was shining brightly over the tents, a doctor visited our camp. Many were already seriously ill. Renu worked late into the night, acting as the doctor's assistant. At one point she came for me; I was lying on my cot, just outside the tent. She had seen my feet earlier in the day and now insisted that I show them to the doctor. Before I knew exactly what was happening, I found myself lying face down on a wooden table behind a patchwork curtain in a dark tent. I was told to lie still and not look as they began to work on my feet with the aid of a flashlight and sharp instruments. I felt great pain as they worked and assumed from the conversation we had had in Bengali that they were cutting open the huge blisters that had developed on the balls of my feet, draining the liquid so I could walk more easily. They then applied some kind of medicine and bandaged both feet with white gauze.

I hobbled back to my cot just before midnight and settled down for what I had hoped would be a good night's rest. I was exhausted from the heat, the walking, and the lack of sleep the previous night. However, just as I began to drift off, someone switched on a loudspeaker and began shouting the names of the divine couple: "Radhe Shyam!" I had seen a few loudspeakers being set up that afternoon, along with several electric light bulbs. These were elevated by bamboo poles and powered by a generator lashed to a bullock cart. Either from lack of time or need, they had not been erected in our camp at Mathura. The loudspeakers had been used earlier in the day to make announcements, but now "Radhe Shyam" blared over the camp every thirty minutes, making continuous sleep impossible. The voice was insistent; from its force it seemed to be demanding that we join in the chant. I was greatly annoyed and felt that this was carrying the devotional element too far; I imagined that they even wanted us to dream of Radha and Krishna. Just let me sleep!

I had been told that we were to rise at three, but at 2:20 someone was shouting over the loudspeakers for us to get up. I resisted for some time, but twenty minutes later I was told that if I did not get my trunk onto the bullock cart soon, there would be no room. So much for another night's sleep. I swore and roused myself groggily from my cot. This was going to be much harder than I thought.

We were on the road by three. It was a beautiful, balmy, starlit night. Crickets and katydids chirped gently; the shouts of the bullock drivers urging on their bulls and water buffalo intermittently broke the melodious rhythm. Two shooting stars suddenly flared across the sky—an auspicious sign. I walked beside Renu, whose strength inspired me. She had stayed up for several hours last night, helping the doctor care for those in need, and must have had little or no sleep, yet her walk showed no sign of fatigue. Her steps were sure. She carried a bamboo walking stick and a fan of woven grass. As she walked, she sang Bengali songs in praise of Radha. Occasionally she would glance at me and a smile would flash across her face. We walked on together.

Our first site of the day was the smallest of the twelve forests, Kumudban, the "Lotus Forest," located about five miles southwest of Madhuban. A pond called Padma Kund, the "Lotus Pond," which is sometimes filled with lotus flowers, is the chief feature of the place. The most prominent building at Kumudban is a baithak of the saint Vallabha. The *Chaurasi Baithak Charitra* explains that a disciple of Vallabha's named Krishnadas Meghan asked Vallabha on this site why this forest was named the "Lotus Forest."[95] Vallabha told him that Krishna and Radha came to these woods on the night of the full autumn moon. Radha asked Krishna to create a forest of Kamoda and Kamodani trees. Krishna carried out her wishes and then added a pond full of lotuses. After explaining that this was the reason this forest was named Kumudban, Vallabha gave his disciples a divine vision which enabled them to see a bower of lotuses and flowering creepers.

We, however, were less fortunate and encountered a simple pond with few trees remaining on its shore. However, the vision of a typical Braj village that presented itself to our sight as the sky began to lighten had a charm all its own. To reach the pond we walked through a small cluster of mud houses with thatched roofs. Several cows were tied up in open courtyards. Dodging puddles of wastewater and fresh cow dung required constant vigilance in such villages. The villagers were just waking as we arrived and peered out at us with apparent curiosity. An old man of the village emerged from his house and told us that Radha and Krishna frolic in this pond after decorating each other with lotus flowers and making love in the surrounding forest. Because of this, he informed us, it is also called Bihar Kund, the "Pleasure Pond."

From Kumudban we marched six miles north through open fields to Shantanukund, where we were to set up camp for the night. Sharp pains shot through my feet with every step. I fought constantly to suppress the thought of giving up and going home. Visions of a comfortable couch in a cool room tantalized me. We arrived at Shantanukund in late morning. This is a beautiful pond where King Shantanu—the great-grandfather of the heroic Pandavas of the battle referred to in the *Mahabharata*—obtained a son by worshiping the sun. Couples desiring a son today come to bathe in this pond. It is surrounded by lush green trees and in the middle is a wooded island. Silvery doves fluttered about the trees of this island, linked to the shore by a red brick bridge. We filed across the bridge and climbed a long flight of stairs to the top of a small hill in the center of the island in order to reach the temple of Krishna as Shantanu Bihari. From here the distant countryside looked very dry. I thought of Narayan Bhatt's words concerning these ponds; for him they were a physical form of Krishna's grace.

The tents were pitched right on the road connecting Mathura and the town of Govardhan. Just behind our tent was a small swamp leading into productive farm fields. There would be no room to sleep anywhere but in the tent tonight. I moved my cot under a nearby tree to escape the afternoon sun. Close by was a small straw hut built on hard, hand-swept ground that a family used for shelter while tending the fields and animals. Several members came and went throughout the day: a woman and her two small children tended a lethargic water buffalo and her newborn calf; an old man with a thin white turban wrapped haphazardly on his head squatted to smoke a hookah. I lay down on my cot and relaxed to the gurgling sound of water as the old man drew on the hookah. I was soon joined under the tree by a horse belonging to a tonga driver. He stood motionless in the shade, slowly grinding his teeth. My feet were hurting so much that I decided to unwrap the bandages applied the night before. What I saw horrified me! I had assumed that the doctor had merely drained the blisters on my feet.

Now, in the light of day, I was shocked to see that he had cut away all the detached skin of the blisters, exposing the raw flesh within. The exposed flesh was very red and new blisters now covered the thin layer of skin that remained. While walking this morning, I had had moments when I actually looked forward with pleasure to visiting some of the sites on our journey which lay ahead. Determined to walk the entire way, I became obsessed with the trial, to push myself, to see what I could do. But that was before I saw the red meat of my feet poking out of the blisters. Now I just did not know. I was angry with the doctor, and I was worried that without the protective layer of skin the wounds would only get deeper and I would not be able to finish at all. Tomorrow we would be traveling fifteen miles, and many were advising me to ride in a tonga. What should I do?

I returned to my tent. After locking my valuables in my trunk, I grabbed my lota and limped across the road to an empty field and relieved myself of the questionable food I had eaten earlier. The flies did not even wait until I had finished before they busily began laying maggots on the gift I had left them. I had practiced using a lota with great apprehension before leaving the States, thinking that this would be the most difficult part of my experience. This now struck me as ridiculous. I then hobbled about half a mile up the road, secured a bucket of water from a deep well with my canvas bag, and bathed. I got great satisfaction out of performing these simple tasks. Their accomplishment somehow assured me that I was surviving. I returned to my cot and dressed my feet with some antiseptic I was carrying. Mohan, my dope-smoking cook, passed by and noticed my feet. When I mumbled something about the trouble they were causing me, he remarked: "Trouble? Lord Rama lived in the jungle for fourteen years and Krishna had to fight Kansa and his demons in these woods, and you speak of trouble." Perhaps he had a point, but I lay back on my cot to fret anyway.

Half asleep, I suddenly heard a voice: "Hello! How are you? Mahesh wants to know if you need anything." It was the voice of a merchant who has a shop in Vrindaban near my friend Mahesh. He and a companion had come in a car to visit some of the pilgrims from Manipur. My mind raced as I stared up at him. How could I ever tell Mahesh all I needed? I was in pain, I was hungry, I was hot, and I was lonely. I decided merely to send a letter to Shrivatsa Goswami through Mahesh telling him of the problems which had developed with my guide, Govinda. As the two drove off, I felt better, knowing that somewhere out there I had a friend who cared for me.

That night I settled down into my tent, my head only three feet from the occasional truck or bus whizzing by on the road, for what I hoped would be a badly needed good night's sleep. I was wrong. The shouting of "Radhe Shyam!" over the loudspeaker began again, this time every fifteen minutes. I had talked with other pilgrims that day; all had assumed that the shouting was mischievious and were as annoyed as I was last night. I covered my head and tried to block out the noise, but this did little good. Finally, in a fit of great anger, I leapt out of bed, determined to confront the source of the racket. On my way I encountered Amar Singh, a tonga driver I had met previously in Vrindaban. "Who is shouting 'Radhe Shyam'?" I asked impatiently. "We are," he replied. "What!" I exclaimed with vehement surprise. "Why?" I then learned that this was not devotional shouting, or at least not merely devotional shouting, but was the means by which our camp was protected. The tonga drivers stayed up all night wandering through the camp shouting "Radhe Shyam!" to each other to ward off dacoits, professional thieves who work this area. The loudspeakers were to discourage the dacoits by letting them know that the camp was being watched. They were not used the first night because we had the powerful protection of Bhuteshwar—and the Mathura police—but here our guards must have been greatly concerned, for the shouting continued all night. I climbed back in bed, but I knew I would not sleep.

We began walking at three the next morning. Before leaving the States, I had placed in my pack Toughskin, a type of bandage I use while hiking in the mountains of my home state of Colorado. It now came in handy; after covering the balls of my feet with a layer of this, I joined my group. Though I experienced great pain with every step, I was determined to complete the entire journey on foot and became obsessed with my vow to finish.

We first wandered north for about four miles, through fertile fields, until we reached Bahulaban, the fourth of the twelve forests. The name of this forest can simply mean "Forest of Plenty" but is more frequently associated with the story of Bahula, a virtuous cow who once inhabited this forest. Dharmaraj, the Lord of Truth, decided to test her and took the form of a lion. Trapping Bahula here in this forest, he roared out that he was going to eat her. Bahula, however, had a young calf hidden at a distance in the forest. She begged the lion to release her just long enough to suckle her calf one last time and promised to return. The lion agreed. After feeding her calf, Bahula returned as promised; at this point Krishna appeared and was so touched by her truthfulness that he rewarded her with the boon of being reborn as one of his wives. The name of this forest can thus also be understood as the "Forest of Bahula."

An old stone relief of Bahula is housed in a small temple perched atop a flight of steps on the southern shore of the pond that dominates this site. Pushti Margis tell the following story about this image.[96] Vallabha visited this site during his tour of Braj and read the *Bhagavata Purana* here for three days. As he was preparing to depart, the villagers came to him and informed him that the Muslim ruler of the area had prohibited them from worshiping Bahula, proclaiming that the worship could resume only after the image ate grass. Vallabha summoned this ruler to the image of Bahula; as the ruler looked on, the stone cow ate an offering of grass. Duly impressed, the Muslim begged to become a disciple of Vallabha. A baithak of Vallabha commemorates this visit to Bahulaban.

Today a village surrounds the central pond. It consists of adobe and brick structures strung out along twisting dirt lanes; cows are everywhere. Cow's milk, the blessing of Bahula, is the major ingredient of the sweets that provide great pleasure to the villagers of Braj. Milk, they say, is the delight of their life; without it life would be much less enjoyable.

As I entered the tiny temple of Bahula, I was joined by a crowd of small children. I took out my camera to photograph the image, and chaos erupted as they fought to get into the picture. I struggled with words and body to clear a path for a good shot.

Leaving Bahula behind, we walked westward toward Radhakund, eight miles away. The pain in my feet was excruciating, but on the way to Radhakund I witnessed an incident that made it well worth the effort. About a mile south of Radhakund is the little village of Mukharai, the residence of Radha's maternal grandmother, Mukhara. Mukhara's house is situated near a peaceful, wooded pond and a temple housing Radha, who stands between her mother, Kirttika, and her grandmother, Mukhara. This site elicited intense reactions in many of the pilgrims; there is an emotional element to this pilgrimage that is difficult to convey. A group of ten Bengali women began dancing wildly at the door of the house, shouting over and over, "Radhe! Radhe!" Suddenly one of the women collapsed and remained motionless. As she did this, five others fell beside her, weeping uncontrollably and rolling in the dirt, crying, "Radha! O Radha!" Many others joined in an ecstatic dance around them. This experience left them with no doubt that Radha had been here.

After this encounter with the presence of Radha, the pilgrims were filled with enthusiasm. All left the village of Mukharai energized, enthusiastically chanting Radha's name. As we walked along a narrow dirt path that wound through the green countryside, peacocks called out from the fields and nearby trees. Pilgrims responded to every call with vigorous shouts of "Radhe! Radhe!" They were primed for a visit to Radha's pond.

NOTES

1. A brahman is told in Sanatana Goswami's *Brihad-bhagavatamrita*: "*Oh fool, do not take sannyasa*. Quickly go to Mathura (Braj). There in Vrindaban you will undoubtedly have your desires fulfilled." I have taken this verse from Maura Corcoran, "Vrndavana in Vaisnava Braj Literature," Ph.D. diss., School of Oriental and African Studies, University of London, 1980, 213.

2. Owen M. Lynch, "The Mastram: Emotion and Person Among Mathura's Chaubes," in *Divine Passions*, ed. Owen Lynch (Berkeley: University of California Press, 1990), 97–98.

3. Ibid., 99

4. Entwistle, *Braj*, 252.

5. *Varaha Purana*, especially 153 and 161.

6. This act of "seeing" the image of a deity in a temple is one of the central practices of Hinduism. It is an act charged with religious meaning and a way for the seer to receive the blessing of the deity. For more, see Diana L. Eck, *Darsan: Seeing the Divine Image in India* (Chambersburg, Pa.: Anima Publications, 1981).

7. A comparable distinction of space is found in Japan, where Allan Grapard has shown that under the influence of Esoteric Buddhism "a clear distinction was made between the plains (the world of the secular) and the mountains (the world of the holy)"; see his "Flying Mountains and Walkers of Emptiness: Toward a Definition of Sacred Space in Japanese Religions," *History of Religions* 21, no. 3 (1982): 205.

8. Diana L. Eck, "The City as a Sacred Center," *Journal of Developing Societies* 2 (1986): 149.

9. This is a common theme in Indian literature; see, for example, Kalidasa's famous play *Shakuntala*.

10. As Freud would have it in "Beyond the Pleasure Principle."

11. These five are *Varaha Purana, Skanda Purana, Narada Purana, Adi Purana,* and *Padma Purana*. For more on this see Entwistle, *Braj*, 232–45.

12. Ibid., 234.

13. See Entwistle, "From Vraja to Braj."

14. *Varaha Purana* 167.2; I have changed Mathura to Braj in these transla-

tions, since the text is referring to the Mathura-mandala, which later came to be known as Braj.

15. *Varaha Purana* 150.15.

16. Ibid., 157.12, 13.

17. Ibid., 151, 152.

18. *Narada Purana*, Uttar Bhag 79.6–18.

19. Rupa Goswami, *Mathura Mahatmya*, ed. Puridas Mahashay (Vrindaban: Shachinatharay Chaturdhurin, 1946), verses 352–98, pp. 22–24.

20. See, for example, Chunnilal Shesh, "Braj-Yatra ki Parampara," in *Braj aur Braj Yatra*, ed. Seth Govindadas and Ram Narayan Agrawal (Delhi: Bharatiya Visva Prakashan, 1959), 91–111; P. D. Mital, *Braj ka Sanskritik Itihas*, 86–87; and Balji Tiwari, "Braj Yatra ki Parampara," in *Braj Vaibhav*, ed. Radheshyam Dvivedi (Mathura: Bharati Anusandhan Bhavan, 1972), 297–300.

21. See, for example, Shesh, "Braj-Yatra ki Parampara," 92. Uddhava's visit to Braj is in *Bhagavata Purana* 10.46–47.

22. *Padma Purana* 5.75 and *Narada Purana*, Uttar Bhag 80.

23. The *Narada Purana* has the lake Pushpasaras, though the two names have the same meaning.

24. *Skanda Purana*, Vaishnava Khanda 6.

25. I hesitate to call the concrete vehicle for conception or tangible form a symbol, as it is typically called, since the radical gap that is present in many Western religious traditions between what is called the signifier and the signified is relatively absent in the context of the religion of Braj. This point will become clearer in the next chapter.

26. Shesh, "Braj-Yatra ki Parampara," 97.

27. *Vraja Bhakti Vilasa*, p. 1 in Baba Krishnadas's introduction.

28. Vaudeville, "Braj, Lost and Found," 203.

29. Corcoran, "Vrndavana in Vaisnava Braj Literature."

30. Ibid., 215.

31. Ibid., 164.

32. Grapard, "Flying Mountains and Walkers of Emptiness," 207. The similarities between Tantric Buddhism and Braj Vaishnavism go beyond shared views of space. Both developed a pilgrimage wherein process was privileged over goal. About Japanese Tantric Buddhist pilgrimage Grapard writes: "The practice of pilgrimage is intimately related to the Buddhist notion that the religious experience was a process (ongoing practice) rather than simply the final goal of practice. . . . The processes involved in the pilgrimage were complex and had to become the basis for a complete change in the pilgrim's consciousness and perspective on the universe" (205–6). In both Japanese Buddhist pilgrimage and the Ban-Yatra, the entirety of the path is seen as sacred. A study exploring the close links between the Mahayana Buddhist notion of emptiness *(shunyata)* and the Vaishnava notion of lila is yet to be done.

33. Ibid., 220.

34. Narayan Bhatt, *Vrajotsava Chandrika*, ed. Krishnadas Baba (Kusumsarovan [Mathura]: Krishnadas Baba, 1960); *Narayana Bhatta Charitamrita*, ed. Krishnadas Baba with a Hindi translation (Kusumsarovar [Mathura]: Krishnadas Baba, 1957).

35. Janaki Prasad Bhatt, *Narayana Bhatta Charitamrita*, 1.25–28, p. 5. Emphasis added.

36. Narayan Bhatt, *Vraja Bhakti Vilasa*, verse 186, p. 100. The Sanskrit word I have translated as "body" is *vigraha*.

37. Narayan Bhatt is declared in Nabhaji's *Bhaktamala* to be well known for recovering all the sites named in the *Varaha Purana*. See Nabhaji, *Bhaktamala*, with commentary of Priyadasji (Lucknow: Naval Kishor, 1977), 589.

38. See Growse, *Mathura*, 75; Hein, *Miracle Plays of Mathura*, 226–27; and Entwistle, *Braj*, 254.

39. *Vraja Bhakti Vilasa*, verse 3, p. 177.

40. This differs from the pilgrimage of the Pushti Marg, which lasts for forty days and begins on the eleventh day of the bright half of the moon of Bhadon.

41. The ideal itinerary for the Pushti Margis was established by Brajnath (1849–1903), a descendant of Purushottam, who is credited with reviving the pilgrimage after it had ceased during the reign of Aurangzeb; see Entwistle, *Braj*, 268.

42. Madhavendra Puri is an important figure in the development of Braj culture. He was the guru of Chaitanya's guru Ishwar Puri. See Friedhelm Hardy, "Madhavendra Puri: A Link Between Bengal Vaisnavism and South Indian Bhakti," *Journal of the Royal Asiatic Society*, no. 1 (1974): 23–41.

43. *Chaitanya Charitamrita*, Madhyalila 17.227.

44. Shrivatsa Goswami, "Charaiveti! Charaiveti," 6.

45. Ibid. (Perhaps via Barbara Miller.)

46. For more on the life of Vallabha, see Richard Barz, *The Bhakti Sect of Vallabhacarya* (Faridabad: Thomas Press, 1976), 16–55.

47. This central event in the development of the Pushti Marg is recorded in a short text written by Vallabha entitled the *Siddhantarahasya*.

48. Entwistle, *Braj*, 263.

49. The Chaubes of Mathura claim that this brahman was a Chaube named Ujagar Chaube. A relationship was thus initiated between Pushti Margis and the Mathura Chaubes through this meeting of Vallabha and Ujagar Chaube.

50. Based on accounts such as appear in *Brihadaranyaka Upanishad* 1.4; see Robert E. Hume's translation, *The Thirteen Principal Upanishads* (Oxford: Oxford University Press, 1921), 81.

51. Much of what is expressed here is based on conversations with Shrivatsa Goswami relating to his article on the Ban-Yatra entitled "Caraiveti! Caraiveti."

52. This seemingly Mahayana Buddhist (first expressed in the Heart Sutra)

statement parallels the philosophical spirit of Gaudiya Vaishnavism, expressed by the phrase *achintya-bhedabhed:* inconceivable difference in nondifference.

53. Turner, "The Center Out There," 191–230; and, with Edith Turner, *Image and Pilgrimage in Christian Culture.*

54. Turner, "The Center Out There," 213.

55. Van Gennep's model is worked out in *The Rites of Passage* (Chicago: University of Chicago Press, 1975).

56. Victor Turner, *The Ritual Process* (Ithaca, N.Y.: Cornell University Press, 1969), 95.

57. Victor Turner, "Pilgrimage and Communitas," *Studia Missionalia* 23 (1974): 307.

58. Victor Turner, "Passages, Margins, and Poverty: Religious Symbols of Communitas," in *Dramas, Fields, and Metaphors* (Ithaca, N.Y.: Cornell University Press, 1974), 231.

59. See, for example, Dale Eickelman, *Moroccan Islam* (Austin: Texas University Press, 1976); Daniel Gross, "Ritual and Conformity: A Religious Pilgrimage to Northeastern Brazil," *Ethnology* 10, no. 2 (1971): 129–48; Morinis, *Pilgrimage in the Hindu Tradition;* Bryan Pfaffenberger, "The Kataragama Pilgrimage: Hindu-Buddhist Interaction and Its Significance in Sri Lanka's Polyethnic Social System," *Journal of Asian Studies* 38 (1979): 253–70; and M. J. Sallnow, "Communitas Reconsidered: The Sociology of Andean Pilgrimage," *Man* 16 (1981): 163–82.

60. These two types correspond roughly to what Jonathan Z. Smith, commenting on the work of Eliade, calls "a centrifugal view of the world which emphasizes the importance of the Center" and "a centripetal world which emphasizes the importance of periphery"; see his "Wobbling Pivot," in *Map Is Not Territory* (Leiden: E. J. Brill, 1978), 101. My typology is certainly not meant to be exhaustive. More types could be added, but my present concern is only with the comparison of these two. Others have developed typologies of pilgrimage—Bharati and Bhardwaj, for example, have developed typologies in terms of the size of the catchment area (see "Pilgrimage Sites and Indian Civilization" and *Hindu Places of Pilgrimage in India*)—but no one, to my knowledge, has developed a typology based on the shape of the journey.

61. Barbara G. Myerhoff, *Peyote Hunt: The Sacred Journey of the Huichol Indians* (Ithaca, N.Y.: Cornell University Press, 1974), 23.

62. Certain Hindu pilgrimages have been viewed as a return to the undifferentiated point of Brahma-bindu, represented by the central lingam in a Shaivaite temple; see the conclusion of Morinis in *Pilgrimage in the Hindu Tradition*, which is based on Stella Kramrisch's symbolic reading of a Hindu temple.

63. Ibid., 15–16.

64. Ibid., 245, where Myerhoff refers to Mircea Eliade's *Myth of the Eternal Return* (New York: Bollingen, 1954).

65. Circular journeys are also found in other traditions, particularly in Mahayana Buddhism. A good example that comes to mind is the Buddhist pilgrimage around the Japanese island of Shikoku. Oliver Statler writes that "this pilgrimage has no goal in the usual sense, no holy of holies to which one journeys and, after celebration in worship, returns home. This pilgrimage is essencially a circle: a circle has no beginning and no end" (*Japanese Pilgrimage* [New York: William Morrow, 1983], 26).

66. See Diana L. Eck, "India's Tirthas: 'Crossings' in Sacred Geography," *History of Religions* 20, no. 2 (1981): 323–44.

67. Entwistle, *Braj*, 106.

68. The notion that ritual space is a framed space has been explored by several interested in ritual. Jonathan Z. Smith, for example, writes of it as a "controlled environment" and "focusing lens" that marks and reveals significance; see his "Bare Facts of Ritual," in *Imagining Religion: From Babylon to Jonestown* (Chicago: University of Chicago Press, 1982), 53–65. Morinis writes of the pilgrimage arena as a space in which the "symbols and images associated with a pilgrimage are invested with a special and distinguishing significance because they are more concentrated, intensified versions of those available elsewhere," and "where the pilgrim sees, hears and imbibes in exceptionally undiluted clarity, the truths and experiences with which he has lifelong familiarity" (*Pilgrimage in the Hindu Tradition*, 209).

69. Owen Lynch found the same thing to be true. He writes that the "*parikrama* is an exercise in seeing things correctly as they really are" ("Pilgrimage with Krishna, Sovereign of the Emotions," *Contributions to Indian Sociology* 22, no. 2 [1988]: 188).

70. Edward C. Dimock, Jr., "Lila," *History of Religions* 29, no. 2 (1989): 166.

71. Lynch, "Pilgrimage with Krishna," 189.

72. Many examples of this can be found in the *Chaitanya Charitamrita*.

73. On the Gaudiya pilgrimage, the Bengalis and Manipuris tended to remain separate; I observed conflicts between various groups over supplies; and the Pushti Margi group arranged their tents daily in strictly hierarchical patterns.

74. Further similarities with pilgrimage in Mahayana Buddhism (often circular) can be noted. Grapard maintains that through pilgrimage practice "a larger consciousness was opened up" which "ultimately resulted in a sacrilization of the total human environment and all of human activity" ("Flying Mountains and Walkers of Emptiness," 221).

75. Eliade, *Myth of the Eternal Return*, 12–17.

76. Myerhoff, *Peyote Hunt*, 255.

77. Ibid., 250.

78. Ibid., 261.

79. The saint Vallabha did not consider Mathura as part of Braj. See, for example, James D. Redington, *Vallabhacarya on the Love Games of Krsna* (Delhi: Motilal Banarsidass, 1983), 188. Entwistle notes the sixteenth-century

transformation from the earlier type of pilgrimage associated with Mathura: "The primary motivation for pilgrimage was no longer to perform rites for one's ancestors, purify oneself and be absolved by bathing in sacred waters, attain liberation, or improve one's prospects in the next life, but to have some kind of vivid aesthetic and emotional experience in the here and now" (Braj, 276).

80. Romila Thapar, "The Early History of Mathura," in *Mathura: The Cultural Heritage*, ed. Doris Meth Srinivasan (New Delhi: American Institute of Indian Studies, 1989), 12–18.

81. Entwistle, *Braj*, 125.

82. Ibid., 117.

83. Thapar, "Early History of Mathura," 17.

84. Doris Meth Srinivasan, "Vaisnava Art and Iconography at Mathura," in *Mathura: The Cultural Heritage*, 390.

85. Cited in Growse, *Mathura*, 32–33.

86. Ibid., 34.

87. Entwistle, *Braj*, 175–76.

88. Growse, *Mathura*, 127.

89. Ibid., 37.

90. Ibid., 129.

91. *Varaha Purana* 158.63.

92. Paulinus of Nola, for example, wrote in the fourth century: "No other sentiment draws men to Jerusalem than the desire to see and touch the places where Christ was physically present, and to be able to say from our very own experience 'we have gone into his tabernacle and adored in the very places where his feet have stood' (Ps. CXXXII.7). . . . Theirs is a truly spiritual desire to see the places where Christ suffered, rose from the dead, and ascended into heaven. . . . The manger of His birth, the river of His baptism, the garden of His betrayal, the palace of His condemnation, the column of His scourging, the thorns of His crowning, the wood of His crucifixion, the stone of His burial: all these things recall God's former presence on earth and demonstrate the ancient basis of our modern beliefs." Quoted by Jonathan Sumption, *Pilgrimage: An Image of Mediaeval Religion* (Totowa, N.J.: Rowman and Littlefield, 1975), 89–90.

93. *Varaha Purana* 158.24.

94. This story is also told in *Bhagavata Purana* 4.8.9.

95. Gokulnath, *Chaurasi Baithak Charitra*, ed. Niranjandev Sharma (Mathura: Shri Govardhan Granthmala Karyalay, 1967), 16–17.

96. Ibid., 17–19.

3

Hungry Mountains and Ponds of Love

The city of Mathura is superior to heavenly Vaikuntha since Krishna took birth there. The forest of Vrindaban is even better because the love dance was celebrated there. Govardhan is even more sacred since Krishna delighted all by raising this mountain with his hand. But Radhakund pond is the best of all places, because it overflows with the nectar of Krishna's love. What sensitive person would not worship this pond situated at the base of Mount Govardhan?

RUPA GOSWAMI,
Upadeshamrita

A fierce demon named Arishta once took the form of a bull and attacked the encampment of cowherds.[1] Krishna met this demon just outside the encampment, ripped out its horns, and beat the demon to death with them. That night Krishna met Radha in the forest. He eagerly reached out to take her in his arms and make love to her. Radha teasingly stopped him, saying, "Hey Shyamsundar, you killed a bull today so you are unclean. Don't touch me!" Taken aback, Krishna asked Radha how he could cleanse himself of this polluting sin.[2] She informed him that he could cleanse himself of the heinous act only by bathing in the waters of every pilgrimage site, and further declared that only after he was completely clean could he touch her. Krishna was much too eager to make love to Radha to leave her for even a few minutes, let alone for the amount of time it would take to make the circuit of every pilgrimage site in the world. So he immediately shoved the heel of his foot into the ground, making a large crater,

100

and then summoned the sacred waters of all the various pilgrimage sites. These combined to make an enchanting pond. When it was full, Krishna quickly bathed in its waters. Radha was very impressed. Feeling rather proud about what he had accomplished, Krishna began to brag. Not to be outdone, Radha and her girlfriends took off their bracelets and dug a cavity of their own. Not a drop of water, however, came into the hole they had dug, so Radha and her girlfriends formed a line to Manasi Ganga, a pond located about three miles away on Mount Govardhan which Krishna had created earlier by mentally transporting water from the Ganges River. There they filled clay pots with water and began passing them down the line to supply water to fill their own pond. This, however, proved to be an impossible task. Seeing Radha in an embarrassing situation, Krishna gave her a wink and began filling her pond with sacred water from his own. Thus the sacred ponds of Radha and Krishna came into existence. The entire complex of the two ponds and the village which sprang up around them is frequently referred to as Radhakund.

We visited Radhakund our fourth day out. The emotions I saw exhibited at Mukharai were even more intensely demonstrated here. Everyone was excited; many of the pilgrims broke into tears as they rushed toward the pond. Radhakund is the most sacred of all sites in Braj for the Gaudiya Vaishnavas because of its associations with their beloved goddess Radha; the name is heard everywhere around this site and is written with mud, taken from the bottom of this pond, on the bodies of many who reside here. Moreover, of all ponds this one is declared to be the favorite of Krishna because it belongs to his dearest Radha.[3] According to the *Chaitanya Charitamrita*, when Chaitanya visited Braj he specifically sought out Radhakund, but no one could show him its exact location. By means of his meditative vision, he eventually found a small pond in a field which he identified as Radhakund and bathed in it with ecstasy. The work of excavating the pond, however, was left to Chaitanya's followers.

On his travels around Bengal, Chaitanya once met the son of a wealthy landowner. The son, later given the name Raghunath Das, had exhibited signs of deep religious feelings since childhood, which greatly disturbed his father, who had ambitious plans for his son. Raghunath's meeting with the charismatic saint produced a resolve; after escaping the vigilance of his apprehensive father, he joined Chaitanya and his band in Puri. Chaitanya gave him a stone from Mount Govardhan, which he worshiped daily with deep devotion. Raghunath stayed with Chaitanya until the latter's death in 1533 and then traveled to Braj, where he joined Rupa and Sanatana. Raghunath, too, was to be remembered as one of the Six Goswamis of Vrindaban. He settled in Braj at Radhakund pond, situated at the base of Mount Govardhan, and there passed the remainder of his life (d. 1582) worshiping the Lord of the Mountain and composing amorous poems about the love affair of Radha and Krishna. As there are no major temples in Radhakund, Raghunath's samadhi, or tomb, serves as the gathering point for many of the activities of the residents and pilgrims.

Raghunath Das, the first *mahant*, or head priest, of Radhakund, seems to have been the first to excavate the pond.[4] Radha's pond was excavated in 1546 and Krishna's pond, called Shyamkund (Shyam is a common name for Krishna), in 1553. While the excavation of Krishna's pond was under way, Raghunath had a dream in which King Yudhisthira revealed to him that the five Pandavas, the heroes of the *Mahabharata*, now resided on the banks of this pond in the form of trees. The pond was thus constructed so as not to disturb these trees, and consequently has an irregular shape. The trees around Radhakund were even protected by the Mughal authorities.[5] Land around the complex was officially purchased in the name of Jiva Goswami, who became the second mahant of Radhakund, and under his influence Raja Man Singh in 1591 had brick containments built for the ponds.[6]

Pilgrims are told another informative story about the excavations of this site, which is situated on the northern end of Mount Govardhan. One day when Raghunath Das was having a well dug so that he did not have to use the water from Radhakund pond for cleaning pots, the workers struck a stone that began to bleed. Raghunath immediately stopped the work. In a dream that night it was revealed to him that the workers had cut off the tip of Mount Govardhan's tongue. He was instructed to remove the stone and install it in a temple. The reddish stone, called Giriraj ki Jibhya, the "Tongue of Govardhan," is now housed in a small temple just to the north of Shyamkund, where it is offered milk daily. The Gopakup well remains on the eastern side of the ponds but has never been finished.

Pilgrims visiting the ponds today find them encircled with many small temples, stone houses, large trees, and meditation huts. Radha's pond is rectangular, whereas Krishna's pond has an uneven shape; the two are separated only by a narrow causeway. Sandstone steps leading down into the water were added in the early nineteenth century through the efforts of a wealthy Bengali merchant who took up the life of a homeless wanderer in Braj at an early age and became known as Lala Baba. A great variety of people can be observed descending the steps and floating flowers on the surface of the pond as an offering to the goddess. When I arrived at Radhakund with the Ban-Yatra pilgrims, the steps and walls surrounding the ponds had been freshly painted pink. With an occasional palm tree rising into the blue sky, it gave the impression of a Florida resort.

It is said here that Radhakund is nondifferent from Radha, and Shyamkund is nondifferent from Krishna. The two ponds are considered natural forms of the divine couple. This is usually supported by the assertion in the *Chaitanya Charitamrita* that "the sweetness of the pond is the same as the sweetness of Radha, and the greatness of the pond is the same as the greatness of Radha."[7] The two ponds, then, serve as concrete forms for theological contemplation of the relationship between Radha and Krishna. A passageway has been constructed under the causeway that separates the two ponds, allowing the sacred liquid which fills them to flow back and forth and intermingle. Radhakund and Shyamkund, then, are two bodies of water which share the same liquid. They are aquatic forms of the divine couple that can be compared to a pictorial illustration of Radha and Krishna attached to the walls of many homes and shops throughout Braj. In this illustration, entitled *ek pran do deha* (one life, two bodies), Radha and Krishna are portrayed standing wrapped in each others limbs so that it is difficult to distinguish where one body begins and the other ends. The real deity of Braj for the Gaudiya Vaishnavas is neither simply Krishna nor Radha but rather the dual divinity Radha-Krishna. One life, two bodies; one liquid, two ponds. These images tell us much about the basic concept of Gaudiya Vaishnava philosophy, which is expressed by the phrase *acintya-bhedabhed*: inconceivable difference in nondifference.

The Puranic expression of the relationship between Radha and Krishna is based on the Upanishadic account of the creative expansion mentioned in chapter 1: "In the beginning, Krishna, the Supreme Reality, was filled with the desire to create. By his own will he assumed a twofold form. From the left half arose the form of a woman, the right half became a man. The male figure was none other than Krishna himself; the female was the Goddess Primordial Nature, otherwise known as Radha."[8] Reality, in the Gaudiya tradition, is accepted as nondual, or *advaita*, and is apprehended as being, consciousness, and joy, or *sat-chid-ananda*.[9] Joy, the highest dimension of reality, however, requires a differentiation between the enjoyer and enjoyed. Love cannot take place in formless unity; love requires a body, in fact, love requires at least two bodies. For the taste of enjoyment, the nondual reality splits and becomes two bodies; in essence they are one, functionally they are two. Contemplation of the interconnected ponds of Radha and Krishna provides an opportunity to understand something of the highest experience of joy which comes from the reunion of two entities that were previously separated. "Separation gives rise to the pleasure of union, and conversely union contains a loving feeling of separation. In such intermingling the separate identities of lover and beloved dissolve into a single whole: two characters flow into each other; two separate entities become interchangeable."[10]

Philosophically expressed, Radha is Krishna's *hladini-shakti*, his power of bliss. She is the source of all joy, the power of all love, the root of all nature, and the embodiment of all sensual beauty. Her claim to divinity lies not in a long historical development but rather in the intensity of her emotion.

Compared with other Hindu deities, Radha's career is somewhat brief; she appears quite late in Hindu scriptures. In the *Bhagavata Purana*, usually dated in the ninth century, one gopi is singled out to receive the special favors of Krishna, though she is never mentioned by name. Contemporary Vaishnavas identify this gopi as Radha and claim that the author of the *Bhagavata Purana* did not write her name because she was too special.[11] Radha is named and the nature of her love is first celebrated openly in the *Gita Govinda*, the famous twelfth-century love poem of Jayadeva.[12] She enters the Puranic literature around the thirteenth century, and her place in Hindu tradition begins to find firm footing. Charlotte Vaudeville argues, however, that "her emergence in the cultic and devotional sphere of Vaishnavism as Krishna Gopala's beloved and *shakti* is known to have taken place rather late, certainly not much earlier than the sixteenth century. . . . It was in Vrindaban, in the heart of Braj country, that the *gopi* Radha, Krishna's sweetheart in popular tradition and the very embodiment of pure love for Krishna, came to be established as the latter's *shakti* and consort in the theological and cultic sphere."[13] The theology of Radha, then, is intimately connected with the cultural developments of Braj.

In Braj, Radha is a simple cowherd girl. Though she may sometimes be shy, she is nevertheless powerfully assertive and proud. Other gopis are more refined, particularly Radha's archrival, Chandravali, but Krishna is irresistibly attracted to the direct demeanor of Radha. Radha will let nothing stand in her way of getting Krishna. Whereas others attracted to Krishna treat him with a deferential respect due to their awareness of his awesomely majestic nature, Radha is not intimidated by Krishna and approaches him with the familiarity of a fellow villager. Because of this, Krishna finds Radha's love more intimate, powerful, and delightful. A verse from one of Rupa Goswami's dramas expresses much about the nature of Braj's beloved goddess:

> Just yesterday she was playing in the dust,
>   her ears newly pierced,
> Her hair, barely as long as a cow's ear,
>   tied with a colored thread;
> Oh, where has this Radha learned such proficiency
>   in the ways of love
> That she has conquered the unconquerable![14]

Radha is given a complete life history in Braj. She was born, or many say "found," by her father, Brishabhanu, at her mother's village of Raval, located slightly upstream from Krishna's childhood village of Gokul. She grew up in her father's village of Barsana, and later married and moved to her husband's village of Javat. There she lived with her husband, Abhimanyu, her mother-in-law, Jatila, and her sister-in-law, Kutila, always trying to escape the watchful eye of this trio to meet illicitly in the forest with Krishna.

Whatever ultimate connection Radha and Krishna might share, on the manifest level their relationship is an illicit affair; Radha is married to another. Vaishnava theologians have analyzed human emotions in great detail to determine which were the most passionate and therefore the most useful for devotion.[15] They concluded that the erotic relationship between a man and a woman is the most powerful, and among these kinds of relationships, the relationship between a man and a woman married to someone else is the most intense kind of love possible, for in this love the lovers risk everything, are free of the burdens of duty, and experience a love that is ever alive because it can never be taken for granted. Illicit love is an edgy affair, which does not take place in the center of domestic life. The boredom that results from assuming that one completely knows one's partner never occurs in the secret meeting of the forest, where the lovers are aware that each meeting may be their last. The love between the illicit lovers Radha and Krishna is, therefore, ever new and vital.

A sixteenth-century poem of Rupa Goswami gives an indication of the most intimate and therefore most special story associated with Radhakund for the Gaudiya Vaishnava tradition. The *Ashta Kaliya Lila Smarana Mangala Stotram* (The Auspicious Praise of the Remembrance of the Love Play Divided into Eight Time Periods) outlines the daily love play of Radha and Krishna in Braj.[16] Two of the eight time periods that make up a day are singled out as particularly significant, since they are twice as long as the other six. These are nighttime, when the couple make love in the forest of Vrindaban, and midday, when the two play their love games in and around Radhakund pond.

Rupa Goswami discloses in this poem that just prior to midday Krishna leaves his village under the pretense of tending the cows. Radha leaves her house in her husband's village, supposedly to perform the sun worship—ironically, intended for the benefit of the husband—and the two meet in secret at Radha's pond for an afternoon of love play. Radha and Krishna are especially fond of sporting in the water. Thus, this site is the most sacred of all in Braj for many Gaudiya Vaishnavas, because in addition to the fact that they believe it consists of the waters of all pilgrimage sites, they also believe it contains the love juice that flows between the divine couple. Rupa expresses this sentiment in the lines from his *Upadeshamrita* quoted at the beginning of this chapter. The very water of the pond itself is considered a concrete form of the love of Radha and Krishna, and is worshiped accordingly. Contact with the water of Radhakund pond is believed to be transformative, and virtually everyone who visits the pond desires to bathe in it.

Radhakund is the favored residence of practitioners engaged in a meditative technique called Raganuga Bhakti Sadhana, in which the practitioners visualize the lilas of Krishna and his intimate companions, and then enter the visualized scene by taking a dramatic role in the lila defined by a subtle double called the "perfected body."[17] Radhakund does not appear the same for one engaged in this meditative practice. Narottamdas Thakur, a leading figure in the development of Raganuga Bhakti Sadhana, described Radhakund as seen through the mind's eye of one trained in this meditative technique in a seventeenth-century text entitled the *Kunjavarnan* (Description of the Love Bowers).[18] This poem makes it clear that there is an important dimension of Braj that is not available to direct observation. Narottam's text is much too elaborate to reproduce in detail here, but the basic structure of the Radhakund shrine as he describes it is as follows.

The core of the shrine is a pond, sacred to Krishna because it is the pond of his dearest love, Radha. The pond is square, bordered on the four directional sides by four bejeweled stairways. At the top of each stairway stands a marvelous pavilion available for the love games of Radha and Krishna. A beautiful tree full of blossoms and hanging ornaments branches above the four pavilions, and at the four corners of the pond are attractive bowers of myrtle decorated with a variety of flowers. The goddess Vrinda serves the pond continually, refreshing it with fragrant waters. Red lotuses and white lilies grow in the waters of the pond, and swans and colorful gallinules float on its surfaces. A jeweled altar stands in the pond's center, and in the middle of the altar is a bed of bright, sweet-smelling flowers. Situated on this magnificent altar is the divine couple Radha and Krishna. A beautiful garden of flowers in which peacocks dance surrounds the entire pond, and the lovely sounds of parrots and songbirds fill the air. The entire shrine is attended by hundreds of female servants. The pond is encircled by eight delightful love bowers which are tended by eight close girlfriends of Radha, called sakhis, who help bring about her union with Krishna. Radha and Krishna make good use of each of these bowers, which are decorated with abundant varieties of fragrant flowers, jeweled ornaments, and colorful songbirds.

There is a tension in the Gaudiya Vaishnava tradition between the worldviews of householders and ascetics.[19] In a sense there are two Radhakunds in this tradition: the first is the physical pond reached through ordinary pilgrimage activity; the second is an eternal transcendent place that is perceptible only to the mind's eye and is reached only through meditative technique. The tension between the two is creative, for the two Radhakunds influence each other, and the division between the two is not firm, since the attainment of the second is aided by the first—those engaged in the meditative practices still believe it is important to reside at the physical site of Radhakund—and the sanctity of the first has much to do with its connection to the second. The distinction does, however, highlight the fact that the religion of pilgrimage is of a down-to-earth nature. Contact with the physical Radhakund is enough for the pilgrims. Pilgrimage is concerned primarily with manifest appearances, and pilgrims move through physical spaces. The ascetic, on the other hand, is concerned with a meditative technique designed to pierce appearances and reach a transcendent reality. Since this can be done anywhere, physical space is less important in the ascetic tradition. Again, this must not be taken as an indication of a rigid dualism in Gaudiya Vaishnava asceticism, since even the ascetics believe there is an important relationship between the physical Radhakund and the meditative Radhakund. They are two different perspectives of reality, not two different realities.

The day we camped at Radhakund was very hot. I found pockets of shade around the ponds where members of our group had sought shelter from the blazing sun. I began to notice increasing numbers of bandages on the feet of my fellow walkers, assuring me that I was not the only tenderfoot among the crowd. These times of hiding from the heat provided everyone abundant opportunity to talk, and as I was trying to meet as many people performing this pilgrimage as possible, I joined a few of the sheltered groups. Besides discussing the heat and the difficulty of the journey, the pilgrims shared stories about Radha and Krishna and the saints who had visited this place. The Ban-Yatra is an occasion to leave behind the regular duties of everyday life and indulge in stories dear to the heart, and what better place to do this than in Braj itself; every place visited evokes a story and provides a stage on which to experience the world of that story.

As I listened in the tremendous heat to the stories about the love play at Radhakund, I was struck by the great contrast between the outer world of physical suffering we were undergoing in this pilgrimage and the joyful, blissful, even erotic, inner world the pilgrims were celebrating. The Ban-Yatra pilgrims were deliberately pursuing the former for the latter. Again I wondered what this seeming disparity could be about. Whether in Bengali or Hindi, the two most common words I heard in discussions about this pilgrimage were *tapasya* and *ananda*. Pilgrims would frequently tell me, "This pilgrimage is very difficult; it is our form of asceticism [tapasya]." They would just as frequently say, and usually as a connected idea, "But we do it to experience joy [ananda]." Contrasts continually appeared: outer versus inner, difficult walking versus enjoyable stories, hard versus soft, ascetic versus erotic, painful versus blissful, suffering versus love, and masculine versus feminine. The relationship between these apparent oppositions still puzzled me.

It was late morning and time for my bath in Radhakund. I felt compelled to take one; everyone would ask me if I had done so. But the stories of this place had also captured my imagination, and I wanted to take a refreshing bath in its cool, sacred waters. Scores of pilgrims lined the edge of the pond, bathing and worshiping the pond of love with the aid of a priest. The priests carried plates on which flowers could be offered to the pond, as incense and small clay oil-wick lamps were waved above its water. As I neared the shores of the pond, a swarm of priests rushed toward me, each offering his respective services. I managed to disentangle myself from this enthusiastic web of entrepreneurs and retreated to an unoccupied corner of the pond to bathe alone. As I emerged from the water I asked Radha to forgive my strange and foreign ways and offered my own thanks to the source of love.

I then found a quiet courtyard overlooking the pond, where I could observe the worship of the pilgrims, reflect on the stories I had heard, and write in my notebook. Two green parrots, perched in a tree shading the courtyard, serenaded me as I worked. I was absorbed for some time, writing about the pond, when suddenly I was startled by the call of "Radhe! Radhe!" and looked up to find a young Bengali woman staring at me. She had smooth olive skin, long black shiny hair, and an alluring smile. Her eyes were deep and dark, simultaneously mischievous and mysterious. She was disarmingly attractive. She wore a yellow sari, the kind that female renunciants wear, and had "Krishna" written in the Bengali script with Radhakund mud on her forehead. She asked me what I was doing. I blurted out in the best Bengali I could muster at the moment that I was conducting research on the Ban-Yatra which had brought many of us to Radhakund. She looked at me with puzzled curiosity but seemed to accept my explanation. When I asked her what she was doing there, she informed me that she was living at Radhakund and conducting "research" on the love of Radha and Krishna. She repeated the word I had used for "research" in an obviously mocking manner. I felt nervous talking with her and did not wish to prolong our conversation. She seemed to understand this and left shortly after telling me her name. She was called Maya.

I continued my observations of the pond. I would be struck repeatedly by the extent to which ponds constituted a focus for this pilgrimage. We visited dozens of them while wandering through Braj, honoring many with a bath or some means of worship. Bathing (*snan*) in the ponds and honoring them by sipping their waters (*achaman*) are two of the most important practices listed in the older texts like the Mathura Mahatmya. Many say that the Ban-Yatra should be performed during the rainy season for the primary reason that this is when the ponds are full of water and are therefore fully manifest. The ponds of Braj are clearly considered to be natural manifestations of divinity.

That evening I met Nirmal Ghosh, a stocky, grizzled man of fifty-five years with a stubbly gray beard and a yellow sectarian mark smeared across his forehead. He used to sell grains and spices in Calcutta, but had now left this business to pursue a religious life in Navadvip, the town in Bengal where Chaitanya was born. He spoke with a loud, rough voice, laughed a great deal, and seemed to have few cares in the world. I liked him immediately; he was one of the most mischievous characters I was to meet. He pulled me around the two ponds, barking out the stories he had heard about each place we came to.

That night I set up my cot in a cow pasture behind our tent and watched a gorgeous sunset. During this season the Braj landscape assumes a special charm. A former British district magistrate of Mathura, Frederick Growse, after disparaging the physical appearance of Braj, wrote: "In the rains however, at which season of the year all pilgrimages are made, the Jamuna is a mighty stream, a mile or more broad; its many contributory torrents and all the ponds and lakes, with which the district abounds, are filled to overflowing; the rocks and hills are clothed with foliage, the dusty plain is transformed into a green sward, and the smiling prospect goes far to justify the warmest panegyrics of the Hindu poets, whose appreciation of the scenery, it must be remembered, has been further intensified by religious enthusiasm."[20] The subtle beauty of the land of Braj was slowly beginning to reveal itself.

It is the land of Braj itself that is the chief focus of this pilgrimage. In an insightful article which examines the origin and development of the Ban-Yatra, the Hindi scholar Seth Govindadas argues that this pilgrimage is rooted in Hindu nature worship traceable to the early Vedic period of some three thousand years ago.[21] He maintains that the natural phenomena of Braj were worshiped first; the forests, groves, rivers, mountains, ponds, and even dust were first considered holy because of their identification with Krishna. Later temples were built on the important sites, and images were installed. Although today the pilgrims worship in these temples, the worship of nature (*prakriti-puja*), he insists, remains more important in the Ban-Yatra than the worship of temple images (*murti-puja*). For many, the Ban-Yatra is a celebration of a divine environment. This can best be seen in the sites and activities situated around Mount Govardhan.

Part of an extension of the Aravalli mountain range of Rajasthan, Mount Govardhan is a long, narrow, crouching hill located on the southern rim of the circuit of Braj. This rocky ridge, whose slopes are covered in many places with shrubs and small trees, is only seven miles long and rises to an average height of only about one hundred feet, but it is one of the most prominent and sacred features of Braj. The anthropologist Paul Toomey has written: "The cluster of sacred places is so great at Govardhan that one gets the impression of having entered a veritable 'Krishna's Coney Island.'"[22] Mount Govardhan has been worshiped longer than any other natural phenomenon in Braj; Entwistle remarks that Govardhan is "almost certainly the oldest sacred object in Braj."[23] The earliest iconographic representations of Krishna discovered in this area feature him holding up Mount Govardhan.[24] As one of the most clearly identifiable markers of the episodes described in Vaishnava scriptures, Mount Govardhan served as a starting place for many of the early activities in Braj. Several stories are told about this important site.

The cowherds of Braj used to worship Indra, the ruler of the gods. Indra lived in a magnificent celestial palace and was in control of the rain clouds. The cowherds under Nanda worshiped Indra, assuming that he protected their cows. As the cowherds were preparing for their annual worship of Indra, Krishna stopped them; he pointed out that they were not settled cultivators but nomadic cowherds who roamed about the forests, and therefore should have little to do with Indra. Instead, he argued, they should worship Mount Govardhan, the true "nurturer" (*vardhan*) of cows (*go*), upon whom they depended. He proposed that they circumambulate Mount Govardhan and offer to it the food collected to worship Indra. Krishna then assumed the form of the mountain and from its summit announced: "I am the Mountain."[25] Brajbasis will often say that Krishna merged with all the stones and said, "I am hungry!" As the hungry mountain, Krishna proceeded to devour, through a crack in the hill, the heap of food assembled by the cowherds.

Needless to say, Indra was not pleased; he unleashed his fury on the cowherds in the form of a violent storm. While incessant torrents of rain poured fiercely from the dark clouds, the frightened cowherds sought shelter with Krishna. Krishna responded by lifting up Mount Govardhan and holding it on the little finger of his left hand, a giant umbrella to protect the cows and cowherds while Indra exhibited the full force of his destruction for a period of seven days. Finally, Indra realized who he was dealing with and surrendered. The cowherds then understood that Krishna was the true protector of cows and from that day worshiped Mount Govardhan as their chief deity.[26]

Mount Govardhan is worshiped today in a variety of ways by the residents of Braj who regularly circumambulate the mountain. Govardhan stones are set up and worshiped in innumerable shrines around the area. Unlike ordinary manufactured images that need to be installed (*pratistha*) by a brahman priest, Govardhan stones do not require such formal consecration; every stone from the mountain is considered to be a natural form (*svarup*) of Krishna. The residents of Braj also feast the mountain during an annual festival called Govardhan Puja, or Annakut. The latter, an early name for Mount Govardhan,[27] means "mountain of food." During the season just after the rains have stopped,[28] the women of Braj construct in the courtyards of their homes cow-dung images of Krishna holding Mount Govardhan.[29] In a hollow at his navel is placed a dish into which is offered milk and sweets. A mountain of rice, called Annakut, is placed before the cowdung figure. Family members then walk around the image singing songs of praise to Mount Govardhan.[30]

According to a story frequently told in Braj, Mount Govardhan used to reside in the Himalayan range far to the north.[31] During the previous age Lord Rama was engaged in battle with the ten-headed demon Ravana, who had abducted Rama's wife, Sita, and carried her off to the island of Lanka. Rama enlisted the aid of a vast army of monkey warriors, who prepared for an invasion of Lanka by building a huge bridge to link the island with the mainland. Some of the monkeys journeyed to the distant Himalayas to fetch mountainous boulders for the bridge. Hanuman, the macho general of the monkey army and eager devotee of Rama, picked up an entire mountain named Giriraj, "King of the Mountains," and flew off with it toward Lanka. Midway, however, Hanuman got word that the bridge had been completed, and so dropped the mountain where he was. Realizing that his golden opportunity had just slipped away, Giriraj addressed Hanuman: "I made myself light for you to carry, because I was pleased to go and be of service to Rama. But now, I am being deprived of the sight and touch of Rama, the very reason I agreed to leave the home of my mother and father." Giriraj then began to complain to Rama, claiming that a great injustice had been done to him. Lord Rama appeared and blessed him, saying, "Do not worry! In the next age I will lift you with the finger of my own hand and will make you worthy of worship." All other mountains carried off to create the bridge would be touched by the Lord's feet, but only Giriraj would be held high above the Lord's head, making it very special.[32] From that time onward, this mountain became identified as one of the main forms of the Lord.

Various stories are told to account for the small size of the mountain today. Here are two: Once the sage Paulastya was wandering about and came to the Vindhya mountain range, where he saw the beautiful mountain Govardhan.[33] Since there were no such mountains near his home in Banaras, Paulastya desired to take Govardhan there so that he would have a peaceful place to meditate. The sage proposed this to Govardhan's father, Vindhya, who out of fear of a sage's curse felt obliged to agree to the proposal. Sadly, Govardhan accepted the plan, but he established a condition. He told the sage: "I agree to stay in your hand, but you must not put me down anywhere. If you put me down somewhere, I will go no farther." The sage agreed, and Govardhan sat on his hand. Soon the two arrived in Braj. Up to this point

Govardhan had been very light, but here he became very heavy; the sage was unable to carry him any further and placed him on the ground. After performing his evening meditations, the sage tried again to pick up Govardhan but failed. The sage then became very angry and began to curse Govardhan: "If you stay here you will decrease in size by the quantity of one sesamum seed each day." Govardhan accepted this curse because he knew that Krishna would manifest himself here and play on his slopes. Govardhan used to be a very high mountain, but for this reason he is now short.

Another version of this story reveals that even mountains desire to go on pilgrimage. Mount Govardhan—or Giriraj—was once located in the Vindhya mountain range.[34] The great sage Agastya had once gone there while touring pilgrimage sites and had recounted his travels to a group of saints who had gathered around him. The son of Vindhya was nearby and overheard the conversation. He soon developed a great desire to go on pilgrimage and requested the sage to take him along on his journey. The sage agreed and set out with Giriraj in the palm of his hand. After touring some of the famous pilgrimage centers the two came to Braj. Early one morning Agastya put Giriraj down with orders to stay put while he went off for his morning toilet. While the sage was away Govardhan heard voices in the sky; the gods were discussing their plans to manifest as cowherds in Braj because Krishna was soon to be born there and perform his lilas. Giriraj became greedy in his heart and began to think that whereas he would see only an image of the Lord at the pilgrimage sites, here he would have a direct view of the Lord in human form; moreover, he thought, there was a chance that the Lord's feet would touch him. He thus resolved not to move from the spot. When the sage Agastya returned he ordered Giriraj to get back on his hand, but Giriraj said: "Maharaj, I told you before that I am immovable. Wherever I am put down, there I must stay. So I will not get back on your hand." Giriraj then became very heavy, and because of this the sage cursed him: "You are foolish. You have a big body. So what! You will decrease by the size of one sesamum seed every year. In the end this body of yours will completely vanish." In the past, they say Govardhan used to stretch to the forests of Vrindaban, and the Yamuna used to flow at its base, but this is no longer the case.

In all these stories Mount Govardhan is conceived of as a living being. There are a number of local traditions regarding the form the hill takes. Some see it as a cow, some as a lion, and some as a snake. A popular Gaudiya view has it that Mount Govardhan is a peacock, with its two eyes at Radhakund and Krishnakund, its stomach at Manasi Ganga, and its tail at Punchari.[35] The most popular view, however, is that the hill is Krishna in the form of a playfully hungry cowherd boy.

We encountered the sites of Mount Govardhan on the morning of the fifth day of our journey. After getting up at three—I actually slept this night—we left the Radhakunda complex and began the fourteen-mile circumambulation of Mount Govardhan. As we began our clockwise journey around the mountain, several of the pilgrims picked up three pinches of dirt from its base and popped each into their mouths. This northern end of the mountain is not much more than a mound covered with a tangle of small trees and bushes. We came first to Kusum Sarovar, the "Flower Pond." This site is uninhabited and remains remarkably quiet most of the year except for the occasional bursts of pilgrims. The square pond is lined with sandstone steps and octagonal pavilions featuring arched windows facing the water, which catch the cool breezes coming off the pond and give a view of the huge turtles that inhabit its waters. Impressively ornate cenotaphs stand in gardens of flowers on its western shore, built in memory of Suraj Mal Singh and his two wives. Suraj Mal was king of Bharatpur, a devotee of Mount Govardhan, and a great patron of Braj; he will be discussed in chapter 4. An attendant arranges fresh flowers on the white marble footprints of Krishna that cover his remains inside a domed chamber decorated with elaborate paintings of the stories of Braj. Shuklaji told me that Radha comes to this pond with her girlfriends to gather flowers for her lover, Krishna. The pond, said to have once been surrounded by a beautiful forest of flowers, is where Krishna, while tending his cows one day, met Radha and after making love to her braided fresh flowers into her hair. A temple on the southeastern corner of the pond named Ban Bihari, or "He Who Sports in the Forest", celebrates this lila, though the images depicting Krishna braiding Radha's hair have been stolen.

Kusum Sarovar is the pond in which the celestial sage Narada bathed to obtain the body of a gopi, which then allowed him access into the intimate lila grounds of Braj. To the southwest of Kusum Sarovar is another pond called Narada Kund; Narada later bathed in this pond to transform himself back into a male. This incident is marked by a temple, which stands on the shore of this pond and houses an image of Narada. A temple to Uddhava, the close friend and adviser of Krishna sent to console the gopis after Krishna left Braj, is located on the southwestern corner of Kusum Sarovar. After being transformed by the gopis' passion for Krishna, Uddhava prayed: "Let me become one of the shrubs, creepers, or herbs of Vrindaban, which are fortunate to have come in contact with the dust from the feet of the gopis, who have left even their families and the path of virtue—both of which are difficult to give up—to pursue Krishna, who is sought by the seekers of the highest knowledge."[36] Uddhava now resides on the bank of Kusum Sarovar in the form of a creeper, ever able to observe the lilas of this pond. A sign from the British period, dated 1866, stands on the southeastern corner of the pond and prohibits the harming of wildlife in the vicinity of Mount Govardhan.

We next came to the town of Govardhan, situated in a wide cleft that slices through the middle of the mountain. This is one of the most popular sites visited by those seeing Braj by bus, since it is on the road connecting Mathura with the Rajasthani town of Dig. Growse reports that the rocks of the mountain had to be covered with dirt before the road could be laid by the British, in order to show respect for the mountain.[37] The town encircles a large pond named Manasi Ganga. Many of the temples and Rajput buildings that surround the pond were built by the kings of Bharatpur, who ruled the area of Braj in the eighteenth and nineteenth centuries. Manasi Ganga was first encased with stone steps in the sixteenth century by Raja Man Singh of Amber, and was repaired and maintained by the kings of Bharatpur. On the night of Diwali, the autumn festival of light, the pond is worshiped and ringed with thousands of small oil-wick lamps. A story is told about how this pond came into existence.

One day when Krishna was grazing his cows at the foot of Mount Govardhan a demon named Vatsasur disguised itself as one of his calves. Krishna recognized and killed this demon before it could do any damage, but in so doing he incurred the sin of killing a cow.[38] In order to expiate this sin Krishna mentally transferred water from the Ganges River into a hollow in the center of the mountain, thus creating Manasi Ganga, the "Mental Ganges." Sometime later, Krishna's father, Nanda, was preparing the cowherds for travel to the Ganges for a sacred bath.[39] Not wanting them to leave Braj, Krishna stopped them, saying, "The Ganges is right here!" Having announced this, Krishna surprised the cowherds by causing the goddess of the Ganges to manifest out of this pond. The cowherds honored the goddess by bathing in the pond and offering a ring of lamps around her shore.

Historically, the most important temple in the town of Govardhan is the Haridev temple, situated on the southern bank of Manasi Ganga. The image is of Govardhan Dhara, Krishna holding Mount Govardhan aloft on the little finger of his left hand. This is one of the four major

Krishna temples said to have been established by Krishna's great-grandson Vajranabh. The present temple is an old structure, built in 1580 out of red sandstone by Raja Bhagawan Das of Amber, who had shortly before joined the service of the Mughal emperor Akbar. It later came under the patronage of the Bharatpur kings, who managed the temple until independence. The Mathura Mahatmya of the *Varaha Purana* and other old pilgrimage itineraries mention that one should begin the circumambulation of Mount Govardhan after first bathing in Manasi Ganga and then visiting the temple of Haridev.[40] Both Chaitanya and Vallabha are recorded as having begun their circumambulation of the mountain in this manner.

The most popular temple in the town of Govardhan today, however, is the temple of Mukut Mukharavind, located in the shallow waters of the eastern edge of the Manasi Ganga pond. This temple was built by one of the kings of Bharatpur, the primary patrons of Govardhan. After independence in 1947, when power was taken away from local kings, the Mukut Mukharavind temple was much more successful than the Haridev temple in competing for the attention of the new patrons—the pilgrims themselves.

The title of this temple refers to two stones that emerge from the pond and are worshiped as Krishna's "crown" (*mukut*) and "lotus mouth" (*mukharavind*). The latter rock has a depression into which pilgrims offer huge quantities of milk. A chaotic crush of pilgrims carrying a wide assortment of containers shoved to get into this temple. As I squeezed in with them one of the attending priests slung a flower garland drenched in milk around my neck. He laughed and waited for a money gift; I observed the lively activity and excess of offerings with milk dripping down my chest.

There is an old temple on the northern side of Manasi Ganga named Chakreshwar, or "Lord of the Circle." This is another of the four main Shiva shrines established by Vajranabh, and houses five lingams. The Shankara priests of this temple say that Shiva is the protector of Braj, here remembered for drinking up all the waters left behind by the violent seven-day storm unleashed by Indra. Other sources say this is called the place of the Chakra because Krishna dried up the floodwaters with the fiery power of his *chakra* (discus).[41] A meditation hut used by Sanatana Goswami, who for a time used to circumambulate Mount Govardhan daily, is nearby. The story is told that mosquitoes were once so thick in this area that they were disturbing his worship. Sanatana had decided to leave when Chakreshwar, disguised as a brahman, appeared before him and promised that mosquitoes would no longer bother him. The local inhabitants claim that this place is still clear of mosquitoes. There is also a baithak on this spot where Vallabha performed a seven-day reading of the *Bhagavata Purana*. The *Chaurasi Baithak Charitra* tells that Shiva as Chakreshwar appeared to hear each day's reading.[42]

We visited the temple of Dan Ghati before leaving the town of Govardhan. This temple is located in the narrow crevice of the mountain where it is said that Krishna once stopped the gopis and demanded a gift (*dan*). Krishna here is Daniray, or "Lord of the Giver," and assumes the form of a large elaborately dressed Govardhan stone, also the recipient of large quantities of milk. Milk-drenched flowers, boxes of sweets, and scores of oil lamps adorned the stone, which is now enclosed in cement walls. The resident priests press the pilgrims for donations. The Mathura road now passes through this crevice, making it another spot popular with those touring Braj by bus. Some buses stop long enough for the passengers to get out and peer over a wall to see the sacred stone below; others whiz by while riders toss coins out of the windows.

Anyor is the first village we encountered on the circumambulatory path after leaving the town of Govardhan. This village, located on the eastern side of the mountain, was once the site of a Buddhist monastery.[43] It now consists of a few brick buildings and mud huts scattered among the shrubs and rocks that lead to the summit of the mountain. A large old temple situated on top of the hill is visible from here. Several of the pilgrims stopped to rest and take refreshments in the local tea shop. The midmorning sun was well into the sky and shimmered off the walls of the temple. Many associate Anyor with the site of the Annakut feast, in which Krishna in the form of Mount Govardhan consumed huge quantities of food.[44] In fact, a popular derivation of the name Anyor is *an or*, which means "Bring more!"—words spoken by Krishna as the hungry mountain when he wanted another helping.[45] It is also a site associated with the discovery of the image of Shri Nathji, which was once housed in the old temple that looms above the village. This is perhaps the most important of all the images of Krishna established in Braj. Both Gaudiya and Pushti Margi sources credit the saint Madhavendra Puri with a key role in the discovery of the image of Shri Nathji and the establishment of the worship of Krishna at Mount Govardhan at the end of the fifteenth century, though their respective sources differ over the nature of his initiative.

Madhavendra Puri was most likely a member of a Vedantic school that followed the monistic teachings of Shankara but drew inspiration from the *Bhagavata Purana* and emphasized devotion. He came to Braj toward the end of the fifteenth century. Whether he came from Bengal or from southern India is unclear, but regardless, he brought with him a form of Vaishnavism linked to the southern Indian bhakti movements that can be traced back to the ninth-century mysticism of the Alvars, which emphasized an intimate relationship with the Lord.[46] His influence on the Gaudiyas is particularly significant, since he was the guru of Chaitanya's guru, Ishwara Puri, who initiated Chaitanya into the "maddened" love of Krishna.

Madhavendra Puri's role in establishing the worship of Krishna at Govardhan is told from a Gaudiya perspective in Krishnadas Kaviraja's *Chaitanya Charitamrita*.[47] After arriving in Braj, Madhavendra approached Mount Govardhan and, becoming mad with love, circumambulated the hill with great reverence. He then took a bath in Govindakund, a pond just down the trail from Anyor, and sat beneath a tree for his evening meditation. While sitting there he was approached by a beautiful cowherd boy who offered him some milk and began pestering him with questions: "Why do you not eat? And why are you meditating?" Madhavendra Puri was surprised the boy knew he was fasting. He asked the boy where he had come from. The boy replied that he was from a nearby village, and further informed him that no one in this area fasts; therefore, the boy had been sent to give Madhavendra milk. The boy then disappeared. That night Madhavendra had a dream in which the boy returned to him and took him by the hand to a bower in a nearby forest. The boy explained that he resided there, suffering cold rains and scorching winds, since a priest had hidden him there long ago out of fear of a Muslim attack. The boy, who revealed himself to be Krishna-Gopal, the one who supports Mount Govardhan, instructed Madhavendra to take the image out of this bower, wash it with water from Govindakund, and install it in a temple on top of the mountain. The next morning Madhavendra Puri uncovered an astonishing life-size image of Krishna with his left arm raised to hold Mount Govardhan and performed the requested tasks with the assistance of the villagers. He then organized a huge Annakut feast to be offered to the deity. After overseeing the temple service for two years, Madhavendra had another dream that sent him on a trip to southern India in search of sandalwood paste to cool Krishna-Gopal. The service of the temple was turned over to some Bengali priests, and Madhavendra set off on his journey. He never returned.

While Gaudiyas portray Madhavendra Puri as the primary agent behind the discovery and worship of the image that was to be established atop Mount Govardhan, Pushti Margi sources tell a different story. According to the *Shri Nathaji Prakatya Varta*, a text attributed to Hariray, a great-great-grandson of Vallabha who lived in the seventeenth century, the image was first discovered by an Anyor villager named Saddu Pande.[48] One day a cow that belonged to Saddu Pande was missing. While searching for the cow on Mount Govardhan, Saddu Pande discovered an arm sticking out of the ground.[49] He was informed by a strange voice that this arm belonged to Krishna, who lifted Mount Govardhan and was now standing in a rock cave beneath the mountain. Saddu Pande and the residents of the surrounding villages began worshiping the arm with milk. Sixty-nine years later, on the day Vallabha was born, the mouth of the image appeared and Saddu Pande was instructed to feed it daily with milk. About this time, Madhavendra Puri arrived at the house of Saddu Pande in Anyor and asked to see the image that had appeared out of the hill. Madhavendra tried to offer the deity solid food, but the deity informed Madhavendra that he would accept his first food only from the hands of Vallabha.

When Vallabha arrived at Govardhan in 1492,[50] he installed Shri Nathji—the name given to the deity by the Pushti Margis—on a pedestal and began offering him solid food. Soon after, a wealthy merchant named Purnamal had a dream in which Shri Nathji asked him to finance the construction of a temple on Mount Govardhan. Hiramani, a renowned architect from Agra who had a similar dream, began laying the foundation of the temple in 1499. When it was finished in 1519, Vallabha initiated the elaborate temple service that has come to characterize the worship of Shri Nathji. Vallabha appointed Madhavendra Puri and some of his Bengali followers residing at Radhakund to conduct the service. The Bengali priests served Shri Nathji in his temple atop Govardhan for fourteen years until they were expelled by the temple manager, Krishnadas, a Pushti Margi who was supported by Todar Mal and Birbal, two powerful Hindu officers serving in Akbar's court in Agra.[51] Pushti Margi sources claim that Shri Nathji was displeased with the Bengali priests because they had installed an image of the goddess Vrindadevi beside him and were sending temple funds to their gurus in Vrindaban. To eject the resistant Bengalis from the temple, Krishnadas set fire to their huts while they were engaged in the worship of Shri Nathji. When the Bengalis ran down the hill to put out the fires, Krishnadas took possession of the temple and blocked their return, claiming that they cared more about their huts than they did Shri Nathji. The expulsion of the Bengalis from the Shri Nathji temple is one of the earliest signs of the developing competition between the two sects in Braj. Shri Nathji was removed from the temple on Mount Govardhan in 1669 because of growing fears caused by the anti-Hindu activities of the Mughal emperor Aurangzeb. After a two-year sojourn, the deity ended up in the Rajasthani desert just north of Udaipur. A new temple was constructed in the desert, and a village sprang up around it that came to be known as Nathdwara. The Shri Nathji temple of Nathdwara is now the most popular Krishna temple in the world.

Vallabha's second son, Vitthalnath, was responsible for the development of the elaborate style of temple ritual that came to be associated with the worship of Shri Nathji. The embellishments included the use of seasonally varied perfumes, jewels and ornate clothing, flowers, and abundant food offerings. Vitthalnath also increased the importance of music in the temple; Pushti Margi sources credit him with appointing eight poets to sing before Shri Nathji. These came to be known as the Ashtachhap, or "Eight Seals." There were four disciples of Vallabha—Surdas, Paramanadadas, Kumbhandas, and Krishnadas—and four disciples of Vitthalnath—Chaturbhujdas, Nandadas, Chhitswami, and Govindaswami. Perhaps best known among them is the blind poet Surdas.

According to the *Chaurasi Vaishnava ki Varta*, an early eighteenth-century work compiled by the important Pushti Margi writer Hariray, Surdas was born blind just north of Braj to poor brahman parents.[52] At age six he left home and soon began to attract followers with his moving songs and rare ability to see things those with normal vision could not. He eventually arrived in Braj and settled on the bank of the Yamuna downstream from Mathura. There he met the saint Vallabha, an event that transformed his life. Vallabha changed Surdas's self-pity by initiating him into the celebration of Krishna's lila. He then established Surdas at Mount Govardhan, where the poet composed songs to be used in the liturgy of the temple. The poems of Surdas demonstrate the important role of poetry in the religion of Braj. Almost every gathering in Braj is marked by poetic celebration. These poems have been called "verbal icons";[53] they convey subtle theology, generate emotional experience, and give access to "a reality that would not otherwise be there."[54]

Pushti Margi sources claim that Shri Nathji, the Lord of Govardhan, showed special favor to Surdas on a number of occasions. One time Surdas was eating his noon meal and the boy who tended him had gone to fetch water. While he was away Surdas began to choke on a piece of food. Gagging, he reached for his water pot, but the boy had yet not returned. Realizing the severity of the situation, Shri Nathji placed his own water vessel within Surdas's reach and allowed the poet to drink from his own golden cup. Surdas continued on, living a life of increasing fame. Pushti Margi sources maintain that Surdas's reputation was so great that the Mughal emperor Akbar paid him a visit in Mathura and tested his devotion by requesting that the blind poet compose a poem in praise of Akbar himself. Surdas passed the test by responding with a poem which declared that there was no room in his heart for anyone but Krishna. When his death drew near, Surdas went to die at Parasoli, a site on the eastern side of Mount Govardhan where Pushti Margis believe Krishna performed the rasa-lila (the amorous circle dance with Radha and the gopis) and caused the moon to stay full for a night which lasted six months. The octagonal pond of Chandra Sarovar, the "Moon Pond," now dominates this site. On the southwestern side of this pond stands the memorial tomb of Surdas, an important station on the Pushti Margi Ban-Yatra.

Leaving Anyor we walked less than a mile to Govindakund. This is a beautiful, serene pond, surrounded on all four sides with sandstone steps. Brilliant green shade trees and the clear blue sky were reflected on the mirrored surface of the pond. When we arrived a small group of colorfully dressed women had just finished washing their clothes; the steps around them were covered with bright pieces of cloth. I had been walking with Shuklaji since spotting him at a tea stall in the village of Anyor. He suggested that we sit on the steps of this pond for a few minutes while he told me its story.

After Krishna had raised Mount Govardhan and defeated Indra's attack on the cowherds, Indra was humble and ashamed, and began praising Krishna. Krishna laughed and told Indra that he had done what he did as an act of grace: he saved Indra from the pride of power and wealth and had made him mindful of the highest reality. As a sign of surrender and respect, Indra bathed Krishna with the celestial Ganges carried in the trunk of the elephant Airavat, Indra's vehicle, and then gave Krishna the name Govinda, or "Procurer of the Cows."[55] The sacred water from this bathing created the pond of Govindakund.

We continued on a rocky path that passed through a tract of flowering trees with beautiful red blossoms. The mountain here consists of stacks of large rocks; several peacocks were dancing atop them, fanning their tails in an attempt to attract an amorous partner. The rocks gradually began to get smaller. Soon we came to the southern tip of the mountain, where there is a village called Punchari, which means the "tail." Whether Govardhan is conceived of as a peacock, cow, lion, or snake, this place is always considered the tail of the body of Krishna. We swung around the tail and started back north. We had now come seven miles.

Along the way we encountered a man doing the *dandavat parikrama*, a particularly arduous way of performing the circumambulation of Mount Govardhan. This man had first collected 108 stones from the mountain. He was proceeding around the fourteen-mile path by repeatedly lying completely flat on the ground. As he prostrated he moved one of the stones forward one body length, repeating this motion 108 times until the entire pile of stones was one body length ahead of him. He then stepped forward and began the process over again. The man was about forty years old, had long black hair and a beard, and wore a thin white cloth around his waist. He seemed totally absorbed in his task. The less ambitious pilgrims made donations to this dusty man by placing coins in a small shrine containing a picture of Radha and Krishna that he moved slightly ahead of the pile of rocks. I was told it takes at least two years to complete the circumambulation by this method. I looked at the man with great admiration—three weeks of normal walking seemed torture enough for me—and deposited a few coins in his shrine before moving on.

Huge rocks began to appear on our right once again as we approached the town of Jatipura. The mountain had a mysterious quality about it here. Rock stacked upon rock rose high into the blue sky, and each rock seemed to resemble the shape of the entire mountain, replicating itself endlessly in an expanding multitude of forms. The sun, now directly overhead, caused the wall of smooth, shiny rocks to shimmer in its brilliant light.

Jatipura is located on the western slope of Mount Govardhan, directly across the mountain from Anyor. This is a very important site, especially for the Pushti Margi pilgrims, who typically camp here for seven or eight days during their circuit of Braj. I spent four days in Jatipura with a Pushti Margi pilgrimage group after completing the entire circuit with the Gaudiya Vaishnava pilgrims and came to the conclusion that this is a town obsessed with food, feeding, and eating. There are three major Pushti Margi temples in Jatipura, but the real focus of the town is the Giriraj ka Mukharavind, the "Lotus Mouth of the Mountain." Members of the Gaudiya Ban-Yatra stopped here long enough to pour some milk over the enshrined stone before pressing on, but Pushti Margi pilgrims make this their longest stop and engage in elaborate rituals, all involving considerable amounts of food.

The Lotus Mouth refers to a crack in the rock at the base of the mountain around which the town of Jatipura has grown. This crack is a huge orifice drawing large crowds of pilgrims and sucking in enormous quantities of food. According to the Pushti Margis, this is the spot where the mouth of Shri Nathji appeared. A round boulder, slightly bigger than a human head, has been fixed atop a large slab of rock just above the crack; this is the focus of much ritual activity in Jatipura. On the first morning I spent at this site, the boulder was wrapped in a pink cloth. A line of pilgrims had assembled to pour milk over the stone. The cloth was removed and bucket after bucket was emptied with shouts of "*Giriraj ki jai!*" ("All Glory to the King of Mountains!"). The milk flowed through a drain to the base of the large slab, where it was eagerly lapped up by a motley collection of fat dogs. Large numbers of the contented beasts could be seen lying in the shade of a nearby building after gorging themselves with milk. Dogs are usually considered very lowly animals in India, but I overheard three pilgrims admiring the situation of these dogs who spend their days in Braj enjoying the remains of Giriraj's milk feasts.

The evening worship is quite different. A row of dim light bulbs illuminates the area under the corrugated tin roof that covers the shrine, as the Mukharavind stone undergoes an elaborate transformation at the hands of the attending priests. Eyes, a jeweled crown, a nosepiece, and earrings are placed on the round boulder, which now becomes the head of Krishna the Cowherd, making the identification between Krishna and the mountain clearly evident. Artificial arms and legs are added to the stone—the left arm is raised in the mountain-holding pose—and ornate clothes and necklaces are draped over the figure. The process of decorating the stone takes nearly an hour, as the head priest carefully selects each ornament from a metal trunk and positions it with loving attention to detail. A dais is placed beneath the feet of the metamorphosed stone, and the mountain is ready for a hearty feast.

I observed two massive feasts while I was staying with Pushti Margi pilgrims at Jatipura: one night a wealthy pilgrim sponsored a *kanvara*, a presentation of large quantities of sweets; another night the maharaj leading the pilgrimage had organized a *chappan bhog*, an offering of fifty-six different kinds of food.[56] The foods were placed in leaf dishes and artistically arranged in semicircular patterns before the freshly dressed stone. Never before had I seen such quantities of food; dishes were crammed into a section of the mountain measuring twenty by sixty feet. A curtain was drawn for about twenty minutes to allow Krishna to devour the offerings in private and then it was opened, with great excitement. The alleys and lanes of Jatipura were jam-packed on these occasions with pilgrims struggling to catch a glimpse of the sumptuously excessive display of food and the mountain of a god to whom it was offered. The pilgrims would return the next morning to receive their share of this feast.

We pushed on in a northerly direction, past the town of Govardhan, to complete our circumambulation of Mount Govardhan. At one point a herd of *nil gay*, large brown deer resembling American elk, burst from a thicket and ran across our path. Sometime later a group of us gathered beneath some trees to rest. While we were sitting a few people got up and started to climb the mountain. When they were noticed, several in the group began to grumble and one man bolted up and shouted: "We Bengalis do not walk on Govardhan. He is our god. You are committing a great offense [*aparadh*]." The offending party immediately turned around and returned to the group, looking rather chagrined. Gaudiya Vaishnavas are not to set foot on the sacred mountain. We pressed on toward Radhakund to complete our circling of the mountain and continued on around to reach our next camp, near the town of Govardhan. We were all yearning to rest our bodies.

Bodies, bodies, bodies. They were on display everywhere: sweating bodies, aching bodies, tired bodies, bodies of hungry mountains and bodies of water. And sore feet! At camp I found that I had developed two more blisters and my left knee was throbbing with pain. A friend of mine once complained that travel writers too often become obsessed with their bodies. I fear repeating this obsession, but it is true that removed from one's habitual world one spends more time thinking about the body, especially when it is in pain. This is particularly true on pilgrimage, where the body is the vehicle of experience. Pilgrimage is not ethereal religious practice. Pilgrims get down into dirt, stones, water, and mud. The Ban-Yatra is an encounter between the body of the pilgrim and the body of God.

Again and again I observed pilgrims embracing the world of nature: A woman approached a tree, wrapped it in her arms, and held it tight. A man bent down, touched his head to a large Govardhan stone, and hugged it for a few minutes. Another smeared mud from the bottom of Radhakund onto his forehead and then threw a handful of the pond's water into his mouth. An elderly woman addressed a soft song to a bird. The saint Chaitanya was exemplary of this behavior,[57] but it is also a frequent occurrence among the Ban-Yatra pilgrims of today. The entire land of Braj, every particle of dust, is considered divine.

The Ban-Yatra is a celebration of nature; the natural phenomena of

Braj are the major foci of this pilgrimage. Lynch points out that the natural phenomena of Braj, particularly Mount Govardhan, are neither symbols nor metaphors for divinity but rather "metonymic divinity."[58] Though Lynch does not develop this notion, I think it is a suggestion worthy of further consideration. In chapter 2 I mentioned the gap between the "is" and the "ought" that is operative in certain kinds of pilgrimage.[59] Another gap related to this one is the gap between what is called in linguistics the signifier and the signified. Assumption of the universal existence of this gap has determined many analyses of religious objects and the interaction with them. Mircea Eliade, for example, writes: "The sacred always manifests itself as a reality of a wholly different order from 'natural' realities. . . . The sacred tree, the sacred stone are not adorned as stone or tree; they are worshiped precisely because they are *hierophanies*, because they show something that is no longer stone or tree but the *sacred*, the *ganz andre*."[60] That is, the tree or stone is a signifier that signifies a reality "totally different" or "wholly other" than the reality of the tree or stone. According to this reading, an "abyss" divides the signifier and the signified; there exists a wide gap between the profane "is" and the sacred "ought." But it is precisely this gap that is in question in the Ban-Yatra and much of the religion of Braj. The rocks encountered in Braj on the Ban-Yatra both point to a reality beyond the apparent *and* are worshiped themselves. Instead of an abyss dividing the concrete form, or the signifier, from that which is beyond it, or the signified, here we find that the two are understood as being intimately related. This is not to say that the Vaishnavas of Braj think Krishna is exhaustively contained within the concrete form of the tree or stone—far from it; by definition Krishna is uncontainable—but rather that the trees and stones of Braj are not ultimately different from Krishna; they are a part of his very body. This, I take it, is what Lynch is getting at by saying that the natural phenomena of Braj are not symbols (i.e., signifiers separate from the signified) but "metonymic divinity."

Behind the celebration of nature in Braj is an environmental theology most explicitly developed by the Founder of Braj, Narayan Bhatt, whose final words were recorded by his biographer, Janaki Prasad: "Devotion to Braj should be performed. The land of Braj is worthy of worship. This very Braj is the highest place. Braj is the body (*vigraha*) of Shri Krishna. Krishna, the son of Nanda, never leaves Braj."[61] Narayan Bhatt's pronouncement that "Braj is the body of Krishna" has become a *mahavakya*, or "great saying" in Braj. It was repeated to me again and again by the pilgrimage guides, participants, and many of the residents of Braj. Much of the advertisement of Braj as a sacred space has hinged on this notion. Dipak Bhatt, the head of Narayan Bhatt's family living in Unchagaon today, put it this way to me: "There is no difference between Braj and Shri Krishna. Krishna is Braj. Braj is Krishna. The forests, groves, trees, ponds, hills, and even dirt are Krishna. Just by living in Braj one is in contact with Krishna. Just being present in Braj is itself a religious practice [sadhana]."

We have already seen that Mount Govardhan is conceived of as a living being. This notion is extended by Narayan Bhatt to all of Braj. He means literally that Braj is the body of Krishna and is prepared to tell us which places in Braj correspond to which body parts. Narayan Bhatt writes in his *Vraja Bhakti Vilasa:* "The Braj Mandal is an essential form of the Lord consisting of organs and limbs."[62] Narayan Bhatt maps out the body parts of Krishna in great detail by identifying them with the twelve major forests and other important sites in Braj: Mathura is his heart; Madhuban is his navel; Kumudban and Talban are his two breasts; Vrindaban is his brow; Bahulaban and Mahaban are his two arms; Bhandiraban and Kokilaban are his two legs; Khadiraban and Bhadrikaban are his two shoulders; Chatraban and Lohaban are his two eyes; Belban and Bhadraban are his two ears; Kamaban is his chin; Triveni and Sakhikupaban are his two lips; Svarna and Vihval are his two rows of teeth; Surabhiban is his tongue; Mayurban is his forehead; Manengitaban is his nose; Sheshashayi and Paramanandaban are his two nostrils; Karhela and Kamai are his two buttocks; Karnaban is his penis; Krishnakshipana is his anus; Nandanaban is his head; Indraban is his back; Shikshaban, Chandraban, Lohban, Nandagram, and Srikund are the five fingers of his right hand; Gadhasthan, Lalitagram, Bhanupur, Gokul, and Baldev are the five fingers of his left hand; Govardhan, Javavat, Sanketban, Naradaban, and Madhuban are the five toes of his left foot; and Mridban, Janhaka, Menakaban, Kajjaliban, and Nandakup are the five toes of his right foot.

Many have characterized Hinduism as a religion of renunciation which turns its back on the world.[63] It is true that some Hindu philosophers view the world of nature, or *prakriti*, as a snare to be avoided, a trap to be escaped. The multiple world of appearance for Shankara's Advaita Vedanta, for example, is not ultimately real. It is an ever-changing cover which distorts and conceals the true stable reality hidden beneath it. From this position the world of nature has no value in and of itself. This position, however, does not include all Hindu philosophies. Operative in the culture of Braj, as theologically expressed by such figures as Narayan Bhatt and acted out by the Ban-

Yatra pilgrims, is a very different view of the phenomenal world of nature. Here we encounter a vital affirmation of the natural world. The natural world of Braj itself is divine. There is no need to close one's eyes to the world and fold one's legs in abstract meditation; rather, one need only open one's eyes to the reality that is ever present and stretch one's legs wandering through the forests of Braj to experience the ultimate joy. Here ultimate reality reveals itself as (not only in) concrete form: "Krishna is Braj. Braj is Krishna."

A contemporary expression of the notion that Braj is a natural form of Krishna appears in an article written by Shrivatsa Goswami of Vrindaban, who along with his father, Shri Purushottama Goswami, led a Gaudiya Ban-Yatra around Braj in 1986.[64] From a Gaudiya Vaishnava perspective, any talk of Krishna is really a talk of Radha and Krishna. Shrivatsa writes that the Ban-Yatra is a journey into "full awareness of nature." Radha, for him, is the root of all nature and Krishna is the highest spirit, and out of their love play the world is created for more love. Krishna, Shrivatsa points out, is dark blue, Radha is a golden yellow, and the intermingling love play of the two produces the green land of Braj. For this reason, he says, this pilgrimage is sometimes called the Hari-Yatra, or "Green Pilgrimage." The timing of the pilgrimage is important. The Ban-Yatra begins just after the celebration of Krishna's birth at Janmashtami. This is the time of year when the dusty, scorching winds cease and the results of the monsoon rains begin to appear; the joyfully frivolous love play manifests itself once again in the form of a new layer of greenery. For Shrivatsa, then, the Ban-Yatra is a journey which provides one with a chance to become aware of what Braj, and by extension all of nature, truly is: the physical expression of the dynamic and mutual love of Radha and Krishna. The purpose of the Ban-Yatra, he says, is to "taste" this love play and experience the resulting joy—ananda—an experience which can be had only from the manifest play of natural forms.

The pressures of a growing population and developing economic expectations have more recently caused conflicting views of the land to appear in this region. In a world which increasingly sees land as a resource to be owned and exploited, the land of Braj is threatened with a number of ecological problems. Many trees in the region of Braj have been cut down, leaving several of the "forests" surviving in name only. The Yamuna River is polluted with raw sewage spilling in directly from many of the towns built on its banks and with industrial waste from the factories upstream in New Delhi. A huge oil refinery in Mathura pours toxins into the air daily. Wildlife has decreased significantly over the past few decades. Although Growse reported that he could not travel between Mathura and Vrindaban without seeing a herd of deer, the sight is very rare today. Even the peacocks of Braj—once protected even by the foreign Mughal and British rulers—are threatened.[65] And many of the pilgrimage sites are falling into ruin due to neglect and plunder by thieves involved in the lucrative illegal art market.

Several who have performed the Ban-Yatra have become involved in efforts to conserve the environment of Braj. Perhaps the most impressive I met was a man by the name of Madhava Das Baba. By the time I met him, Madhava Baba was a frail old man, dying of cancer, but he had come from his native state of Tamil Nadu as a young man long ago to see the sites of Braj. He fell in love with this "form of Krishna" and spent the remainder of his days wandering in Braj, researching its sites, and dedicating his life to restoring and protecting its environment. And he did so with the firm belief that the land of Braj was nondifferent from Krishna. He was introduced to me, only half jokingly, as the present incarnation of Narayan Bhatt, who had also come to Braj from Tamil Nadu. Madhava Baba struggled against great odds, frequently fighting one-man battles to save some natural feature of Braj he found threatened. He was particularly fond of the trees. He told me that when he first came to Braj some fifty years earlier there were great tracts of forest composed of large trees, some measuring over four feet in diameter. It is now illegal to cut trees in much of the area, but the law is difficult to enforce. Madhava Baba told me how on a number of occasions he would catch people cutting trees, but by the time he could get the police there they were gone. Many trees have also been cut down legally, to support what Madhava Baba called a "greed for more goods." As an example, he narrated the story of a man who owned a grove of huge, ancient trees near Mount Govardhan, which yielded abundant fruit every year with little work. The owner, however, was not content with the natural profits from the annual crop. He wanted immediate funds to finance the weddings of his three daughters, and so the trees were cut down and sold for lumber. Not long after, one of the daughters and the husbands of the other two died. Madhava Baba used this as one of innumerable incidents to illustrate how an obsession with short-term profit is resulting in long-term destruction.

The government has planned to build a railroad line across Mount Govardhan since the late 1960s. Madhava Baba, viewing Govardhan as a living being, was instrumental in stopping this plan. In 1973 Madhava Baba got the government to pass legislation to protect eleven sacred hills to the west of Mount Govardhan, which had been auctioned off to be crushed and used as road-building material. In 1975 he was able to secure government protection for the water and fish of a sacred pond near Nandagaon, both of which were being taken in excess by local farmers. He personally restored another pond, sacred to the goddess Vrinda, near Nandagaon and has battled hard to save many other sites. The welfare of the wildlife of Braj also greatly concerned him. As he faced impending death, I asked him what he considered his greatest achievement. He replied, "I planted trees at the foot of Mount Govardhan." Madhava Baba died shortly after I interviewed him. He had accomplished much, but he was one of a very few who are trying to save the land and sites of Braj at a time when environmental pressures are nearly overwhelming and traditional values are being significantly challenged. In many ways the forests that the Ban-Yatra pilgrims travel through are in such sorry condition that unless the work carried out by such figures as Madhava Baba continues, they will soon be reduced to a memory.

Maganlal Sharma, my pilgrimage guru, visited our camp in Govardhan that night. I had just lain down on my cot and was thinking about some of my motivations for coming on this journey. I realized that besides my academic concerns I was looking forward to a contemplative experience, a quiet time removed from the demands of the ordinary world. Although such times were occasionally to be had while wandering in the countryside, in camp I was never alone. I was always being watched. I had set up my cot outside our tent to gaze at the stars. Within a radius of fifteen feet, some thirty people curiously observed every move I made as I got ready for bed. I had the sensation of being on a stage, performing some strange drama for their entertainment. Flossing my teeth provided particular amusement. A member of my audience remarked, "But isn't that harmful?" I tried to assure him that in my country it was considered beneficial. Two feet from the head of my cot a man was squatting, preparing tea on a small kerosene burner for late-night customers. His stove hissed and sputtered noisily. A group gathered around him, enjoying the drink, laughing and talking. One of my young "cooks" sat at the foot of my cot, cheerfully preparing his nightly chillum of hash. The importance of the inner world in Hindu culture began to take on a whole new meaning!

Amid this spirited scene I somehow drifted off to sleep. I was suddenly awakened by the voice of Maganlal: "Radhe Shyam!" He was now standing over my bed. He had come to see how his clients were faring. Inquiring about my health, he examined my blistered feet. "You should finish the journey in a tonga," he insisted. I resisted. I was determined to walk the entire way. I had become obsessed with the trial of the journey and felt that riding a horse-drawn tonga would be tantamount to failure.

I resisted for yet another reason. Those who rode in the tongas passed us each morning, barely awake, missing the sites along the way that can be reached only on foot. These sleepy tonga rides looked to be continuous with those times from the late morning to late afternoon when we lounged about drowsily waiting for the heat of the day to pass—time that had an unreal quality compared with the time we spent walking. The stationary, sultry afternoons were something most of the travelers merely endured while waiting to move, waiting for the next morning's walk. These pilgrims lived to walk, came alive while walking, were eager to walk, despite the pain and discomfort. Moreover, the walkers were much more alert to the novel sights, sounds, and sensations encountered on the road. Pilgrimage is about movement, a movement that revels directly in the surrounding environment, and the forests of Braj are best relished by walking, not sitting.

After leaving the environs of Mount Govardhan, we ventured into the deserts to the west, where the trees were even scarcer and the sun hotter. I would continue to walk.

NOTES

1. I have enhanced the story I heard from Shuklaji while at Radhakund with the account of the ponds' creation found in Krishnadas Baba's *Braj Mandal Darshan* (Kusum Sarovar: Krishnadas Baba, 1958), 24–25.

2. The killing of a cow in any form is a grave sin for a Hindu.

3. *Chaitanya Charitamrita,* Madhya-lila 18.7.

4. This account of Raghunath's involvement with Radhakund is taken from Navadvipdas, *Shri Radhakund Itihas* (Vrindaban: Shri Krishna Press, n.d.), 25–31.

5. See Mukherjee and Habib, "The Mughal Administration and the Temples of Vrindaban," 297.

6. Although it appears that Jiva was involved in land sales around Radhakund at a much earlier date (Navadvipdas says in 1546), records of the sales show up in Mughal documents in 1579. See Mukherjee and Habib, "Akbar and the Temples of Mathura," 236. The nature of this land sale is discussed in

detail in Mukherjee and Habib, "Land Rights in the Reign of Akbar: The Evidence of the Sale-deeds of Vrindaban and Aritha," *Proceedings of the Indian History Congress* 50 (1989): 237–39; 245–49. For Man Singh's involvement with Radhakund, see Navadvipdas, *Shri Radhakund Itihas,* 35.

7. *Chaitanya Charitamrita,* Madhya-lila 18.11.

8. Summary translation by C. Mackenzie Brown, "The Theology of Radha in the Purana," in *The Divine Consort: Radha and the Goddesses of India,* ed. John S. Hawley and Donna M. Wulff (Berkeley, Calif. Graduate Theological Union, 1982), 57.

9. Jiva Goswami, *Bhagavata Sandarbha,* ed. Chinmayi Chatterjee (Calcutta: Jadavpur University, 1972).

10. Shrivatsa Goswami, "Radha: The Play and Perfection of Rasa," in *The Divine Consort,* 83.

11. See, for example, ibid., 88.

12. See the fine translation by Barbara S. Miller, *Love Song of the Dark Lord* (New York: Columbia University Press, 1977).

13. Charlotte Vaudeville, "Krishna Gopala, Radha, and the Great Goddess," in *The Divine Consort,* 2, 11.

14. Translated by Donna M. Wulff from the *Vidagdhamadhava* of Rupa Goswami, "A Sanskrit Portrait: Radha in the Plays of Rupa Gosvami," in *The Divine Consort,* 35.

15. See my *Acting as a Way of Salvation: A Study of Raganuga Bhakti Sadhana* (New York: Oxford University Press, 1988), 40–60.

16. I have translated this poem in *Textual Sources for the Study of Hinduism,* ed. Wendy Doniger O'Flaherty (Manchester: Manchester University Press, 1988; Chicago: University of Chicago Press, 1990), 163–65.

17. The *siddha-deha;* see my *Acting as a Way of Salvation.*

18. Narottam Das Thakur, *Kunjavarnana,* in Niradprasad Nath, *Narottam Das o Tahar Rachanavali* (Calcutta: University of Calcutta, 1975), 644–58.

19. Louis Dumont has suggested that "the secret of Hinduism may be found in the dialogue between the renouncer and the man-in-the-world" ("World Renunciation in Indian Religions," *Contributions to Indian Sociology* 4 [1960]: 37–38).

20. Growse, *Mathura,* 73.

21. Seth Govindadas, "Braj-Yatra ka Uday aur Vikas," in *Braj aur Braj Yatra,* 85–90.

22. Paul M. Toomey, Ph. D. Dissertation from University of Virginia, *Food from the Mouth of Krishna: Sacred Food and Pilgrimage at Mount Govardhan* (Ann Arbor, Mich.: University Microfilms, 1986), 31.

23. Entwistle, *Braj,* 286.

24. John S. Hawley, "Krishna's Cosmis Victories" *Journal of the American Academy of Religion* 47, no. 2 (1979): 201–21.

25. *Vishnu Purana* 10.47, and *Bhagavata Purana* 10.24.35.

26. For a history of the development of the Krishna-Govardhan cult, see Charlotte Vaudeville, "The Govardhan Myth in Northern India," *Indo-Iranian Journal* 22 (1980): 1–45.

27. *Varaha Purana* 162.24.

28. This is celebrated in the Hindu calendar on Karttik II.1.

29. I had occasion to observe this ritual in Vrindaban in the home of Mahesh Kumar and in the temple of Radharaman after I had completed the pilgrimage.

30. For more on this festival see Vaudeville, "The Govardhan Myth in Northern India," and Toomey, *Food from the Mouth of Krishna.*

31. I have taken this particular account from Mohan Das "Narad Baba," *Sampurna Braj Darshanam* (Vrindaban: Shri Radha Mohan Satsang Mandal, 1987), 52; and from *Vraja Bhakti Vilasa* 5.1.

32. This point is made clear by Narayan Bhatt in *Vraja Bhakti Vilasa* 5.1.

33. Krishnadas Baba, *Braj Mandal Darshan*, 44–45.

34. Mohan Das, *Sampurna Braj Darshanam*, 53–55.

35. Vijay considers Govardhan a cow, with Radhakund and Krishna Kund as the eyes (see *Braj Bhumi Mohini* [Vrindaban: Shri Prem Hari Press, 1985], 132); Krishnadas Baba calls Govardhan a peacock (see *Braj Mandal Darshan*, 40); many who reside in the town of Govardhan consider the mountain a snake with Manasi Ganga as mouth (see Toomey, *Food from the Mouth of Krishna*). Entwistle suggests that this adds support to the theory that the current Govardhan cult is the result of a transformation of a previous cult of a spirit who controlled the rain and could take the form of a mountain or animal (*Braj*, 281).

36. *Bhagavata Purana* 10.47.61.

37. Growse, *Mathura*, 301.

38. Many accounts name the threatening demon as the bull Arishta.

39. This particular version is taken from Krishnadas Baba, *Braj Mandal Darshan*, 43.

40. *Varaha Purana* 162.12.

41. See, for example, Vijay, *Braj Bhumi Mohini*, 116.

42. Both of these incidents are referred to in ibid., 117.

43. See Entwistle, *Braj*, 130.

44. This is particularly true of the Bengalis, see Narahari Chakravarti's *Bhaktiratnakar*, 5.

45. See, for example, Mohan Das, *Sampurna Braj Darshanam*, 57.

46. Hardy, "Madhavendra Puri," 23–41.

47. *Chaitanya Charitamrita*, Madhya-lila 4.21–109.

48. This account is taken primarily from Charlotte Vaudeville's translation of this text in "The Govardhan Myth in Northern India," 15–45.

49. See Vaudeville, "The Govardhan Myth in Northern India," for an argument which links the worship of Shri Nathji with early forms of snake worship.

50. Entwistle points out that this date is too early (*Braj*, 141).

51. For the Pushti Margi account of this incident see the *Varta* of Krishnadas translated in Barz, *The Bhakti Sect of Vallabhacarya*, 216–22.

52. For a fuller account of the life of Surdas, see John S. Hawley, *Sur Das: Poet, Singer, Saint* (Delhi: Oxford University Press, 1984). Hawley claims that we know very little about the real life of Surdas from the surviving hagiographical literature, but he argues that Surdas was an independent figure who was later adopted by the Pushti Margis. He even questions the blindness of Surdas.

53. Bryant, *Poems to the Child-God*, 72–112.

54. Hawley, *Sur Das*, 177.

55. This story is also found in *Bhagavata Purana* 10.27.

56. For more on these feasts see Toomey, *Food from the Mouth of Krishna*.

57. We read in the *Chaitanya Charitamrita* that Chaitanya embraced the trees and creepers of Vrindaban (Madhya-lila 17.204), bathed ecstatically in the waters of Radhakund (Madhya-lila 18.5), and threw himself on the ground upon arriving at Mount Govardhan and hugged a stone (Madhya-lila 18.16).

58. Lynch, "Pilgrimage with Krishna," 176.

59. See p. 75 in this book.

60. Mircea Eliade, *The Sacred and the Profane: The Nature of Religion* (New York: Harcourt Brace, 1959), 10–12.

61. Janaki Prasad Bhatt, *Narayana Bhatta Charitamrita*, p. 100, verses 185–86.

62. Narayan Bhatt, *Vraja Bhakti Vilasa* 1.93. Though Narayan Bhatt claims there are fifty-five forest sites to be discussed, four of the body parts and corresponding forests of Braj are missing from the list. A verse appears to have been lost from the original text.

63. See, for example, Louis Dumont, *Religion, Politics and History in India* (Paris: Mouton, 1970).

64. Shrivatsa Goswami, "Charaiveti! Charaiveti!"

65. Menaka Gandhi has recently taken up the cause of protecting the peacocks of Braj. The World Wide Fund for Nature has also begun sponsoring the reforestation of the Vrindaban area (Vrindaban Forest Revival Project).

4

Into the Desert

How can you make demands on our hearts?
  That would be insulting him!
When he was here our hearts did not burn,
  but now the yearning crackles hot,
For he has left our hearts abandoned
  and ablaze: will they never cool? . . .
No yogic cure can bring us life, says Sur:
  we're scorched with separation.

SURDAS, from *Sur Das*

We rose at two-thirty in the morning and marched twelve miles into the desert state of Rajasthan. Much of the surrounding land was barren and dusty. We passed few trees as we walked along a road that stretched before us as level and straight as a gun barrel. Halfway between Govardhan and the town of Dig we stopped to rest in a small village on the Rajasthani border. The thatched veranda of a tea stall sheltered a few wooden benches. I sat down to rest my feet and ordered a cup of tea. The tea stall stove was constructed of brick and mud and covered with a layer of cow dung that had dried to a concretelike hardness. There was a round hole on top of the stove, slightly smaller than the diameter of the pan in which the tea was being boiled, with another hole at the bottom to draw air. The shopkeeper stoked the fire with a few fresh pieces of wood, and I was soon enjoying a cup of sweet, milky tea spiced with cardamom, ginger, cloves, and cinnamon. It was served in a lightly baked clay pot that would disintegrate shortly after being tossed to the ground, India's ancient answer to the world's problem with disposable Styrofoam cups.

I let out a deep sigh and relaxed, enjoying every minute of our brief stop. Three wooden carts pulled by camels rolled past; I was astonished by the softness of the huge feet of these humped animals. Suddenly, I spotted Maya, the young Bengali woman I had talked with briefly at Radhakund. I was surprised to see her and wondered why she had joined us. While I stared at her with great curiosity, she glanced my way; as our eyes met she smiled. I looked away quickly, embarrassed and shy. I finished my tea and stood up. My legs had already stiffened and cramped, so I began to stretch them by hobbling slowly up and down a side street lined with adobe houses. Two small boys were rolling a steel hoop with a wooden stick in the narrow lane. Several women sat in the shade of a tree, swinging a cradle that was suspended from its limbs. When I returned, Maya was standing at the tea stall with three other Bengalis. She said something to me I did not understand. She motioned me closer and told me that she did not have enough money for tea. Slowly it dawned on me that she was indirectly asking me to buy her a cup of tea. When I asked if this was what she desired, she said something which I again did not understand, but it provoked an explosion of laughter from the group she was with. One of them remarked, "Don't. He may be a Vaishnava." I had no idea what was really going on, but I gave Maya a rupee for the tea anyway. By that time, however, the shopkeeper had run out of tea and it was time to move on. Maya kept the rupee.

Our destination that day was the town of Dig. Dig is not associated with any playful activity of Radha and Krishna but is identified in some of the guidebooks as Dirghapur,[1] a town built by Krishna's great-grandson Vajranabh in memory of the wide-striding Vishnu who once took the form of a dwarf to defeat a particularly pesky demon.

Long ago there was a demon king named Bali who had performed a special sacrifice and had thereby acquired an unworldy strength. He proceeded to attack the city of the gods, drive out its inhabitants, and occupy heaven. By these actions he came to control the entire universe. Aditi, the mother of the gods, was greatly distressed for her children. She performed a difficult vow, winning from Vishnu a boon: he would take birth as her son and restore heaven to the gods. Soon Aditi gave birth to Vishnu as the tiny dwarf Vamana. Vamana approached Bali, who was sufficiently impressed with the little fellow's nerve to inquire what he might like. The dwarf asked only for the amount of land he could cover in three paces. Amused by this seemingly modest request, Bali granted it. The dwarf then began to grow to such gigantic proportions that he filled the entire universe. With his first stride he covered the whole earth; with his second he stretched across the heavens so that not an atom of space remained; with the third stride Vishnu crushed the head of Bali, thereby releasing him from his wicked ways.

In more recent history Dig was the center of a princely state which played an extremely important role in the development of Braj. The Mughal patronage of Braj started by the emperor Akbar declined significantly during the reign of Aurangzeb. Still fighting the Marathas in the Deccan, Aurangzeb died a sad man in the town of Ahmadnagar in the year 1707. That same year there was born near Dig a remarkable man who would come to have considerable influence on the developments in Braj. His name was Suraj Mal Singh.

Suraj Mal was a Jat. The Jats, people closely related to the Rajputs, are the most important ethnic group living in the Yamuna River valley between Delhi and Agra. They claim to be the descendants of the Yadavas, Krishna's own clan, which ruled over Mathura.[2] The word *Jat* may mean "unionist," owing to the democratic and collective nature of these groups.[3] Jats are primarily farmers, known for their fierce spirit of freedom and fighting. The historian Khushwant Singh writes of them: "The Jat was born the worker and the warrior. He tilled his land with his sword girded round his waist."[4] As Mughal power began to decline, the Jats in the area grew in strength and boldness. "Within a few years of Aurangzeb's ascending the throne the Jats first became an irritant, then a nuisance and finally a thorn in the aging body of the Emperor and Empire."[5] Organized under a powerful landowner named Gokal Ram, the Jats were responsible for the rebellion which caused the attack of imperial troops on Mathura in 1669. Gokal and his forces were eventually defeated by the well-armed and disciplined imperial troops. Gokal was taken prisoner and was publicly executed in Agra, his limbs hacked off one by one,[6] but his fame lived on to serve as inspiration for the Jats.

Shortly after the death of Gokal another leader appeared among the Jats. Raja Ram began building small forts which were protected from artillery by thick mud walls. From these forts he carried out raids against imperial caravans and villages. To avenge the killing of Gokal, it is said that sometime between 1688 and 1691 the Jats under Raja Ram looted Akbar's tomb at Sikandra just outside of Agra and cremated his bones. The historian Vincent A. Smith claims, "The pilgrim to Akbar's tomb now visits, although he does not know it, an empty grave."[7] Outraged, yet occupied with his military campaign in the south, Aurangzeb sought the aid of Bishan Singh, the Rajput king of Amber who ruled over the territory adjacent to the western boundary of Jat lands. Bishan Singh was made ruler of Mathura and commanded to contain Jat ambitions. Raja Ram was killed in battle shortly after the desecration of Akbar's tomb.

A guerrilla fighting force was soon thereafter organized by a nephew of Raja Ram by the name of Thakur Churaman. His military band of Jats traveled light, avoiding the less mobile and heavily encumbered troops of the Mughal army, and continually harassed the imperial convoys traveling between Delhi and Agra. The looting Jats managed to establish several strongholds west of the Yamuna River and all but closed the imperial highway between the two capitals. After Aurangzeb's death in 1707 his two sons became embroiled in a war of succession. Churaman skillfully looted the forces of both sides, acquiring enough wealth to pay his troops and build a secure fortress at Thun, a town a short distance to the southwest of Dig. Bahadur Shah, Aurangzeb's eventual successor, was forced to recognize Churaman as the unofficial ruler of the western bank of the Yamuna River; he later requested Churaman to accompany him on his military campaign against the Sikhs in the north. Churaman is reported to have died in 1721 by swallowing poison during a heated argument with his eldest son.[8] Churaman's rebellious nephew, Badan Singh, lost no time in seizing leadership of the Jats; aided by Sawai Jai Singh, who would soon build the royal "pink city" of Jaipur on the plain below Amber, Badan Singh attacked and destroyed the fortress of Thun.

In 1725 Badan Singh began building a fort, palace, and gardens at the site of Dig, which was to be the new capital of the growing Jat kingdom. Badan Singh wanted to transform the Jats from rebels into rulers, and so struck an alliance with Sawai Jai Singh of Jaipur. Jai Singh first asked him to subdue the Meos, a looting band of Muslims inhabiting the hilly regions to the north of Dig, and Badan Singh sent his able teenage son, Suraj Mal, to lead the troops. The results so pleased Jai Singh that he put Badan Singh in charge of patrolling the royal highways between Delhi, Agra, and Jaipur and awarded him with the title of raja. Thus, Badan Singh became the first ever to be called Braj Raja, or the "King of Braj."[9]

Now that Badan Singh had acquired land, wealth, and the prestige of a title, as no other Jat leader before him had done, he set to work building his palace at Dig. The Mughal empire was in serious decline, leaving many talented artists and craftsmen unemployed. "In droves the master builders from Delhi and Agra sought employment at the courts of Badan Singh and Suraj Mal."[10] These craftsmen built a court that rivaled the great Mughal courts of Delhi and Agra. The gardens of Dig are particularly known for their delightful fountain pavilions. "At the height of his glory, Suraj Mal erected the fountain palaces called Bhawans which are surpassed in India for elegance and perfection of workmanship only by the Taj Mahal at Agra."[11]

Badan Singh's eyesight began to fail, and slowly he turned over the responsibility of ruling the kingdom to his favored son, Suraj Mal. In 1732 work was started on a new palace thirty miles south of Dig which was to become the site of the capital town of Bharatpur. After worshiping the family deity, Mount Govardhan, Suraj Mal began construction of a fort which, when completed, would be the most formidable in northern India. It was protected by deep moats and high, thick stone walls which were impenetrable by artillery. In 1805 British troops under the command of Lord Lake laid siege to the Bharatpur fort for four months before admitting defeat—one of the most humiliating setbacks experienced by the British during their conquest of India.

Sawai Jai Singh of Jaipur had taken great interest in the religious affairs of Braj and was viewed as one of the major protectors of the area. It is very likely that the performance of the Ban-Yatra declined during the reign of Aurangzeb, but in 1722 Jai Singh was appointed governor of Agra and the pilgrimage flow into Braj once again began to increase. It is reported that Jai Singh himself performed a Ban-Yatra just after Janmashtami in the year 1724.[12] He built a residence in Vrindaban, an observatory and headquarters in Mathura, and a temple in Govardhan. He became involved in the temple affairs and settled many religious disputes among the competing groups of Braj. He was particularly sympathetic toward the Gaudiya Vaishnavas and used the name of Govindadev on his seal.[13] With his death in 1743, Badan Singh and Suraj Mal lost a patron but gained the worthy responsibility of protecting the land of Krishna. After defeating an imperial army sent to subdue him in 1750, Suraj Mal arranged a peace treaty with the Mughals by which they agreed not to harm any of the temples or sacred trees in the region of Braj. "The terms of the treaty were a public recognition of the Bharatpur rulers' superior position in Braj Mandal, justifying their title of Braj Raj."[14]

Badan Singh died in 1756. Suraj Mal's dealings with the unstable Mughal court in Delhi were so skillful and successful that by this time he had more wealth than any other king in northern India.[15] He had sacked Delhi in the year 1753, carrying away many treasures to his palace in Dig, and later helped determine who wielded power within the Mughal court. His own military power and reputation could not be ignored by anyone operating in the central plains. Braj culture gained a great deal from the patronage of Suraj Mal, but in 1757 it also suffered a devastating blow because of his association. The Afghan ruler Amad Shah Abdali invaded India in 1756; by January 1757 he had taken Delhi. After plundering that city, Abdali turned his attention south, his eyes on the wealth and power of Suraj Mal. He demanded that Suraj Mal surrender his territory and pay him tribute; the latter refused to meet Abdali's full demands and began preparing the fort at Dig for war. Abdali, however, was hesitant to attack the well-defended fort at Dig and decided instead to send his troops into the less protected areas of Braj. He gave his commanders orders to "move into the boundaries of the accursed Jat and in every town and district held by him slay and plunder. The city of Mathura is a holy place of the Hindus, and I have heard that Suraj Mal is there; let it be put entirely to the edge of the sword. To the best of your power leave nothing in that kingdom and country. Up to Agra leave nothing standing."[16]

Abdali's troops arrived in Mathura as Holi, the spring festival of love, was under way. Many pilgrims had come to Braj for this popular celebration. Trying desperately to stop the invading troops, ten thousand Jats had lost their lives several miles north of Mathura at the town of Chaumuha. When the Afghan soldiers entered the city of Mathura, they were told that any booty they could find was theirs and that five rupees would be paid for every head they delivered to the chief minister. Indiscriminate slaughter was carried out for two days. The following report of a witness survives:

It was midnight when the camp followers went out to the attack. It was thus managed: one horseman mounted a horse and took ten to twenty others, each attached to the tail of the horse preceding it, and drove them just like a string of camels. When it was one watch after sunrise I saw them come back. Every horseman had loaded up all his horses with plundered property, and atop of it rode the girl-captives and the slaves. The severed heads were tied up in rugs like bundles of grain and placed on the heads of captives. . . . After afternoon prayer an order was given to carry the severed heads to the entrance gate of the chief minister's quarters, where they were to be entered in registers, and then built up into heaps and pillars. Each man, in accordance with the number of heads he had brought in, received, after they had been counted, five rupees a head from the State. Then the heads were stuck upon lances and were taken to the gate of the chief minister. It was an extraordinary display! Wherever your glance fell nothing else was to be perceived but severed heads stuck upon lances, and the number could not be less than the stars in the heavens.[17]

The ravaging troops then proceeded to Vrindaban, where the massacre continued:

> Wherever you gazed you beheld heaps of the slain; you could only pick your way with difficulty, owing to the quantity of bodies lying about and the amount of blood spilt. At one place we reached, we saw about two hundred dead children lying in a heap. Not one of the dead bodies had a head.[18]

These were certainly the darkest days in the history of Braj. From Vrindaban, Abdali's troops moved on to Mahaban, the site of Krishna's childhood. The site was defended by four thousand militant ascetics, all of whom died fighting the Afghans.[19] Abdali then proceeded to Agra, but here his troops were devastated by an epidemic of cholera and began to demand that they return to Afghanistan. Abdali had no choice but to call off his campaign and leave the Rohilla leader Najib-ud-daulah in control of Delhi.

Suraj Mal's power and influence continued to grow after Abdali left India. In 1761 he captured Agra, the city of the Taj Mahal, and added it to his territory. The contents of the Red Fort were promptly transferred to the forts at Dig and Bharatpur. Suraj Mal was now the undisputed ruler of the Yamuna tract between Delhi and Agra. The only power that could challenge him was Najib-ud-daulah. On Christmas Day 1763, the forces of Najib-ud-daulah encountered the forces of Suraj Mal just south of Delhi. During the fierce battle that ensued Suraj Mal himself was killed. His troops withdrew undefeated, but they had lost their leader. Suraj Mal's body was never recovered, but one of his queens produced two of his teeth, which were cremated at the edge of Mount Govardhan.[20] The pond of Kusum Sarovar was encased with sandstone steps, and on its western bank a beautiful shrine was built in memory of the great King of Braj. The site remains popular with Ban-Yatra pilgrims yet today.

After the death of Suraj Mal, his sons first suffered defeat by the forces of the Jaipuri king Madho Singh and were then crushed by the imperial troops of Delhi, now supported by the powerful Marathas. The Marathas under Mahadji Sindhiya took possession of Delhi, Agra, and Mathura in 1771 and remained the most powerful military force in the area of Braj until the ascension of British power in the early nineteenth century. In 1785 Mahadji established a camp in Vrindaban, which remained his headquarters for six years. He built ghats on the bank of the Yamuna in Vrindaban and the steps of Potarakund, the "Diaper Pond" in Mathura.[21]

At the time of his death, Suraj Mal's kingdom stretched from Delhi to Agra, extending sixty miles on each side of the Yamuna River. The circle of Braj formed the heart of his kingdom. Suraj Mal was a great patron of Braj, particularly of Mount Govardhan, his own "chosen deity," or *ishta-devata*. After he sacked Delhi in 1753, he made Govardhan the state deity.[22] Though the sons of Suraj Mal were forced to acknowledge the superior power of the king of Jaipur and the emperor in Delhi, throughout the eighteenth and nineteenth centuries the successors of Suraj Mal continued to play an influential role in Braj. The Jat kings of Dig and Bharatpur remained the patrons of the town of Govardhan until they lost their power just after independence. Among the many buildings they financed in Govardhan was the famous Mukut Mukharvind temple. Cenotaphs of later Bharatpur kings were erected in the town of Govardhan, on the northern shore of Manasi Ganga.

The palace and gardens of Suraj Mal and Badan Singh today provide much pleasure for the Ban-Yatra pilgrims. We arrived at the palace, now a state museum, after the long walk from Govardhan. The grassy lawns of the palace grounds are flanked on the east and west by two large stone-lined reservoirs called Rup Sagar and Gopal Sagar. These supply the water for the fountains, numbering around five hundred, which make these gardens famous throughout the region. The gardens, laid out according to the fourfold Mughal design, are divided by four canals radiating from a central tank. The palace buildings, which were all given names related to Krishna, are constructed out of a light pink sandstone. Gopal Bhavan, situated on the western edge of the gardens, is the largest and most attractive of the mansions; its delightful arched windows and balconies extend over the water of Gopal Sagar. The architectural beauty of Gopal Bhavan is best appreciated by viewing the mansion's rose-colored reflection on the surface of the surrounding water. The mansion is flanked on the north and south by two ornate symmetrical pavilions known as Savan and Bhadon, the rainy months, respectively, of July–August and August–September. These are two-storied structures capped with a hut-shaped roof that is crowned with a row of spikes. The upper story is an open hall; the lower story is visible only from the reservoir onto which it opens through a finely carved arched veranda. A curtain of water can be made to flow through copper pipes, creating the mood of the rainy season. The Jat architects were masters at artificially producing the charms of the rainy season, a development most likely inspired by the poetic traditions of Braj.[23]

On the opposite side of the gardens is a charming pavilion known by the name Keshav Bhavan, which looks over the reservoir of Rup Sagar. It is an open square pavilion, again designed to create a sense of the amorous mood of the monsoons. Surrounded by a stone canal that is lined with water jets, this pillared pavilion has a double roof filled with water that can be released through pipes on its outer boundary. Round boulders were placed inside the double roof so that when water flows through the system they roll about and imitate the sound of thunder. The interacting pattern produced from the lower jets and upper pipes creates an intricate curtain of water that cools any existing breeze and completes the fantasy with a colorful rainbow.

I sat for a while inside this pavilion with Mr. Nath. We looked out over Rup Sagar and fantasized together about the past glories of the palace of Suraj Mal and Badan Singh. After exploring the remaining buildings, we proceeded to a small pond named Lalakund just outside of town, where camp was being set up. Judging from the sandstone steps and platforms that surround the pond, it must have once been a grand site, but these structures are now crumbling into the water and the shores are overgrown with hardy shrubs and bushes. Brown bodies bathed among the foliage, now littered with red cloths laid out to dry. After locating my tent I joined this activity, pouring buckets of warm water over my head. Splinters of light reflected off the falling drops; a warm breeze rippled against my body. The water dried quickly, and I returned to my tent. There I gulped down a few *chapatis*, locked my valuables in my trunk, and climbed a hill overlooking the pond in search of a cool resting spot.

A group of pilgrims had gathered beneath a large shade tree growing on the hill beside a decaying temple. I was part of this afternoon shade club which assembled each day to sweat out the heat. The group always included Mr. Nath, the driver's license officer from Calcutta; Nirmal Ghosh, the ex-shopkeeper from Navadvip; and Mr. Ibomcha Singh, a seventy-two-year-old man from Manipur who was performing this pilgrimage for the fifth time. The members of the group would lazily discuss various religious topics, bolting up from their straw mats from time to time to make a point forcefully when the conversation strayed into argument—as it frequently did. From our shady perch we could see far in all directions. The terrain that we had been walking through had been extremely flat. Now, however, light brown hills appeared on the northern horizon. We would be heading that way the following day.

No flat plain surrounding the pond was spacious enough to hold all the tents of our pilgrimage party. A few had to be pitched in a separate area next to some fields just north of camp. My own tent was on the far edge of these. Our first hint that this was not the most suitable location came shortly after we had arrived. A huge swarm of hornets attacked our camp, stinging many people. Nirmal Ghosh was stung on the tip of his nose; he thought this rather hilarious. I was sitting in my tent later that afternoon filtering water with my Katadyn pump when five unfamiliar men appeared at the doorway. I didn't like the looks of them. One spoke to me in rough Hindi; the other four surveyed the contents of our tent. My trunk was open and a knife lay on top. The one addressing me demanded that I give the knife to him. I refused, mumbling in English just where I would like to give it to him. After thoroughly scrutinizing our tent, they left. A tonga driver promptly approached me. He was visibly upset and told me that if these men returned I was to force them to leave immediately. He informed me that they were dacoits. I began to look around and realized that our tent was in an unprotected part of the camp. Worse, it was pitched right next to a dense field that would provide good cover for anyone wanting to slip in and out of camp unnoticed. Remembering stories that I had read in local newspapers of poor, isolated farmers being killed by dacoits for a few brass pots, I became very nervous. What would they do for the camera equipment I was carrying? I decided to sleep inside the tent that night. For the first time I desired the presence of the lights and loudspeakers, and understood why the wealthier pilgrimage parties hire armed guards to accompany them. Feeling extremely vulnerable, I placed the coveted knife under my pillow, providing at least the illusion of protection. I slept very lightly that night.

Our guides also must have been quite fearful at this site, for they had us up well before two o'clock. We hurried out of camp and headed into the dry desert hills to the north. The starry night formed a canopy over our path. It was still quite dark when we arrived at our first stop, the village of Paramadana. Our trail wound through shadowy lanes lined with mud-walled houses. We passed sleepy villagers who, from their rope beds that had been set outdoors, groaned and mumbled at our enthusiastic cries of "Radhe! Radhe!" The dogs of the village were the only ones awake to greet us at this early hour. Their barking, however, aroused the village priest, who appeared to open the doors of the temple we had come to see. Within the village of Paramadana is the house of Sudama, the poor childhood schoolmate of Krishna who was later rewarded with great wealth for his steady devotion.

When the temple doors were opened, the pilgrims pushed and shoved to get a glimpse of Sudama standing between Radha and Krishna.

From Sudama's village we turned west, walking single file through dry fields. Occasional sugarcane crops provided relief from the open stretches of land and reflected the dancing rays of the rising sun. We passed an open well crowded with women in brightly colored saris—reds, yellows, even fluorescent green—chattering noisily as they awaited their turn. They offered brass and earthen pots of water to us with wide smiles. A nearby peacock added its welcoming call, and many of the pilgrims responded with shouts of "Radhe! Radhe!" The pilgrims were always jubilant as the sun appeared on the horizon, painting everything with its rose-colored light.

All too soon, however, this source of beauty became a threat. There is nothing gradual about dawn in the desert. We pressed on in the rising heat; the long line of marching feet raised a wall of dust. By midmorning we had arrived at our next camp in a barren field near the Rajasthani village of Khoh, situated at the foot of the Aravalli Hills. On this dusty plain I began my daily routine. I took my trunk and cot off the bullock cart and carried them to my tent. After the long, thirsty walk of the morning, I was anxious to get more water. Renu had just arrived, and we exchanged tired greetings. She informed me that she had just come from a tent pitched in the shade where Rajarani was resting. Although Rajarani had been riding in a tonga the entire way, she was feeling worse by the day. We were both quite worried about her and talked about the possible need for her to abandon the pilgrimage. I locked my cameras and other valuables in my trunk and set out to secure a bucket of drinking water for our tent from a nearby barrel. Returning to the tent, I began pumping filtered water into my two plastic bottles. I guzzled down the first cup I produced, celebrating a fresh supply of water. It is remarkable how preoccupied one becomes with water in a desert climate.

I then removed my shoes and inspected the latest damage. There seemed to be some improvement, but I was still applying seven medicated bandages a day. These would have to wait, however, for I was hot and sweaty and eager for a bath. About a quarter of a mile from my tent was a well. Plastic bucket, lota, and Dr. Bronner's soap in hand, wrapped only in a gamcha, I headed through empty fields in that direction. The circular well was encased in stone and cement, creating a platform of about fifteen feet in diameter raised approximately ten feet off the ground. When I arrived, two dozen people had already crowded onto the platform and were competing for water. The water table was low, making it difficult to draw up the water. I climbed the stone steps leading up to the platform and presented myself to the workers in charge of hauling water. I talked one of them into filling my bucket and then moved to the edge of the platform to join a line of bathers. Turning my back on the busy crowd and squatting, I began to bathe as if I were the only one present. As I poured satisfyingly cool lotas of water over my body, I looked out onto the distant hills shimmering in the heat. Below me stretched a muddy pond. Black, frisky water birds darted among sluggish water buffalo. The warmth of the sunshine and the dry desert breeze felt good on my skin.

While I was bathing, one of the ropes used for hauling up water suddenly broke, leaving a bucket at the bottom of the well. I looked on with horror as one of the workers grabbed onto another rope and descended into the deep hole. Several tense minutes later, he emerged, smiling, bucket in hand. Mr. Nath was waiting for me when I returned to my tent. He had observed me taking notes and greeted me enthusiastically: "You must write about the madness. There are old people here who have difficulty walking, but they are running to meet their god. Have you marked it?" I had indeed marked it. The rush and excitement of the pilgrims as they entered a particular site was remarkable. This pilgrimage is certainly an occasion for divine madness.

Mr. Nath and I talked further about the pilgrimage. Examining his hand he said, "I wonder what it will look like after I finish this pilgrimage."

"What do you mean?" I asked. "Do you expect this pilgrimage to change your hand?"

"It must," he replied. "This pilgrimage changes one's life. The change must be evident in the lines of one's hands."

Later that afternoon I was strolling out of a field of *chara*, a tall crop used for cattle fodder, when I noticed a Jeep coming toward me. My initial thought was that it belonged to the compound of Shrivatsa Goswami, but I quickly dismissed the thought as tormenting wish fulfillment. I kept walking, but the Jeep pulled alongside me and I saw that it was indeed Shrivatsa's. I was greeted by the driver; my guru, Maganlal Sharma; a friend, Asim Krishnadas, who bore gifts of sweet, succulent papayas; and Dr. Umesh Sharma. Umesh had recently finished a doctorate in philosophy from the Institute of Oriental Philosophy, a college in Vrindaban affiliated with Agra University. He was now conducting research on the local arts and crafts of Braj and therefore had an interest in many of the villages through which we would be passing. My letter sent to Shrivatsa had produced results. Since I had been abandoned by Govinda, Shrivatsa and Maganlal thought Umesh would be a useful traveling companion.

Umesh and I were close in age. He had a stocky build and a glowing round face. I was quite happy to have the additional companionship and welcomed him. I soon learned that he wrote plays, was a popular actor in his college days, and had aspirations of being a film star. So far his talents and good looks had landed him only a minor part in a Bombay film. At first he was relatively quiet and very serious, but after some time he began to reveal another side of himself, suddenly serenading me with a recent Hindi film song, punctuated with the movement of his dark expressive eyes. We shared the fruit brought by Asim with great pleasure and decided that he should join my tent. There was room now, as Rajarani had decided to quit the pilgrimage and return to Vrindaban in the Jeep with Maganlal. She had suffered greatly. Although she could chatter away as if she were not in full control of her mind, there was a calming beauty about her that I would miss. This pilgrimage is hard; about a third of the participants were unable to complete the entire circuit. Two days later a woman was taken back to Vrindaban and died that night. Several people informed me that death on a Ban-Yatra was considered blessed.

Umesh and I walked into Khoh, a typical eastern Rajasthani village. Most of the houses are constructed with mud walls and thatched roofs. The region is dry, and fruits and vegetables are scarce. We met the local tailor and cloth merchant, a thin man of about fifty years of age. His face was creased and weatherworn, his cropped, stubbly hair mostly gray. White teeth flashed in a warm and friendly smile, and his bright eyes looked directly into ours with apparent ease. He invited us onto the veranda of his house, where we perched on a rope bed and were served cups of delicious tea. As we relaxed and sipped the tea, he recounted how three years before he and several other villagers had performed the Ban-Yatra in the month of July. They had no tents or carts of any type, but took only what they could carry, obtaining food and shelter from other villagers along the way. They started and finished at their own village, demonstrating that the Ban-Yatra is essentially a circle. The place of beginning and end is of little importance for many; there is no real destination. The point is merely to close the circle. We said our good-byes—"Ram! Ram!"—and walked back to camp under a beautiful red-dust sunset. The pungent smell of the evening's cow-dung fires greeted us.

That night there was a dramatic performance called a *rasa-lila* in our camp. The stage was a crude construction with a picturesque cloth backdrop. A group of young boys from a nearby village enacted the story of the poor brahman Sudama who had trouble keeping his wife clothed and fed, and so journeyed to Krishna's court at Dvaraka seeking financial assistance, with nothing but a small bag of flattened rice to offer his friend. When Sudama entered the palace, Krishna received him gloriously, personally washing his feet and making him sumptuous offerings of food. Sudama was too embarrassed to show Krishna what he had brought for him, but Krishna snatched the bag of rice away from him anyway. Krishna was delighted with the simple gift. Sudama left Krishna's palace the next day, having failed to make the request for assistance as his wife had begged him to do. However, when Sudama arrived back home, he could hardly believe his eyes. Where his shack had stood, there now rose a magnificent palace. His wife, arrayed in jewels and a luxurious sari, stepped out of the gate to welcome him into his new home.

The next morning we rose at what had now become our usual time. At three o'clock we began walking toward the hills to the north. We wandered along soft dirt trails at the bottom of deep ruts cut into the dry terrain and then slowly worked our way to the top of a rocky red pass. The going was especially difficult for those without shoes. The guides—all clad in shoes—urged those in pain to pray for Radha's kindness. From the top of the pass we dropped down into a narrow, fertile valley hidden from the surrounding countryside. A small stream trickled through the valley and a few trees appeared, providing a sharp contrast to the rocky hills nearby.

At the upper end of the valley the trees thickened and we came to the temple of Badrinath. "Badrinath?" those who are familiar with Indian geography might ask. "Isn't that in the Himalaya Mountains?" And indeed it is. Badrinath is a famous temple and pilgrimage site located high in the mountainous region of Garhwal. The main shrine, which houses a black stone image of Vishnu, has been a focus for pilgrimage activity for well over a thousand years. However, for the four months of the so-called rainy season, the pilgrimage guides informed us, Badrinath dwells not in the Himalayas but in Braj. In fact, so do all the other famous pilgrimage sites of the Himalayas. The priest of the Badrinath temple told us that one day Nanda, Yashoda, and the cowherds wanted to visit the Himalayan pilgrimage sites. Krishna, however, could not bear the thought of being separated from them for the time required to perform the journeys—he wanted to continue playing with them in Braj. He therefore caused all pilgrimage sites to come to Braj for the four months of the rainy season so that the cowherds could visit them in his presence. For this reason they all exist in Braj today.

The priest of the Badrinath temple took me to the rooftop and pointed out Hardwar, Rishikesh, Gangotri, Yamunotri, the Ganges River, and other famous Himalayan sites in the surrounding hills. He explained through his long, woolly gray beard that to worship Badrinath in the Himalayas during the four months of the rainy season would be useless, since the deities were dormant then everywhere except in Braj, where they remained actively present. He said that a visit during the monsoon period to Badrinath and the other Himalayan sites reproduced in Braj has the same effect as performing pilgrimage and worship at these distant sites during the other eight months of the year. Thus, the benefits of the Ban-Yatra include those of all these Himalayan pilgrimages. Lord Vishnu declares in the Mathura Mahatmya: "All pilgrimage sites and holy places situated on the seven continents come to Braj when I sleep" (156.3). This is why Narayan Bhatt declares that the Ban-Yatra is to be performed during the rainy season for the greatest benefit. Although all pilgrims I talked with agreed that this is a very difficult pilgrimage, they also agreed that it is easier than making the combined journeys to all other sites.

The notion that Braj is alive while the gods sleep elsewhere highlights two important aspects of this pilgrimage and its conceptual space. First, as with other Indian pilgrimages,[24] the Ban-Yatra is a coincidence of place and time. It is a time out of ordinary activities, but the timing is important. Pilgrimage experience in South Asia is related to the notion that special powers are available at particular places at particular times. The benefits of all other pilgrimages are most powerfully available in Braj during the four rainy months. More importantly, however, this notion highlights the fact that once again the religion of Braj involves reversals. Elsewhere the gods sleep during this season; here in Braj they revel and dance enthusiastically with Krishna. The rainy season is the customary period for ascetics to remain settled in some ashram;[25] during the rainy season the Ban-Yatra pilgrims walk. Braj bhakti is religion in motion. Moreover, one often hears that in Braj everything is mixed up and that the gods' behavior is different here from elsewhere (Shiva is a good example). Braj is a land marked by the desire of a deity who breaks laws more like a child innocently unaware of the rules than an adult who is reacting against them. Therefore, the ways of Braj are not bound by ordinary protocol or patterns of expectation. Krishna simply wished for the pilgrimage sites to join him in Braj, showing a disregard for convention and a playful indifference toward rules. Nothing in Braj is quite the same as it is in the habitualized world. Braj is a carnivalesque playground set apart from the commonplace; it is a special place where Krishna's play undermines all established routines.

The temple of Badrinath in Braj is nestled in a pleasant grove of large flowering shade trees, some known for their sweet plums. Colorful birds inhabit the dark green branches that reach high into the clear, azure sky. This grove is called Tapovan, the "Forest of Asceticism," because it is said that in this forest many famous sages practiced austerities. In fact, the entire surrounding desert area is known to be conducive to the practice of asceticism and is therefore known as Tapasya-Kshetra, a "Field for Asceticism." In the center of the grove, just below the temple, is a deep pond named Taptakund, the "Pond Heated by Ascetic Activity." This desert terrain is clearly associated with ascetic activity; we were soon to learn why.

The temple of Badrinath is an unusual one. It was constructed with a variety of stones, most of which are now painted green and white, and is reached from the grove by a steep set of stone stairs. Inside are numerous images. The central shrine features three old black stone images, which are elaborately decorated and peer out of a gold curtain that has holes cut out for their faces. The temple priest informed me that the central figure is Badrinath, who is standing between Nara and Narayan, the two Himalayan mountain ranges that flank Badrinath. To the right of the three central images stands the divine couple, Radha and Krishna, for all are gathered here to be with them. Further to the viewer's right is a small shrine for Ganga Ma, the goddess of the Ganges, which is said to flow just behind the temple. On the left is a shrine for the ever-present Shiva, featuring a lingam and Shiva's family of Parvati, Ganesh, and Nandi.

We spent a lot of time here, the grove seducing us with its pleasures. After bathing in the deep pond we rested in the cool shade of the dense trees. Brilliant saris were laid out to dry on the steep steps leading down to the pond. Mr. Nath was inspired by the ascetic stories of the grove and requested me to take a picture of him sitting in yogic posture. "Maybe I will sit here for a thousand years," he joked. But after a few minutes he got up and we went to a cart where a man was selling tea and vegetables dipped in a spicy batter and fried in mustard oil. Perhaps we enjoyed ourselves here too much, for it was now quite hot and long past time to be pushing on to our next camp. On the way down the mountain we were to learn why this area was called the field of asceticism or *tapas*: tapas can also be translated as "heat."

By ten o'clock the sun was so intense that many in our group were forced to stop frequently and rest in whatever scant shade could be found. Several were vomiting from the heat. Renu, who appeared to be holding up quite well, helped two elderly women who were having trouble walking. Their saris were wet with perspiration, and their hair stuck to their faces. When we finally reached our camp Umesh was ill. He spoke of returning to Vrindaban. This was his first day out, and I wondered if he was going to be able to bear the difficulties of the journey. The words written in a note by Shrivatsa Goswami and sent with the Jeep the previous day suddenly came back to me. A Japanese scholar visiting a rather luxurious Ban-Yatra two years before had remarked to him, "Why has loving Krishna made Ban-Yatra so difficult?" My thoughts exactly. The pilgrims on this journey suffer intensely; this pilgrimage clearly has something to do with asceticism.[26] Once again I was struck by the extreme contrast between the soft inner world of the passionate stories and this hard ascetic activity. What was the relationship between them, and what is the role of asceticism in the religion of Braj?

We camped near the village of Pasopa. Towering on a hill above Pasopa stands the temple of Pashupati. The latter is Shiva as "Lord of the Animals," who is usually thought to dwell in the holiest Hindu shrine of the Katmandu valley of Nepal. Pashupati, however, also responded to Krishna's summons and resides on the western rim of the circle of Braj during the rainy season, though now images of Radha and Krishna have replaced the original Shiva lingam, lost or stolen some time ago.

I attempted to wash the sweat and dirt out of some of my clothes in this camp. A few children from the village gathered at a well to watch the strange foreigner try to imitate the pounding technique used in India. I soaped my formerly white shirts and slapped them on a stone slab but was unsuccessful at removing the yellow and brown stains. When finished, I held up the shirts; the children giggled at my failure. I returned to my tent and laid the clothes on top of it to dry, hoping no one else would comment on my inept washing abilities. Umesh was kind; he only smiled. After forcing down another bad meal of gritty rice and a few poorly prepared potatoes, we collapsed in bed praying that the Lord of Animals would protect us from the dacoits known to haunt this area. I fell asleep gazing at the black silhouettes of the mountains to the north.

The next day was even more difficult. When we rose from our dust-covered beds at a quarter of two, the stars were brilliant. We would walk until eleven o'clock this day and cover eighteen miles. Heading north, we passed through several dry valleys. As the sun hovered like a big red balloon in the eastern sky, it became obvious that the heat was again going to be fierce. Mountains rose off the desert floor ahead of us. As we pressed on toward their shimmering silhouettes, I found myself daydreaming of the ease and comfort of travel in the compact air-conditioned station wagon I had stashed away in a barn in southern Vermont. I returned to the present with a jolt, and the car's cool comfort slipped back into the dream. It seemed to me, however, that there was something lacking in the kind of travel its memory evoked. We pay a price for the comfort of a controlled environment. For those within a closed car, the outside world whizzes by in a vague and muffled manner. Walking through Braj, one experiences the land directly. The pounding sun produces sweat, rocks cause one to stumble, flower scents reach the nose, the song of a bird delights the ear, dust can be tasted, and the breeze touches the body; one has time to sense and study the shape of the world as it is encountered on the road.

We came upon a herd of white and reddish brown goats. The vastness of the desert slowly absorbed the sound of their jingling bells. They were accompanied by a dark, lean, white-turbaned shepherd who carried a fifteen-foot-long bamboo staff with a scythe tied to one end for cutting foliage from the hard-to-reach branches of the occasional tree. Four camels burdened with turbaned riders and large bundles of cotton came loping past us. They stirred the air, filling our nostrils with dust. Gas-powered water pumps chugged steadily nearby, bringing refreshing water to the earth's parched surface. We zigzagged through fields of tall chara plants nurtured by this irrigation technique and pressed on toward another series of hills rising off the desert floor in the distance.

Ahead, twelve-foot-tall elephant grass lined both sides of the soft dirt of our pathway. The weight of these plants causes them to bend at the top, creating a cool tunnel through which travelers can pass in complete shade. These were the favored thoroughfares—now rapidly disappearing—before the advent of the modern highway. When the tall plants dry out after the rainy season, they are used to make hourglass-shaped stools, rimmed and held together with old bicycle tires. These can be seen scattered about the many roadside tea stalls throughout Braj. We encountered a bullock cart full of villagers in this tunnel of grass. The women peered curiously at us through peepholes fashioned from the saris that covered their heads. Shouts of "Radhe! Radhe!" produced bright smiles on the uncovered faces of the men.

The dusty soil soon gave way to rocky terrain. We eventually came upon a shallow body of water called Gaurikund, the "Pond of the Fair-Colored Goddess." High above the pond, on the peak of a rocky ridge capped with large, light-colored rocks, stood the temple of Kedarnath. Kedarnath is the site of a highly renowned Shiva temple in the distant Himalayas, which houses one of the most famous self-manifested lingams of India. Here Shiva is also called Sada-Shiva, the "Eternal Shiva." Kedarnath, too, joins the other pilgrimage sites in Braj for the four months of the rainy season.

After a refreshing bath in the pond of the goddess, we started up the long flight of stone stairs leading up the mountain to Kedarnath. A red flag marked our destination. From below, the temple appeared to be constructed of white stone. Mohan, my "guide/cook," intercepted us at the base of the mountain, insisting that we remove our shoes and leave them with him, along with a "donation" to cover his services. The blisters on my feet were still raw enough that the climb up the stone steps was very painful. As we approached the summit it became evident that the temple was not man-made at all, but was a natural formation caused by a large white boulder with a deep crevasse on its underside, creating a small cave. The opening was big enough to allow only one person at a time to enter by crawling on hands and knees. From this humble position it was easy to bow to the dark brown lingam of Shiva within. This is said to be a natural lingam, summoned by Krishna to give the residents of Braj the benefits of the Kedarnath pilgrimage without ever leaving Braj. Inside the cave there was just enough space for the attending priest to squat on the floor of alternating black and white marble squares and bless each pilgrim making the passage through the cave with red *sindhur* powder and water made holy from contact with the Shiva lingam. Emerging from the other side, I climbed an outcrop of large boulders just behind the cave temple and sat down to rest. High above the surrounding plain, the view was magnificent; the spot was peaceful, conducive to reflection.

Once again we had come into the presence of Shiva. While I sat thinking about how frequently one encounters Shiva on this "Krishnaite" pilgrimage, the image of a fierce Shiva meditating in the Himalaya Mountains flashed through my mind. This image was immediately followed by another: the figure of Shiva as a beautiful gopi. Suddenly these two contrasting images seemed to represent the tension between the outer world of asceticism and the inner world of eroticism that I had been pondering throughout much of the pilgrimage. I recalled a conversation I had had with Shuklaji. While walking together earlier that same morning I asked him about his daily religious practices. He mentioned that he began his day in Vrindaban with a visit to the Gopishwar temple. Why this particular temple instead of one of the temples of Radha and Krishna? "Because Shiva is the way to Radha and Krishna," he replied. "Shiva is first among the devotees. One enters the lila of Krishna only by way of Shiva. This is why we begin the pilgrimage at Gopishwar."

I was now beginning to understand more about who Shiva is in the culture of Braj, and why he is so important for this pilgrimage. On the one hand, Shiva is understood to be Yogeshwar, the "Lord of the Yogis," who sits naked on a tiger skin high atop Mount Kailash in the distant Himalayas, his body smeared with ashes, performing acts of strenuous asceticism. Shiva, the model male ascetic, is the form that dominates the desert regions around Kedarnath. On the other hand, Shiva is Gopishwar, the "Lord of the Gopis," who dances on the bank of the Yamuna River as a female lover, her body beautifully dressed and decorated with jewels. Here Shiva is the model gopi; it is this form that is declared to be the highest form of Shiva by the residents of Braj. This complex Shiva, hard male ascetic on the outside, soft female lover on the inside, is—as Shuklaji confirmed on a number of occasions—the model pilgrim. Entrance into the world of the Ban-Yatra requires one to make both moves exemplified by Shiva. The order of and relationship between these two moves is important, but it is initially clear that the bliss which the pilgrims seek is found not by avoiding the ascetic move but by going *through* it.

The name Sada-Shiva, an alternate for Kedarnath, brought another relevant image to mind that provided clues regarding how to understand the relationship of these two forms of Shiva and the two moves they represent. Reflection on this image made me realize that it was a mistake to view the asceticism and eroticism of Braj as polar opposites. A couple of years before this, I had had the opportunity of visiting yet another cave in which Shiva is encountered. The Elephanta cave temple, located on a small island off the coast of Bombay, houses one of the most aesthetically powerful sculptures ever produced in India. The temple features an iconographic image of Sada-Shiva which is composed of three heads.[27] One head faces right; another is diametrically opposed to it and faces left; the dominant central head faces forward and appears to emerge out of the borderline created by a boundary of tension which joins the opposing heads. The right-facing figure, wearing a crown with skulls, stares at a cobra it is clutching in its hand with willful determination. It is masculine in form and has been identified by art historians as Bhairava, the fierce, ascetic, destructive side of Shiva. The left-facing figure is feminine and gazes lovingly at a lotus blossom; this has been identified as Uma, the graceful, passionate, creative side of Shiva. These two opposing figures represent the tension of polar opposites. Reflecting on this image, the art historian Stella Kramrisch writes: "Right and left of Mahadeva's 'face of eternity,' the contorted virile visage of Bhairava and the dreaming femininity of Uma represent the mystery of the coexistence of the absolute together with the fundamental pair of opposites of male and female as they exist in God."[28]

We would not be wrong to associate tapas (asceticism) with Bhairava and kama (passion) with Uma. It would be wrong, however, to think of the seemingly opposite states of tapas and kama as mutually exclusive. As Wendy Doniger O'Flaherty has so aptly demonstrated in her *Asceticism and Eroticism in the Mythology of Shiva*: "*Tapas* (asceticism) and *kama* (desire) are not diametrically opposed like black and white, or heat and cold, where the complete presence of one automatically implies the absence of the other."[29]

To understand something very important about the relationship of these two forces, we must shift our attention to the middle head, Mahadeva's face of eternity, for the third head suggests a different way of viewing the opposition of asceticism and eroticism which characterizes much of the Ban-Yatra. The central face is absolutely sublime. Mahadeva's content smile, weighty eyelids, and broad forehead radiate composure, tranquillity, and bliss. The composed face of Mahadeva appears out of the oscillating boundary of the two opposing faces, yet it represents something that goes beyond both of them. The third head of Shiva expands our conceptual framework and opens up possibilities beyond the world defined by polar oppositions. "Mediation is always achieved by introducing a third category which is 'abnormal' or 'anomalous' in terms of ordinary 'rational' categories. . . . This middle ground is abnormal, non-natural, holy."[30] The holy middle ground is represented in the Elephanta cave by the blissful face of Mahadeva. In Braj, however, Shiva's highest form is understood to be Gopishwar; it is precisely this form that Shiva assumes to enter into Krishna's lila and experience ananda (bliss), the elusive point of perfect balance between tapas and kama.

The stated aim of the Ban-Yatra is to realize that everything is Krishna's lila, and the subjective experience of this is ananda. The way to this experience is exemplified by Shiva. While Gopishwar is the highest form of Shiva for the Vaishnavas of Braj, it is important to understand that this form does not eliminate Shiva as the ascetic

Yogeshwar but rather encompasses this aspect. The blissful state of ananda is approached only after ordinary desire has been given up. Desire, in its ordinary condition, driven by willful intent or egoistic concerns, strives to control the show of life, thereby blocking appreciation of the lila that is beyond such control. Satisfaction occurs only when one is united with the object of desire; this results in the samsaric cycles of happiness and pain. To escape such illusory cycles, the ascetic renounces passionate desire. Shiva moves from the passionate Uma to the fierce Bhairava or the ascetic Yogeshwar. But we have already seen that Shiva is unable to enter and enjoy the love forests of Braj in this form. In order to accomplish this, Shiva had to return to the realm of desire; passion, or kama, is necessary to experience ananda, but Gopishwar's kama is not unrelated to tapas.

In Shaivite theology, Bhairava is associated with fire and Uma with water.[31] The fiery Shiva (Bhairava) had to undergo an experience in water to get in touch with his passionate feminine nature (Uma) in order to achieve the gopi form that allows entrance into the lila. It is Shiva as Gopishwar, an erotic form that encompasses both the tapas of Bhairava/Yogeshwar and the kama of Uma, which points the way to the highest experience of ananda. Uma without Bhairava is ordinary troublous desire; Bhairava without Uma is the total suppression of desire; whereas Gopishwar is Uma and Bhairava in perfect balance, desire in which control has been surrendered to Krishna. In the Bansi Bat compound in Vrindaban Gopishwar holds the lotus of Uma and is still decorated with the cobra of Bhairava. By beginning the Ban-Yatra with a significant imitative encounter with Gopishwar, the pilgrims are provided with a potent image to contemplate throughout the pilgrimage the ambiguous move of love.

Our present concern, however, is the role of asceticism in the religion of Braj. We have seen that Gopishwar is not unrelated to Yogeshwar but encompasses this aspect of Shiva. The experience of ananda involves passion (kama) but not a passion divorced from asceticism (tapas). This suggests, ironically, that something can be truly enjoyed only after it has been given up. Attachment limits an object, whereas detachment allows its full nature to shine forth. Before the pilgrims are truly able to play with Krishna, they must renounce ordinary desire through ascetic activity. Ordinary desire is transformed by passing through Tapasya-Kshetra, the "Field of Asceticism." The desert of western Braj is dominated by symbols of asceticism; here reigns Shiva as paradigmatic ascetic. Significantly, however, the pilgrimage does not end in the desert; this is not the final destination. Asceticism is merely the penultimate move which prepares the pilgrims for the highest experience of Krishna's lila.[32]

Most Indian pilgrimages are governed by a set of ascetic rules and regulations called *niyamas*; this one is no different. Though the degree to which any particular pilgrim follows these rules is left to individual choice, I was told by one of the older guides that the standard set of rules is based on the rules established for a stage of life called the *banprastha*, the period of "dwelling in the forest."[33] A Hindu life is ideally divided into four stages, according to scriptures known as Dharma Shastras. The first stage of a celibate student begins around the age of six and lasts for a period of twelve years. After that one enters into the second stage, that of a householder. At this point one takes a marriage partner and begins the business of raising a family. When gray hairs appear on the head, and when one's children themselves have children, one can enter the third stage, the stage of the forest dweller, in preparation for the fourth and final stage of complete renunciation of ordinary life. Since the name of this pilgrimage is the Ban-Yatra or the "Forest Pilgrimage," many understand it to be an appropriate practice for the forest-dwelling stage, here frequently interpreted as a preferred position occupying the interstice between the domestic concerns of the second stage and the preoccupation with moksha of the fourth stage. Indeed, many making up the pilgrimage party I joined were at the stage of life when they had grandchildren and could leave the business of tending the family to their children.

Rules that various individual pilgrims told me they were observing for the duration of the pilgrimage included refraining from the following: sleeping on anything but the ground, sitting on chairs, oiling the hair and body, shaving, wearing shoes, using soap, engaging in sex, speaking ill of others, eating salt, feeling anger, harming living creatures, eating meat, or ingesting intoxicants. Some of these were overlooked by many pilgrims, especially by the pandas, the professional pilgrimage guides. All, however, agreed that at the very least one was to meditate as much as possible on the stories of Krishna encountered on the pilgrimage.

There is one more very important rule governing the Ban-Yatra, and this rule tells us much about the particular form of ascetic activity involved in this pilgrimage. As one guidebook expresses it: "In this pilgrimage all devotees should maintain the emotional state of a female companion of Shri Radha and Krishna; they should not think of themselves as a male."[34] The anthropologist Lynch writes: "In the *pari-*

krama, the model of the mystic is not the person who gives up all for Christ to understand the mystery of redemption through the *via crucis*. Rather, it is the love-sick milkmaid, who, entranced by a flute-playing trickster, abandons home and family to dance with him in the mystery of *lila*, god's play and sport."[35] The type of asceticism experienced in the Ban-Yatra is neither a suffering endured to overcome sin nor a suffering endured to withdraw from the world; it is a suffering endured in pursuit of love and bliss. The passionate asceticism of the forest is the asceticism Radha endures to accomplish a secret tryst with Krishna.

Several pilgrims explained to me that the only way to experience the full benefits of the Ban-Yatra was by taking on what they called the *gopi-bhava*, that is, by imaginatively entering into the emotional state of a female lover of Krishna or a companion of Radha. Only in this way, they insisted, could one enter into Krishna's play. There is much to this last statement. To fully enjoy the forests of Braj, one must be careful not to get stuck in the desert of asceticism.

NOTES

1. See, for example, Krishnadas Baba, *Braj Mandal Darshan*, 52. The story of Vamana and Bali is found in *Bhagavata Purana* 8.18–23.

2. See Kalika Ranjan Qanungo, *History of the Jats* (Calcutta: M. C. Sarkar, 1925), 18–23. Qanungo suggests that it was during the reign of Badan Singh that this claim was first made, since it legitimated his attempts to maintain political control over the region of Braj (See also p. 62 in the same volume).

3. Ram Pande, *Studies in History: The Jats* (Jaipur: Chinmaya Prakashan, 1981), 3–4.

4. Khushwant Singh, *History of the Sikhs*, vol. 1 (Princeton, N.J.: Princeton University Press, 1963), 15.

5. K. Natwar-Singh, *Maharaj Suraj Mal* (New Delhi: Vikas Publishing House, 1983), 2.

6. Qanungo, *History of the Jats*, 39.

7. Vincent A. Smith, *Akbar the Great Mogul* (Oxford: Clarendon Press, 1902), 328. See also Natwar-Singh, *Maharaj Suraj Mal*, 11.

8. Natwar-Singh, *Maharaj Suraj Mal*, 19.

9. Ibid., 22.

10. Ibid., 23.

11. From Thornton's *Gazetter of India*, cited in ibid., 26.

12. Entwistle, *Braj*, 190.

13. Ibid., 191.

14. Natwar-Singh, *Maharaj Suraj Mal*, 36.

15. Ibid., 64.

16. Qanungo, *History of the Jats*, 99.

17. See William Irvine, "Ahmad Shah, Abdali, and the Indian Wazir Imad-ul-Mulk (1756–57)," *Indian Antiquary* 36 (1907): 60.

18. Ibid., 62.

19. Entwistle, *Braj*, 198.

20. Natwar-Singh, *Maharaj Suraj Mal*, 105.

21. Entwistle, *Braj*, 204–11.

22. Toomey, *Food from the Mouth of Krishna*, 52, note 29.

23. M. C. Joshi, *Dig* (New Delhi: Archaeological Survey of India, 1982), 12.

24. See John M. Stanley, "Special Time, Special Power: The Fluidity of Power in a Popular Hindu Festival," *Journal of Asia Studies* 37, no. 1 (1977): 27–43.

25. Most likely following the early Buddhist precedent.

26. Victor Turner has made the claim that all pilgrimages are a form of temporary asceticism; see his introduction to *Image and Pilgrimage in Christian Culture*. Though this is true in part of the Ban-Yatra, we must again be careful not to allow general statements to overshadow the specificity of a given tradition. The asceticism of the Ban-Yatra is a very particular kind of asceticism.

27. My interpretation of Sada-Shiva at Elephanta follows the interpretations of J. N. Banerjea, "The So-Called Trimurti of Elephanta," *Arts Asiatiques* 2 (1955); Kramrisch, *The Presence of Siva*, 443–68; and Heinrich Zimmer, *Myths and Symbols in Indian Art and Civilization* (Princeton, N.J.: Princeton University Press, 1972 [1946]), 148–51. Kramrisch explains that this representation really has five heads, although one is beyond representation and the other is not depicted since it faces into the rock background of the sculptural image. Nevertheless, she develops her interpretation of this form from the three heads that are visible.

28. Kramrisch, *The Presence of Siva*, 448.

29. O'Flaherty, *Asceticism and Eroticism*, 35.

30. Edmund Leach, as quoted by O'Flaherty, *Asceticism and Eroticism*, 36.

31. See Kramrisch, *The Presence of Siva*, 183. I have heard it said in Braj that Shiva was able to become a passionate gopi by identifying with the feminine side of his androgyne nature through his dip in the Yamuna.

32. The moves represented by the stories of Shiva are also expressed in the philosophical systems of Braj. The three positions described above are perhaps explained most clearly in the philosophical system of the Pushti Marg. The move from the world of ordinary and problematic desire to the world of supreme love is expressed with three hierachical terms. The ordinary state, characterized by the problematic desire for control, is called *adhibhautika*. The intermediary ascetic state, wherein desire is given up in pursuit of the formless One (called in Pushti Marg *akshar Brahman*), is called *adhyatmika*. This move

prepares one for the highest *adhidaivika* state, which consists of love *(prema)* for Bhagavan, who can take any form and is clearly recognized as being beyond control. See Barz, *The Bhakti Sect of Vallabhacarya*, 62.

33. Seth Govindadas claims that the niyamas were established for all sampradayas in Narayan Bhatt's *Vraja Bhakti Vilasa;* see his "Braj-Yatra ka Uday aur Vikas," 89.

34. Mohan Das "Narad Baba," *Sampurna Braj Darshanam*, 18.

35. Lynch, "Pilgrimage with Krishna," 189.

5

Playing Around

After seeing him the eyes fled off the face:
    it seemed as if the lotus, having discarded
    the sun was running away.
The moon and the lily met each other. I could
    hide the expression of love with a trick.
O lady, I saw Madhava today. Having forsaken
    its gravity my bashfulness vanished away.
The knot in the lower garment became loose and
    fell on the ground. I was hiding my body
    under my body.
Even my heart seemed to be of another person.
In all directions I saw Krishna and Krishna alone.

> VIDYAPATI, from *The Songs of Vidyapati*

Shiva, the mighty ascetic, was once lost in meditation upon his tiger-skin perch high in the snowy Himalayas. He had been there for eons, no one caring or daring to disturb him. One day, however, the gods faced a problem for which they required the service of Shiva: a powerful demon named Taraka was terrifying the universe. The god Brahma had given him the boon that he could be killed only by a son of Shiva. Assuming that the hardened ascetic would never sire a child, the demon was confident that he had achieved immortality and so began tyrannizing the universe. Desire, therefore, had to be awakened in Shiva.

Early Hindu texts inform us that kama, or desire, is the root of all action, the moving force behind the differentiating process of creation.[1] Those who view the created world as a dangerous trap to be escaped eschew desire as a way of disengaging and freeing themselves from

160

the disintegrating process. Shiva as the ascetic Yogeshwar exemplifies this move. Those, however, who view the created world as an emanation of divinity embrace desire as the means of engaging in and enjoying the beautiful gift of the creative process. Much of Hindu tradition is a fascinating blend of these two seemingly opposite tendencies.[2] Since the creative process is itself seen as part of Krishna's lila in Braj Vaishnavism, Shiva must return to the realm of desire in order to participate in the play of the world.

To accomplish their scheme of seducing Shiva into action, the gods sought the aid of Kamadev, the "God of Desire," who is usually pictured in Hindu traditions as a handsome youth armed with a sugarcane bow and arrows tipped with beautiful flowers. He rides a parrot and is accompanied by his dear friend Spring. Fearing the dreadful ascetic, Kamadev at first refused the mission, but finally agreed once he understood what was at stake. Kamadev stealthily approached Shiva and released a potent arrow. It found its mark; Shiva's tranquil meditations were shattered by the stirrings of desire. He was furious. A blinding ray of light emerged from Shiva's third eye, located between his eyebrows, and reduced Kamadev to ashes. Because of this act, Shiva is commonly known as the destroyer of desire (Kamanashan). Kamadev is the enemy of Shiva, for desire is the destroyer of the ascetic's withdrawal.[3] But Kamadev's arrow had pierced Shiva's heart, thereby causing him to forsake his previous life, fall in love with Parvati, the enchanting daughter of the mountain, and produce the required son, Skanda, who eventually killed the threatening demon Taraka.

This, however, was not the end of Kamadev. After meandering some fifteen miles to the northeast of our last campsite, we came upon the fifth of the twelve forests, Kamaban, the "Forest of Desire." The *Skanda Purana* claims that in this forest all desires are fulfilled.[4] This is one of the reasons it is called the Forest of Desire. But there is another: our pilgrimage guides told us that in this forest Krishna (or by some accounts Shiva himself) restored Kamadev to life. Kamaban is an important site of Krishna's love play with the gopis, and it is said that Krishna attracts hundreds of Kamadevs here to participate in this performance.[5] The restoration of Kamadev is necessary since Braj Vaishnavism does not aim for freedom from emotional involvement but enlists the services of Kamadev in pursuit of the highest love. Whereas the great philosopher of yoga, Patanjali, defined yoga as the cessation of the fluctuations of the heart/mind, the Gaudiya Vaishnava philosopher of bhakti, Rupa Goswami, writes that the highest love manifests in the fluctuations of the heart/mind.[6] Far from renouncing desire, Braj bhakti uses it as Manmath, the "One Who Churns the Heart."

Desire has a prominent place in the religion of Braj. Many Gaudiya Vaishnavas daily recite a mantra called the Kama Gayatri: "We meditate on Kamadev, who is armed with flowery arrows; may that disembodied one inspire us."[7] This mantra, which invokes the god of desire, is said to have come from the sound of Krishna's flute. Moreover, the Kamadev of Braj is typically identified with Krishna. In his commentary on the *Bhagavata Purana*, Vallabha identifies the highest spiritual form (*adhidaivik*) of the worldly Kamadev (Manmath) as none other than Krishna, who dances with the gopis in the forests of Braj.[8] Krishnadas Kaviraj makes a similar identification in his *Chaitanya Charitamrita* and says that the Krishna of Braj is the uncommon (*aprakrita*) and ever new (*navin*) Kamadev.[9] The name he uses for Kamadev is Madan, the "Intoxicator." Krishna, however, is not to be confused with the ordinary Madan, for in a popular play staged in Braj Krishna defeats this Madan—or, more precisely, the ordinary Madan exhausts himself in his encounter with Krishna.[10] In Braj, Krishna is Madan-Mohan, the "Enchanter of the Intoxicating Cupid," and this particular form of Kamadev is considered more powerful than and superior to the previous one. The Kamadev who attends Krishna's love play has been tempered by the fire of asceticism, which has burned away all egoistic desire. Here desire has been transformed into pure love.

We can understand more about the important distinction between ordinary desire and the highest love, and between Madan and Madan-Mohan, by looking more closely at the terms Krishnadas Kaviraj uses to characterize the Kamadev of Braj: aprakrita, or "uncommon," and navin, or "ever new." In contrast, ordinary desire is common and exhausting. Common love is said to diminish over time. Common love, which is focused on ordinary objects, aims to penetrate, master, and completely know an object. But absolute knowledge kills love. Lovers lose each other, become bored with one another, at the moment they assume they know each other. Common love is easily exhausted, and exhausts one with disappointment. Uncommon love, on the other hand, is ever new because, since it is directed toward an eternal object (*nitya vishaya*) that is ever-changing and completely beyond mastery, absolute knowledge never comes into play. It is a nonpenetrating love that has surrendered control and is content to play with the ever-changing surfaces. The uncommon Kamadev—who is nondifferent from Krishna—inspires a love which is ever new and never diminishes over time, but remains ever bright and intense. This love is called *prema*.

The theologians of Braj maintain that an understanding of the relationship between ordinary desire (kama) and the highest love (prema) is extremely important. Krishnadas Kaviraj, for example, writes in the *Chaitanya Charitamrita* (which summarizes much of the philosophy of the Six Goswamis of Vrindaban) that kama and prema are as different as iron and gold.[11] He goes on to say that an act of kama is done for the purpose of pleasing only oneself, whereas an act of prema is done solely for the pleasure of Krishna, the one who needs no pleasure. That is, kama is egoistic, useful desire, whereas prema is egoless. Kama aims at a purposeful, orgasmic end (the child Skanda is the result of Kamadev's attack on Shiva), whereas prema involves ongoing excitement (the gopis are never impregnated in prema). Krishna's lovers are just playing around. John Hawley says it well: "Kam bears children, prem does not. Kam supplies much of the motivating force that brings the world of family and social obligation into being; prem builds nothing. And if kam can build, it can also exhaust itself, but prem cannot. It has only the most mystical relation to time; it is eternal."[12]

Ordinary desire, associated with love in the city, is a selfish love motivated by a sense of purpose which aims to feed the ego; it is governed by social conventions. The ascetic (represented by Shiva) renounces the tumultuous swings of desire (represented by Kamadev) and retires to the forest, giving up love. But the higher state of prema involves a return to love after all purpose has been abandoned in the fire of asceticism. This is the love of the forest. Here the desire for control is renounced and the ego dissolves in the aimless play of Krishna.

It is also important to realize that prema is not exclusive of kama; prema stands on the borderline between ordinary desire and renunciation. The place of asceticism in the religion of Braj was explored in the desert; Kamaban provides an opportunity to explore the place of desire. Desire is not suppressed in the religion of Braj; bhakti theorists claim that it is spiritually too potent to be so wasted. The terms Krishnadas Kaviraj uses to characterize kama and prema are well-known alchemical elements: iron is turned into gold in an alchemical process of heating. Kamadev is transformed in Shiva's fire, the disciplinary heat (tapas) of asceticism. Shashibhusan Dasgupta writes: "There is no categorical distinction in kind between human love and divine love; it is human love transformed by strict physical and psychological discipline that becomes divine love."[13] The difference between these two kinds of love has to do with the motive behind the passionate force, not with the force itself. Prema is kama in which egoistic control has been surrendered. Dasgupta continues: "*Prema* is but the purified form of *kama*, and hence, *prema* cannot be attained through the absolute negation of *kama*; it is to be attained rather through the transformation of *kama*."

Although Dasgupta made these statements in a discussion of an unorthodox (Sahajiya) position, I think they well represent a dominant view in Braj. I heard several stories there which expressed the notion that kama becomes prema with a shift in motive and object. This transformation is perhaps best illustrated by the life story of Nandadas, one of the famous eight poets of Braj associated with the Pushti Marg.[14]

According to the *Chaurasi Vaishnava ki Varta*, Nandadas was the younger brother of Tulsidas, the saintly devotee of Rama who lived in Banaras. Nandadas was passionately attached to things of the world and one day decided, against the advice of his elder brother, to join a group of people traveling west. En route he saw a beautiful woman who had just bathed and was drying her hair. He fell hopelessly in love with her and declared that every day he would not eat or drink anything until he had had sight of the woman's face. When the woman's husband discovered what was going on he objected, but Nandadas silenced him by threatening to commit suicide. In despair, the husband of the woman decided to move his family to Gokul, since they were disciples of Vallabha's son Vitthalnath. Nandadas followed the family to Gokul, however, refusing to give up the object of his desire. When the family reached the Yamuna River the husband bribed the ferryman not to take Nandadas across. Later that day, their guru, Vitthalnath, invited the family to enjoy a meal in his temple. Curiously, he had set an extra place. When the husband inquired why he had done so, Vitthalnath asked him what was to be done with the man they had left on the other side of the Yamuna? Vitthalnath then informed them that Nandadas was a divine soul whose lust for the woman had drawn him to Krishna. The moment Nandadas saw the Yamuna—an attractive, feminine form of Krishna—his lust had been transformed into an ecstatic love for Krishna. From that day on he began producing passionate poems about the love of Braj.

According to local tradition, Tulsidas eventually learned that Nandadas was staying in Braj and traveled here to convince him to return to Banaras and worship Rama. After experiencing much pressure from his older brother, Nandadas finally quipped: "Why should I give up Krishna for Rama? Rama had only one wife and couldn't even keep her; Krishna had sixteen thousand and managed to satisfy them all."

As the story of Nandadas illustrates, passion is very useful for the life of bhakti; it is a powerful force that is neither to be wasted in complete suppression nor to remain in its ordinary state. It is to be used for the ultimate realization. Passion, in the hearts of passionate yogis such as the gopis, leads to the highest realization: Krishna is all. In their intense longing for Krishna, the gopis see Krishna everywhere. They use their powerful, single-minded passion to experience Krishna in everything. In so doing they are on a par with the Upanishadic mystics who strive to realize that everything is Brahman.

Three hierarchical positions with respect to kama emerge from these considerations. The lowest state is love in the city, which consists of remaining in the realm of Kamadev and following the ways of ordinary desire. A better state is to move to the realm of Shiva, asceticism in the forest, and renounce desire altogether. But the highest of all states is to use desire, now transformed through ascetic surrender, for establishing a relationship with Krishna and thereby enter his joyful realm of love in the forest.[15]

Shiva is once again present in Braj as an illustrative example. In the middle of the town of Kamaban is a small Shiva temple, referred to in historical documents dating from the eighth century.[16] This is another of the four famous Shiva shrines said to have been established by Krishna's great-grandson Vajranabh. The temple houses a smooth, broad, reddish lingam that was wrapped with a bright pink cloth on the day I visited the temple. Here resides Kameshwar, "Lord of Desire;" this is the Shiva who uses desire. We have seen that Kamadev is able to participate in the love play of Braj because of his fiery encounter with Shiva; here Shiva is able to participate in the love play because of his upsetting encounter with Kamadev. Asceticism (tapas) and passion (kama) meet and mix on the borderline that is the love (prema) of Braj. At this temple I was told that having burned up kama, Shiva accepts it back here in the forest of Kamaban to play with Krishna. Having renounced kama as an ascetic, it returns as prema to Shiva the lover of Krishna; a Shiva, as we have seen, who surrenders his controlling lingam to become a gopi. In Braj, Shiva—along with those who follow him—learns that renunciation is not the final goal but only a penultimate resting station on the way to the highest experience of ongoing prema.

The trek from Kedarnath to Kamaban was a long one; we would walk for over nine hours this day. Emerging gradually from the desert climate that surrounds Badrinath and Kedarnath, we headed east, back in the direction of the Yamuna River valley. Flat brown expanses stretched in all directions as far as the eye could see. Both the stillness and the pounding energy of the noon sun impressed me. My shirt was soaked with perspiration. The weight of my pack cut into my shoulders, and I questioned the wisdom of carrying so much camera equipment, particularly because I was frequently too tired to use it. I walked with Umesh; he, too, was burdened by our sweltering labor but could still come up with a few good Bombay film songs to enliven our spirits. We arrived in Kamaban, where we would camp for two nights, too tired to do any more exploring for the day. We ate what we could of the cooks' potatoes and chapatis and then sweated out the afternoon in the shade of a compound wall. The next day we would traverse the fourteen-mile path around Kamaban.

That night I had plenty of time to talk with more people about why they were performing this pilgrimage. I met a mathematics professor and an electrical engineer, both from Calcutta, who had been sent by their guru. They told me that he had sent them to Braj saying, "The Ban-Yatra is the best way to come to know Krishna deeply." They emphasized the last word. I spoke also with a retired railway manager from Calcutta. His children were all settled with families of their own, and his wife had died ten years ago. He had taken up residence in Vrindaban and had been living there for the past two years. He said that many of the people he had encountered in Vrindaban who had impressed him had told him again and again, "You will not really understand Krishna until you do the Ban-Yatra." Repeatedly, I heard such statements, confirming the notion that the best way to understand something of Krishna's nature is by performing the Ban-Yatra.

My cot continued to be a focus for social activity. I had placed it outside my tent that evening, and Maya, the young Bengali woman I had first seen at Radhakund, who later on the road asked me to buy her a cup of tea, came by and started a conversation with me. Her long hair fell loose about her shoulders, and she was dressed in a yellow robe. Eventually she sat down on my cot and began telling me about her life. She was thirty-six years old, though I would have guessed that she was much younger. Eighteen years before she had been widowed without any children. The status of many widows in Bengal is very low. A woman is held responsible for the life force of her husband, and when a man dies his wife is sometimes blamed, her position in the family falls dramatically, her economic situation changes, and her living conditions may become wretchedly poor.[17] Her situation is even worse if she has had no children. Rather than endure such a situation, Maya decided to renounce domestic life altogether and pursue a spiritual life. She had spent years traveling around the holy towns of Bengal before making her way to Braj. Over the past eighteen years she had met some remarkable men and women who had taught her much about spiritual matters. But, she explained, all signs pointed to Braj. Soon after arriving in Braj, she heard of Radhakund and knew immediately that was where she wanted to be. She has been living there for the past three years. I asked her why she had joined us on the Ban-Yatra. She shot me a quick glance and then replied, "To have an experience of the 'dancing land' of Radha and Krishna." She smiled seductively, got up, and walked away, leaving me to ponder this last statement.

An old man from Assam had joined us while Maya was talking and had begun massaging my arms and legs. I had no idea why he was doing this, but after days of hard walking and aching muscles, I did not really care. It felt great. After finishing, he offered to fetch a bucket of drinking water for me. When he returned he informed me that he needed a place to sleep. Since I was sleeping outdoors anyway, there was plenty of room in my tent. I welcomed him and he joined our tent. Six days later he stole my pair of rubber sandals; my unhappy reaction caused him to seek shelter elsewhere, though he kept my sandals.

Kamaban is now more important for the Pushti Margi denomination of Vaishnavas than it is for the Gaudiyas. In fact, the Pushti Margis, whose temples dominate Kamaban, consider it to be the original Vrindaban. This claim is further enhanced by the fact that today the red-faced image of the goddess Vrindadevi resides in the Govindadev temple of Kamaban. The original images once housed in Vrindaban's Govindadev temple were taken out of Vrindaban just before imperial Mughal forces attacked the area during Aurangzeb's reign. Govindadev was eventually moved to his present residence in the city palace of Jaipur, but the story is told that Vrindadevi refused to move out of Braj and desired to remain in Kamaban. This is where pilgrims come to see her today.

On the southwestern edge of town is the most important pond in Kamaban—Vimala Kund, the only site at Kamaban mentioned in the Mathura Mahatmya of the *Varaha Purana*. There Vishnu, in the form of the boar Varaha, declares: "One is freed from all impurities in the pond of Vimala; one who gives up life here goes to my world."[18] Vimala Kund is an attractive square pond, encased in stone steps and surrounded by numerous temples, ashrams, and large shade trees. When we arrived, the branches of these trees were filled with noisy white-necked storks, and monkeys raced about their trunks. Light played on the surface of the pond, causing a shimmering reflection to pulsate on the surrounding buildings.

Umesh and I wandered into the temple of Vimala Devi, the presiding goddess of the pond, seeking shelter from the near-noon heat. Thick walls shut out the strong light. At one end of the room was the shrine of the goddess, who was dressed in bright clothing and decorated with flowers. The soft, sweet breath of incense filled the air. Four pilgrims entered the temple and walked up to the shrine; they stood for several minutes looking at the beautifully adorned goddess, then tossed a few coins and left. The priest of the temple produced three burlap sacks, laid them on the floor, and invited Umesh and me to sit with him. The marble floor was cool. He stroked his long beard several times and then began to tell the following story.

There was once a king from the northwestern region of Sindh named Vimala. King Vimala had a problem: he had no children. One day the king met the sage Yajnavalkya in a forest and, in the course of conversation, revealed his problem. Yajnavalkya took pity on him and blessed him, foretelling that he would not have a son but would have many daughters, all destined to surrender to Krishna. The six thousand wives of the king soon gave birth to twelve thousand daughters. When these had grown into beautiful women, a messenger was sent to find suitable husbands. The messenger arrived in Braj and found Krishna, who was quickly judged to be man enough for all. The king's daughters were soon sent to Braj to join Krishna. In the forest of Kamaban, Krishna met and began dancing with them all in the circular love dance in which he multiplies himself to equal the number of women. As Krishna made love to each of them, tears of joy flowed profusely from their eyes. The pond of Vimala Kund was formed from these tears.

Ban-Yatra pilgrims also encounter many significant rocks around Kamaban. On the way to Kamaban we had visited a hill called Charan Pahari, the "Mountain of the Foot." Atop this small mountain rests a white boulder with an indentation in the shape of a foot. The boulder is bathed with water and smeared with red powder. Attendants kept the crowds moving; one of them informed us that this footprint was left by Krishna after the rock had softened, while listening to the sound of his flute. Such claims are naturally met with some doubt on the part of the outsider, especially considering the economic benefits gained by the attendants busily collecting money from the pilgrims. But upon observing several women bow down and touch their heads to this stone, come up with tears streaming down their faces, and hug each other crying, "O Sister! O Sister!" I began to think that questions such as "Is this really Krishna's footprint?" were inappropriate. I realized that these women and I simply experienced the rock before us very differently.

Reality is not set for human beings; multiple realities or worlds of meaning are available to us.[19] Judgments of realities are difficult, because there is nowhere to stand that is not situated within a particular reality, which by its very nature regards other realities with suspicion. The conceptual framework by which we consider the conceptual framework of another culture is itself a cultural product with an implicit definition of reality. The historian of religions therefore brackets judgmental considerations and accepts all realities as potentially valid.[20]

Such questions as "Did this really happen here?" are really concerned with the issue of historical authenticity, but this way of thinking is somewhat alien to the religious thought of Braj. For most of the people with whom I discussed this problem, it had more to do with the issue of *bhava*, that is, with the investment of a certain kind of emotional and imaginative energy. In this context the place is not as important as the emotional investment. Talking with a priest who had set up a new shrine at a particular pilgrimage site when the old one no longer proved to be convenient, Entwistle observed: "The Panda presiding at the new shrine was unperturbed when asked about the pre-existing Kalidaha further upstream. 'No problem,' he said, 'we can make a third one if we want.'"[21] One can talk about this as a "fabrication," as Entwistle does, but I think this misses an important point.

There is frequently a sophisticated philosophy operative in Braj that is perhaps best expressed in a work written by Vallabha entitled the *Siddhantamuktavali*.[22] In this work Vallabha outlines three different perspectives by which one can view the world; the world is ultimately nondual, but the form it takes depends on one's perception. Vallabha presents the three perceptual possibilities by using the example of the Ganges. The first level is a perception of the water or physical form of the river; most anyone can see this form. The second is a perception of the Ganges as a power of the undifferentiated reality which underlies all forms; this form is perceived through meditative insight and is approached for spiritual benefits. The third level of perception enables one to see the Ganges as a goddess; this form is perceived through bhakti and is approached with no purpose in mind other than to praise the Goddess Ganges.[23] Vallabha compares the physical world to the first form, the undifferentiated Brahman pursued by the ascetic to the second form, and the full manifestation of Krishna to the third. Vallabha's point, however, is that all three forms are Krishna. Though it is the result of a more limited perception, the world of physical forms is still divine. Thus every rock is a form that is nondifferent from Krishna and potentially can evoke this realization. Not every rock, however, reveals the higher reality of Krishna; only rocks invested with bhava do so. The highest reality is perceptible in a particular object only when one invests that object with the emotional imaginative energy that is called bhava. This process is greatly enhanced when the object has been marked as special and emotionally invested by a large number of people. The investment of bhava, then, not historical authenticity, is the real issue in considering the value of a site for the residents of Braj. In a sense, all shrines are fabrications, but they are fabrications that help one see what is already there. As a tour of these shrines, the Ban-Yatra can be viewed as a process of cultivating bhava, an emotional perception that allows one to become aware that everything is Krishna. What I was witnessing, on the part of these women, was an intense emotional experience that was the result of a very different perception of the rock at Charan Pahari than I had.

Richard Niebuhr writes: "Pilgrims are poets who create by undertaking journeys. . . . Pilgrims see symbols everywhere. Each particular thing beckons the pilgrim as a potential icon and cipher of what is to come."[24] The world of the pilgrim is marked in a peculiar way, and the pilgrim's landscape is charged with meaning. Pilgrims see signs in the ordinary world of a world beyond the ordinary. Again, we can use the word *symbol* only if we realize that the ontological gap between the signifier and the signified has collapsed; the duality of profane and sacred is out of place in this context. The rock of Charan Pahari is both the foot of Krishna and the footprint of Krishna. The world of forms in which Krishna is present is marked with signs of a Krishna who is absent. Where I saw only a rock, these women saw a window into another reality. The rocks of Braj are the words of a poem that paint a picture of another world, and the Ban-Yatra is a way of reading those words and evoking the world of Krishna. The rock before us was an ordinary rock, but for those who saw Krishna's footprint in it, it was also a doorway into another reality.

The process by which religious participants cross a threshold into another reality is usually called ritual. The anthropologist Clifford Geertz has written: "In ritual, the world as lived and the world as imagined, fused under the agency of a single set of symbolic forms, turn out to be the same world, producing that idiosyncratic transformation in one's sense of reality to which Santayana refers in my epigraph ('another world to live in—whether we expect to pass wholly over into it or no—is what we mean by having a religion')."[25] In this regard, the Ban-Yatra is ritual. Contact with the physical forms of Braj that have been invested with emotional energy, such as the rock at Charan Pahari, cultivates an enhanced emotional experience that affirms the presence of Krishna.

This was not the only significant rock we visited. During our circumambulation of Kamaban, we came to a site on the northeastern rim called Bhojan Thali, the place of the "Eating Dish." On the side of a mound just above a small pond lies a rock with a shallow circular indentation. Here, we were told, Krishna once met the gopis and wanted to enjoy a meal with them. The gopis had plenty of food but no plates. Krishna easily solved this problem by making a dish out of stone. The stone seemed to delight the pilgrims, who gathered around it discussing its shape and imagining how one would eat from it.

Another stone at another site delighted them even more. To the west of Bhojan Thali is a site known as Khisalini Shila, the "Rock Slide," a large slab of stone perched at a sharp angle on the side of a hill. A smooth groove approximately fifteen feet long runs down the middle of it. Krishna and his friends enjoyed sliding down this rock, and the pilgrims did the same. They positioned themselves in the groove, let go, and squealed with delight as they slipped down the slide used by Krishna—a form of rump communion, one might say. One by one, and in trains of three to five, they took turns sliding down the rock again and again. Here was an opportunity to participate physically in Krishna's play. The text of Braj is not to be read with the eyes alone but with the whole body. The texts of Braj, these signs in stone, are touched, kissed, hugged, caressed, crawled over, and slid down. The entire body is the vehicle of the sensual experience of pilgrimage.

The next morning we were up by three and walking along a narrow road that followed an irrigation canal. The moon had already set, and it was very dark. Large trees lined the canal, cutting out even the starlight. Katydids and crickets chirped loudly. The road was cracked and pitted by erosion. I had foolishly left my flashlight in my trunk, which was now somewhere on the bullock cart, and I was stumbling terribly. Several times I cursed fiercely, glad that those around me could not understand my language. I could tell from the groans and stumbles ahead that others were also having difficulty. An old Bengali woman walking just in front of me suffered the trail while softly singing songs to Radha. Once again I marveled at the presence of Radha in the midst of such suffering.

Our destination that day was Barsana, Radha's hometown. As we approached Barsana we were met by a cool breeze—and a most impressive sight. A tall, thickly wooded hill stood on the horizon. Poking out of the top of the green trees was a magnificent temple; from this distance I remember thinking that it looked something like a Disneyland castle. On our way to this hill temple we stopped at a small pond near the village of Unchagaon for our morning bath. A dip in this pond is said by some to be a prerequisite for entering the area of Barsana; it cools one down after the heating in the asceticism of the desert. The pond is known as Dehakund, the "Pond of the Body." The body referred to is the gopi body, the body of a passionate female lover acquired by bathing in this pond. If the bath in the Yamuna had somehow failed, this one was guaranteed to work.

Beautiful reflections began to appear as the morning light slowly illuminated the surface of Dehakund. Lush green bushes with yellow flowers lined the distant shore. An island emerged in the center of the pond; anhinga birds rested in the upper branches of its trees, wings outstretched to catch the rays of the morning sun. Several buffalo slurped water from a nearby bank, and a tonga driver led his tired horse to the pond for a drink. Bathers began to descend the steps leading into the pond. A woman standing beside me held her arms close to her body; for the first time there was a chill in the air. This was a pleasant break from the heat of the desert. Dipping and splashing in the water, brushing teeth, drying limbs, combing long black hair, putting on fresh clothes, applying religious marks on foreheads, the pilgrims were now ready to visit the temple of Lalita perched on top of a knoll beside the pond.

Lalita is foremost of the close girlfriends of Radha and Krishna called sakhis by Vaishnavas. These intimate friends aid the trysts and thus have access to the love play of the amorous couple. Lalita is the sakhi who introduces one to the scenes of the intimate encounters. Unchagaon, the village that has grown up below the knoll, is celebrated as Lalita's birthplace. It is here that one day Krishna, moved by Lalita's devotion, secretly married her. So Lalita, though greatly devoted to Radha, has her own amorous relationship with Krishna. In the charming white temple situated on top of the knoll, Lalita stands beautifully bedecked beside Krishna. Unchagaon is also the village in which Narayan Bhatt lived and constructed a temple for Balarama and his consort, Revati. Housed also in this thick-walled sixteenth-century temple is the image of the boy Krishna who helped Narayan Bhatt recover the lost sites of Braj. Near the temple, still maintained by Narayan Bhatt's descendants, stands the memorial tomb of the Great Founder of Braj, who contributed more than any other figure toward establishing the physical culture of Braj.

Lalita's temple was an attractive site, but Radha's temple at Barsana was our destination for the day, so we pushed on another mile east, walking along a wooded canal. The cool breeze continued to blow. It felt good to be moving; with every step we drew closer to the town of Radha, and excitement increased. I was walking with a man from Calcutta who said that he could feel the growing presence of Radha's joy. The temple now loomed high above us on the highest hill in Braj.

The name Barsana is typically explained as having been derived from the word *Brahma-sanu*, which means the "mountain of Brahma."[26] The popular belief is that the god Brahma manifested as this mountain in order to witness the love play that took place on it. The four peaks of the mountain are said to be the four faces of Brahma. It is also referred to as Brishabhanupur, since it is the residence of Radha's father, Brishabhanu. Many claim that it was here that Radha was born.

Barsana was once a tiny village where Narayan Bhatt had established a temple to Radha under the name Larliji (Darling) in the sixteenth century. The priests of the present temple are descendants of one of Narayan Bhatt's disciples. Barsana flourished in the mid-eighteenth century under the guidance of King Suraj Mal's brahman priest and adviser, Rup Ram Katari, who was a resident of Barsana. Rup Ram built large mansions and extensive gardens and turned Barsana into a wealthy town. He also built a new temple for Larliji on the hill. Much of the town, however, was destroyed soon after Rup Ram's projects were completed, when imperial forces from Delhi plundered Barsana in 1775 while fighting the Jat successors of Suraj Mal.[27] A cenotaph commemorating Rup Ram still stands among the buildings of the town. In 1812 the entire town was sold for 602 rupees (worth about thirty dollars today) to an eccentric Bengali millionaire who became a holy wanderer in Braj under the name Lala Babu.[28] Since then, a new temple, financed by the wealthy Seth family of Mathura and completed in the 1950s,[29] has been built on the site of the older temple, believed to mark the residence of Radha's father, Brishabhanu.

Tired from another day's walk but eager for a glimpse of Radha, the pilgrims ascended the long stone stairway that winds through the town to the peak of the mountain. Villagers came to the doors of their white,

plastered brick homes and peered out at the passing crowd; "Radhe!
Radhe!" was ready on their tongues. Several small shrines were set up
on the edge of the steps, with loud attendants encouraging us to make
donations. One man assured us that our money would be turned into
love. Beggars asking for alms were also arrayed along our pathway.
Some chased the pilgrims aggressively; others sat with admirable pa-
tience. Pilgrims too weak to climb the long stairway could ride in a
small palanquin, carried by two men who ran swiftly up and down the
stone stairs.

One enters this wonderful temple topped with numerous spires and
ornate cupolas through an impressively carved sandstone gateway. Inside is a beautiful courtyard checkered with black and white marble
slabs. Sandstone railings and arches, decorated with carved Rajasthani
lotus buds, surround the airy courtyard, framing the picturesque views
of the plains and town below. Near the inner sanctum, bright paintings
depicting the love games of Radha and Krishna decorate the walls,
and an expressive mural of Krishna's amorous dance with the gopis
floats on the ceiling. Behind a wooden rail in the inner sanctum stand
Radha and Krishna as Larli-Lal. The pilgrims eagerly pressed forward
to get a sight of the beautifully adorned couple.

This temple is the traditional starting place in Braj for Holi, the
springtime carnival and feast of love celebrated in northern India.[30]
This colorful festival is usually celebrated for one day throughout
much of India, but here in Braj, the place of its origin, it is celebrated
for a period of ten days. I had the chance to observe Holi celebrations
in Braj during the spring of 1989.[31] The festivities begin around sunset
in Barsana with a mass gathering in the temple to sing sensual love
songs of Radha and Krishna. An orgy of colored water and powder,
dancing and singing, the courtyard is a riot of color, sound, and jostling
bodies. Pounds of powder are hurled from cloth pouches, creating red,
green, yellow, and pink clouds that drift through the courtyard and
settle slowly on the chanting crowd. Streams of water colored with dye
from flower petals and propelled by long pumps crisscross in the air
and spray the rowdy crowd. People wear garlands of flowers and a wild
assortment of clothing and headgear, frequently left over from previous
Holis. Friendlier members of the huddle hug those they bump into.
Everyone is plastered with color and is very excited.

A messenger arrives from Krishna's residence of Nandagaon, a village located six miles to the north. He is pushed through the crowd to
the front of the temple and garlanded. He then announces that the
following day Krishna's representatives will come to play Holi with

the women of Barsana. The crowd cheers. On the following day men from Nandagaon arrive, wearing thick bandages on their heads and carrying shields made of tough leather. They make their way up to the temple through crowds swelling in the streets and weighing down every roof, sending out a barrage of colored water and powder. Inside the temple the men energize themselves with impassioned songs about the love of Radha and Krishna. The women of Barsana gather in the streets below. They are dressed in bright cotton saris pulled over their heads to provide anonymity and are armed with heavy bamboo sticks, six feet long. They form a menacing line in the narrow, spectator-lined streets.

Their songs completed, the men from Nandagaon leave the temple and force their way down the crowded streets. They taunt the women with licentious songs and dance provocatively. The women respond with vigorous whacks of the bamboo poles. The men hold the leather shields over their heads, but the women are strong. They have fortified themselves for weeks with a special diet of milk and ghee and are used to hoisting large pots of water and fuel onto their heads. Throughout most of the year women are dominated by men, but during the play of Holi all ordinary behavior is reversed and many ill feelings are beaten to a pulp.

The Barsana temple is also crowded during the Ban-Yatra season, but the crowd is in a different mood. After a very long walk, the pilgrims were anxious for sight of the queen of love. As I entered the temple I felt a flood of emotions. I had little idea who or what Radha really was—for the pilgrims, for myself—but suddenly I had the urge to follow the example of those around me and bow to her who reigns over the hearts of all drawn to this land. Not knowing exactly what I was doing, I felt pulled, lured, attracted by the world I had walked into, and experienced a desire for Radha's loving joy. I was deeply moved as my forehead touched the cool marble floor.

I got up from the floor feeling very light and found my way to the nearby camp below. Renu was inside our tent. She was lying on the ground beneath a line of freshly washed clothes and seemed to be in low spirits. She complained about the difficulties of the journey, said that it was not what she had expected, and announced that she was thinking of returning to Vrindaban early. She was strong-willed and a hard worker but seemed unable to let go and play. I tried to cheer her up, but I sensed that my efforts did little good.

Our tent was pitched in an empty field with beautiful views framed by the two triangular openings. Out one door was a row of whitish tents, their orange pilgrimage flags fluttering in the breeze. Swaying gently behind them was a thick grove of lush green trees. A small temple dedicated to Shiva was nestled among these. Pilgrims dressed in colorful clothing moved about, preparing the noon meal over open fires. Bullocks and water buffalo lay peacefully chewing their cuds.

Out the other door of the tent stretched a series of fertile fields, leading into the trees which gave way to the bright green hill of Barsana. The view of the temple from here was magnificent. The spires crowning the hill pierced the blue sky, which for the first time was punctuated with fluffy clouds. A group gathered near my tent explained that the white clouds were Radha and the dark ones Krishna. They said that when Krishna sees the white ones he knows that Radha has come, and when Radha sees the dark ones she knows that Krishna is present. The two meet in the sky to the cry of the peacock. The clouds brought with them a cool evening. I settled down inside the tent for a restful night's sleep. I awoke sometime around midnight to the gentle sound of rain falling on the tent.

We rose the next morning to greet a clear day made fresh by the rain. Since today was the beginning of the celebration of Radhashtami, Radha's birthday, we would be staying at this site for a second day. The celebration of Radha's birthday would not get underway in the temple until evening, so we had the day to perform the circumambulation of Barsana. Because this takes only a couple of hours we were allowed to sleep until sunrise—a real luxury! We began our clockwise circling of Barsana by moving slowly up a stone-lined path. A few smiling sadhus emerged from an ashram nestled in the hillside to cheer us on with shouts of "Radhe! Radhe!" After about twenty minutes we approached Sankhari Khor, the "Narrow Passage," which cuts through the ravine dividing the light, northern mountain of Brahma from the dark, southern mountain of Vishnu. The sides of the opening are lined with steep crags, and it is so narrow that only one person at a time can pass through it. Here Krishna plays with Radha by blocking her path, demanding that she and her friends give him some of the curds they are carrying in the pots balanced on their heads. Radha and the gopis refuse. Teasing them suggestively, Krishna breaks their pots and steals their treasure. During some pilgrimages a dramatic performance of this lila is staged in the narrow passage by young brahman boy actors.[32] Thousands of pilgrims cram into the ravine to witness the event.

Having passed through Sankhari Khor, we came to the village of Chiksoli. Here lived Chitralekha, one of the eight main sakhis (girlfriends) of Radha. In fact, each of the eight sakhis has a village near

Radha's town of Barsana. Lalita's village is Unchagaon; Vishakha's is Anjanokhar; Rangadevi's, Dabhala; Sudevi's, Sonehara; Indulekha's, Indroli; Tungavidya's, Kamai; and Chanpakalata's village is Karhela. There is a temple for these eight sakhis in the town of Barsana. The sakhis are frequently understood to be an extension of Radha and are very involved in making the arrangements for the love play of Braj. In fact, the *Chaitanya Charitamrita* declares that the love play of Radha and Krishna could not go on without them.[33]

We walked through the twisted lanes of the village of Chiksoli, passing a woman who was crying because her cow had stopped giving milk. We then climbed a hill above Chiksoli and visited Mor Kuti, the "Peacock House." Inside this small temple is a picture of Krishna dressed as a peacock, since this is the site where he, disguised as a peacock, danced for Radha and her friends.[34] Radha had been very angry with Krishna, who used this as a tactic to approach her. Spellbound by the wonderful dancing peacock, Radha forgot her anger and cried out, *"Mor! Mor!"* The latter means "Peacock! Peacock!"; but in the language of Braj it also means "Mine! Mine!" At this moment Krishna dropped the disguise and declared to Radha that he was indeed hers. The painting inside the temple is said to have been produced by a blind saint who had a vision of the peacock episode on this site.

We came next to Gahwarban, the "Deep Forest," a thickly wooded area on the western slopes of the hill where it is said that Radha and Krishna would slip away to make love in private. There is a small square pond with steep steps in the center of this forest. A Gaudiya temple dedicated to the amorous couple stands on its bank, and nearby is an important baithak of Vallabha. Peacocks glided in and out of the trees.

From Gahwarban a rocky wooded slope leads up the western side of the mountain to its crest. On top, one first enters the compound of a huge sandstone Jaipuri temple, which from the outside looks more like a fortress than a place of worship. Inside is a shrine for Radha and Krishna, surrounded by the family dwellings of the attending priests. This temple was built by the Jaipur king Sawai Madho Singh II and was completed in 1914. It is now under the care of the Nimbarki Vaishnavas.[35] A beautiful flowering garden lines the path connecting this temple with the main temple on the peak of the mountain. Along the garden path is the site where the image of Radha in the Larliji temple was revealed to Narayan Bhatt in the sixteenth century. A small shrine marks the spot where she emerged. Our circumambulation of Barsana culminated with another visit to the temple of Larliji.

I was fetching a bucket of drinking water after returning to camp when I again met Maya. She told me that just down the road leading to Nandagaon was a pond named Prema Sarovar, the "Pond of Love." She suggested that I visit this pond; an alluring smile followed her words. I assured her that I would but went about my tasks not really intending to do so. Many people recommended I visit many places. Back at camp, however, I found myself thinking about the encounter. In particular, Maya's smile had intrigued me; it had seemed so knowing and seductive. Late that afternoon I decided to visit the pond.

The mile walk to Prema Sarovar was a pleasant one. I arrived to find the place deserted, a fairly unusual condition for such a site. Except for the chatter of several flocks of bright green parrots, the pond was quiet and strangely peaceful. Huge bats hung from several trees near the pond, beginning to stir now that sunset approached. I walked slowly around the pond, admiring its construction. The pond is octagonal and is surrounded by sandstone encasements which consist of eight steps leading down into the water. Eight elaborate walkways and meditation platforms extend into the center of the pond at each of the eight corners. These platforms, too, are octagonal. A tree stands on the bank of each of the eight sides, though two are now dead. I marveled at the imagination of its architect and later learned that this was another of the projects of Rup Ram, the remarkable priestly adviser of Suraj Mal Singh.

I walked out onto the meditation platform on the northern side of the pond and sat down to rest. I looked into the water. It was a dark green color and appeared to be very deep. Something about it attracted me. I stared into its depths, lost in silence. Suddenly, I became aware that I was no longer alone. I started and turned around. Standing behind me was Maya. Before I could ask her why she had come she sat down beside me. She looked into my eyes; I felt vulnerable, like she was looking right through me. Finally, she spoke, instructing me with a firm voice, "Look into the pond. Fix your eyes on the surface of the water."

I did as she said. The first thing I noticed was the reflection on the surface of the pond. The slightest breeze created ever-changing patterns of shapes and colors. The visual designs, momentarily appearing and disappearing, were something like an impressionist painting viewed up close. I also observed that the patterns looked different depending on whether I focused my attention on the crests or the valleys of the ripples. "You must use the eyes of the body given to you by Yamuna Ji," Maya insisted. A shiver ran up my spine. I wondered what she was referring to; I had never mentioned to her that I had participated in the preliminary bathing in the Yamuna with my group. I asked her more. She told me that she could see that I had another body but that I seemed completely unaware of its existence, and said that it remained dormant because I was too intent upon my "research." She encouraged me to let go of my "research eyes" and see with my "lila eyes."

She instructed me to return my gaze to the surface of the pond. My attention went back to the creation and destruction of the random patterns produced by the crests and valleys of the ripples. I shifted my focus back and forth between these two scenes. I was not certain what I was supposed to be looking at, when Maya bent over and whispered something into my ear. Suddenly, a third scene appeared, neither on the crests nor in the valleys but out of the plain created by the oscillating motion of the two. A whole new world became visible.

I was looking at a dense forest of flowering trees in which stood a woman and a man. She had a golden complexion and was dressed in a blue sari; he was of a dark color and wore a yellow dhoti. She had flowers braided into her long black hair; he wore a garland of flowers around his neck and had a peacock feather stuck in his hair. They stood facing each other, tense, trembling slightly. They seemed anxious, unsure of each other, hesitant, as if meeting for the first time. But their stare suggested that they longed for the same thing. Slowly, he reached out a vulnerable hand and touched her. She surrendered to his advance and all uncertainty dissolved. The two embraced and suddenly the image was gone. Once again I was looking at the surface of the pond. I turned around, seeking an explanation from Maya. She had vanished.

I was shaken and sat on the platform for some time. When I could stand I hurried back to the tents. I searched the camp for Maya and found her sitting in a circle of women. I approached awkwardly and began to tell her what I had seen. She cut me off abruptly, acting as though what I said was unimportant. She simply remarked, "Prema Sarovar is where Radha and Krishna first experienced love for each other." She then resumed her conversation with the other women. Greatly confused, I slipped away and wandered back to my tent. Umesh and Shuklaji were there resting on the cots. I blurted out my story. They stared wide-eyed. When I had finished recounting the incident, Shuklaji bolted upright and said, "Prema Sarovar is a powerfully confusing place. Even Radha became greatly confused there by the madness of love." To make his point, he narrated the following story.

Some time after their initial encounter, Radha and Krishna met again at the site of Prema Sarovar. Though Radha was married to another and such meetings were prohibited, they could not resist meeting again. On this occasion Radha was sitting on Krishna's lap, tenderly embracing him and playing with his hair, when a bumblebee appeared and began buzzing around Radha's face. Krishna's friend Madhumangal was present and saw that Radha was being harassed by the bee. He chased it away. Then he proclaimed, "Madhusudan has gone away." Madhusudan means "conqueror of honey," and is therefore a fancy name for a bee. However, besides meaning honey, Madhu is also the name of a demon that was killed by Krishna. When Madhumangal said that Madhusudan the bee had left, Radha understood him to mean that the destroyer of the demon Madhu—that is, Krishna—had left. Hearing these words, Radha became lost in an intense mood of separation and was completely unaware of Krishna's presence—even though she still sat on his lap. Greatly distressed, she began to cry. Seeing the intensity of Radha's torment, Krishna became amazed. He was so deeply moved that he, too, was reduced to tears, and the pond of Prema Sarovar was produced from the excessive tears of the romantic couple.

That evening we ascended the steep stairs leading to the main temple for the joyous celebration of Radha's birth. It was a beautiful night; the moon and the stars played in and out of the clouds. The temple was jammed with people. A group of musicians sat in the middle of the courtyard singing poems in praise of Radha, the source of all bliss. The climax of the celebration would take place the next morning with the bathing of Radha in a sacred liquid consisting of milk, honey, yogurt, butter, and sugar. Whoops of "Radhe! Radhe! Jai Shri Radhe!" pierced the air.

I observed another celebration in Barsana while I was with the Pushti Margi pilgrimage. I was sitting around after dinner one evening during our four-day stay in Barsana when a young man delivered an invitation from the maharaj to join the wedding procession of the bridegroom Krishna. The Pushti Margis more frequently emphasize the marriage of Radha and Krishna; this is one of the points that distinguishes them from the Gaudiyas. The participants assembled after dark in the streets below the temple. The music of a shehnai player and drummer, who sat in a bullock cart in the front of the line, announced the beginning of the procession. Behind them a red tractor pulled a vehicle painted with white swans and designed to carry a wedding band; it now contained an electric organ and huge loudspeakers. A young singer, dressed in a red silk shirt and white pants and wearing dark sunglasses, was plugged into the loudspeakers. He danced ener-getically as he sang into his microphone. Following him was a loud wedding band featuring drums and brass instruments. Their sounds blared through the streets and echoed off the surrounding buildings. On either side of the wedding band marched a line of young men bear-ing gas lanterns on their heads. A wild assemblage of dancers wove in and out of these lanterns. Behind them walked the maharaj and his entourage, who were very somber in appearance. A group of invited guests followed the maharaj; I was among these. Directly behind us Krishna—a young boy from the drama troupe' traveling with the group—rode a horse decked out in traditional wedding garb. A forest of light bulbs and fluorescent tubes, planted in pots carried on the heads of older men, illuminated his way. The electricity was supplied by a generator in a bullock cart taking up the rear of the procession.

Throngs of people pressed on us from both sides. Fireworks ex-ploded above our heads as we broke out into open ground and headed toward the stage where Radha was waiting. The density of the proces-sion increased as we drew nearer. When we reached the stage there was nowhere for the assembly to go. At one point my feet no longer touched the ground, yet the crowd continued to press forward. Sud-denly, police appeared and turned the crowd back into itself. Chaos ensued as the divine couple were joined in matrimony to shouts of "Jai Radhe Shyam!"

I very much enjoyed "wandering" the next morning. Shuklaji used the word *wandering*, which to him seemed more accurate than *walking*, to describe our peripatetic movement. Walking is more direct, more purposeful, whereas we wandered from place to place, never taking the most direct route between two places but rather the route marked by Krishna's play. The distance between Barsana and Nandagaon, our next camp, is only six miles; however, we were to wander for more than seven hours, covering a distance of over fifteen miles, before we stopped for the day. The sites we wandered through were the scenes of the sneaky, illicit rendezvous of Radha and Krishna.

We left Barsana before four o'clock and headed north in the direction of Nandagaon, the village in which Krishna and his family lived after moving from Gokul, where they were continually harassed by demons sent by the wicked king Kansa. Halfway between the two villages is a small forest called Sanketban, the "Forest of the Signal." When Radha lived in Barsana and Krishna lived in Nandagaon, there were days they desired each other so intensely that they could not wait for the cover of darkness, yet they had to be very careful. On such occasions they would stand on their respective rooftops and merely signal each other. This signal meant that they were to steal from their homes unnoticed and meet in a small grove located midway between them for a passionate tryst. Their meeting place was Sanketban.

A heavy, thick-walled temple providing shelter for the couple now marks the spot. The temple, which dates to the time of Akbar, appears in the 1598 document listing the temples of Braj under imperial patronage.[36] The temple is thought to have been built by Todar Mal, Akbar's famous finance minister, though it was later rebuilt by Rup Ram.[37] The images of Radha and Krishna are said to have been established by Narayan Bhatt. When we arrived at Sanketban, the village encircling the temple was still covered with a brilliant canopy of stars. We were in time for mangal-arati, the auspicious first viewing and worship of the day. As the priest waved the oil lamps before the waking lovers, sleepy villagers from the nearby adobe houses staggered in to join us.

The morning that slowly emerged was a glorious one—completely cloud covered! Peacocks announced this welcome change with joyful cries. Even my feet felt better. I was now very glad that I had not quit the pilgrimage those first few trying days. I was being rewarded for my perseverance with these delightful morning walks and visits to amazing places.

We continued in a northerly direction past the hill of Nandagaon, admiring its towering temple from the plains below, and then veered northeast toward the town of Javat, another site of secret meetings. We walked for two miles through grassy marshes and lush rice fields. A pair of Saras cranes was feeding in a nearby field. These long-legged cranes stand five feet tall. Their heads and upper necks are bright red, with an ashy crown, and their large bodies are covered with bluish gray feathers. They are nimble dancers. When disturbed or flying they give a loud, shrill, trumpeting call. Saras cranes are always found in pairs, for they mate for life. They are devoted and close companions, feeding only a few feet from each other. The people of Braj say that if one is killed the other will soon die of a broken heart. So famous is their affection in this area that they are never harmed by humans. They seemed unafraid as we passed near them.

Javat is the hometown of Radha's husband, Abhimanyu. When Radha reached a marriageable age, her father, prompted by her great-aunt Purnamasi (this name means "full moon," and it is she who later frequently conspires to bring Radha and Krishna together), arranged for her to marry the son of a woman named Jatila.[38] Radha's love for

Krishna, however, remained steadfast. When her desire for him became excessive, she would go to the rooftop of Abhimanyu's house and signal Krishna to come to her from nearby Nandagaon. Krishna would come, sneak into her bedroom, and there they made love.

One time, however, a servant of Abhimanyu saw Krishna enter the house; Krishna's eagerness had apparently made him careless. The servant ran and warned Abhimanyu that a strange man was with Radha. Abhimanyu immediately stormed to Radha's room, intending to beat her and the unknown intruder. But Krishna had a way out of the sticky situation. Abhimanyu was a worshiper of the fierce goddess Kali. After he married Radha, he continually pressured her to devote herself solely to Kali, but he found her obstinate. Knowing this, Krishna quickly turned himself into Kali, so that when Abhimanyu burst into the bedroom he found Radha worshiping Kali and left quite pleased.

The resident priest narrated this story to a small group of pilgrims gathered on the rooftop of Abhimanyu's three-storied house in Javat. He showed us white marble footprints where Radha stood as she signaled to Krishna in the distant hill town of Nandagaon. He then took us below and directed us to the three-room shrine located on the ground floor. To the viewer's right is the shrine of Krishna disguised as the goddess Kali. In the shrine to the left are the images of those Radha must circumvent: her husband, Abhimanyu, flanked by her mother-in-law, Jatila, and sister-in-law, Kutila. All have very sour expressions. The central shrine houses the divine couple Radha and Krishna, successfully united and smiling in loving satisfaction.

This cast of characters is featured in yet another story told just down the road. After we left the village of Javat, we turned westward and walked an additional three miles to an enchanting forest called Kokilaban, the "Forest of the Cuckoo Bird." This was the sixth of the twelve forests on our itinerary and one of the most beautiful, for the trees have been well preserved and it is inhabited by many animals and birds, including Saras cranes, peacocks, green parrots, and, of course, cuckoo birds. Though this forest is included in Narayan Bhatt's list of the twelve major forests of Braj, many Ban-Yatra itineraries feature Khadiraban as the sixth forest. Khadiraban, named after the flowering *khadira* tree, is a small forest located four and a half miles southwest of Kokilaban. There Krishna killed a demon who took the form of a heron. Kokilaban, however, was the sixth forest visited on our particular pilgrimage, and it was here that one of the older guides in our party told me the following story.

Krishna wanted Radha very badly. Unfortunately, she was in her husband's house, and, furthermore, she was angry with her lover. Krishna knew, however, that Radha could not resist the call of the cuckoo, so he changed his voice into that of a cuckoo and called invitingly. Radha slipped out of her house, assuming that she had left undetected. Her ever-watchful mother-in-law and sister-in-law saw her leave, however, and followed her to Kokilaban. What they saw in this thick grove shocked them: Radha was embracing Krishna passionately. They hurried back to inform Abhimanyu of what they had seen. Abhimanyu was furious and rushed to the forest, Jatila and Kutila in tow. This time Krishna cleverly turned himself into a cuckoo. When Abhimanyu erupted into the forest, he merely observed Radha gazing lovingly at a cuckoo. Abhimanyu knew that this was her favorite bird. Outraged over being disturbed with such nonsense, Abhimanyu now turned on Jatila and Kutila and demanded an explanation: "Where is this dark one?" Krishna, however, could not resist a tease; he remained visible in his human form to Jatila and Kutila. They pointed to him, saying, "There he is!" "But that is not a man," shouted Abhimanyu, "that is a bird!" During the fierce quarrel that ensued, the eager lovers slipped away into the forest.

There is something very dissatisfying about home. One leaves home, a place entrenched in the domestic structures and routine of the city, and travels to the forest in pursuit of the unknown, an unknown which promises something different. There is in the Ban-Yatra a coincidence of travel and the illicit affair. The Ban-Yatra is a circular journey in which forbidden love is celebrated. The pilgrim and the lover are both playing around. The illicit affair is an adventure into the unknown, a wandering into uncertain territory, and that after all may be its strongest attraction. In illicit love, taboos that inhibit desire are cast aside, leaving the lovers outside social containment. Marriage, the foundation of social stability, settles into the static home and becomes habitualized, encrusted with structures of duty, purpose, responsibility, and expectation. Love is frequently lost in such structures, and dissatisfaction ensues. Desire promises to be fulfilled only elsewhere, in some unknown place, by some unknown person. Both travel and the illicit love affair are attempts to free oneself from these stagnating structures and move toward the unknown forest which promises something new. Whereas boredom can kill love in marriage, a love affair with the Unknown can never be boring. The uncertainty of forbidden love arouses desire and keeps things interesting. Desire for Krishna never becomes stagnant, as Krishna can never be fully contained, can never be fully conquered, can never be fully known. Krishna plays with his lovers, teases his lovers; they must accept that they can never be sure what they will get. He never stands still but is always on the move to yet another forest. There is no final destination "out there."[39] A love affair with Krishna does not end in a purposeful climax but leads on and on to yet another forest in a state of ongoing excitement.

From Kokilaban we moved south to our next camp, situated on a large plain at the base of the Nandagaon hill. By the time we arrived, I was tired but in a cheerful mood. I sat watching a group of young boys swim naked in a pool of water behind my tent; their laughter rippled across the water as they took turns diving off a stone wall. The day had been moderately cool and cloudy. I seemed to be moving further and further from the mood of despair I had experienced early in the journey. At one point in our morning walk we were traveling along a path lined with tall elephant grass and padded with a deep layer of soft dirt. The opportunity of experiencing this terrain with my bare feet proved to be too tempting. I peeled off my canvas shoes and felt the earth squeeze between my toes. I realized that I had been missing much of the direct contact with the land that the barefoot pilgrims experienced. Although I had two new blisters by the time we arrived at camp, my feet were not bothering me so much. I was happy. I was getting to know the land of Braj in a way that I had not imagined. I simply had not known that I would have to go through so much to gain access to it. I now felt that that process was beginning to happen, and I was enjoying each day more and more. I was even hungry for the boys' cooking and eagerly went in search of my noon meal.

That evening Shuklaji, Umesh, and I climbed the hill of Nandagaon to visit the temple of Krishna's father, Nanda. To reach this temple one climbs a long flight of sandstone steps that winds through the town and leads to a large courtyard. The courtyard is surrounded by a walled walkway with ornate pavilions in the four corners. From the walkway one has a magnificent 360-degree view of the countryside surrounding Nandagaon—forested land that has been preserved, since this is considered an important place for Krishna to graze his cows. Inside the courtyard is the main temple of Nandagaon, built on the site of Nanda's residence. Nandagaon is another of the sites developed by the Jats. According to Growse, the present temple was built in the mid-eighteenth century by a Jat ruler named Rup Singh.[40] Suraj Mal's priestly minister, Rup Ram, had constructed a mansion here, and a square designed to accommodate pilgrims below the temple was built by one of the wives of Suraj Mal. The stone stairway leading up to the temple was added in 1818 by one Babu Gaur Prasad of Calcutta. Like Barsana, this town was also purchased in the early nineteenth century by the wealthy ascetic Lala Babu.

The first thing one encounters on entering the temple compound is a small shrine containing a Shiva lingam; the latter is covered with an eight-pillared white marble canopy. In older literature this hill is called Nandishwar, the "Lord of the Bull Nandi," a name referring to Shiva. The entire mountain is frequently considered a manifestation of Shiva, and the number of famous Shaivaite shrines in Braj is often expanded to five to include this important temple. It is likely that this hill was previously a sacred site for Shiva that was transformed during the sixteenth century. Shuklaji narrated the story now told about the Shiva who resides in the Nandagaon temple.

Shortly after Krishna's birth, Shiva desired to see him. Shiva came down from Mount Kailash and presented himself at Nanda's door. Krishna's mother, Yashoda, was so frightened by the sight of the wild, ash-smeared ascetic that she refused to let him near her baby and turned him away. At the moment Shiva left, however, Krishna began to cry, for Krishna perceived Shiva as a devoted lover. Nothing Yashoda did could stop Krishna from crying. She consulted some elders and soon came to realize her mistake. She immediately sent for Shiva. Upon his return the baby Krishna stopped crying and greeted Shiva with a delightful smile. Yashoda begged Shiva's forgiveness and asked how she could rectify her error. Shiva replied by requesting that he be allowed to reside in the courtyard near Krishna and eat the remnant food from his table. The temple priests offer Krishna's remnants daily to the Shiva lingam situated within the walls of the compound.

The central temple is a large, thick-walled vault capped with two heavy pyramidal spires that are visible from a great distance. Inside is the palace of Nanda's family. Nanda and Yashoda flank the children Krishna and Balarama. Nanda and Yashoda are life-size brass figures; Nanda sports a saffron-colored turban, and Yashoda is dressed in a beautiful sari. The smaller figures of Krishna and Balarama are made out of black stone and wear crowns of peacock feathers. All are garlanded with flowers. Radha and two of Krishna's cowherd friends are also present. This temple too is an important site for the celebration of Holi in Braj. The day after the festivities in Barsana, Holi moves to Nandagaon and the women of Nandagaon beat the men of Barsana under a riotous explosion of colors.

Nandagaon is a particularly important site for the Pushti Margis, who favor the child Krishna. I later spent three days here with the Pushti Margi pilgrimage. We passed two days wandering in the forests that have been preserved around the town of Nandagaon; here the troupe of rasa-lila actors traveling with the pilgrimage party staged a play of Krishna and his cowherd companions frolicking in these forests with their cows. The play featured a real white calf, which was doted on after the performance by members of the audience who took turns petting it. The last night we were in Nandagaon, the maharaj arranged for a Nandotsav—Nanda's joyful celebration of Krishna's birth—to be celebrated in the temple. Thousands of pilgrims crammed into the courtyard of the temple and waited for two hours before the maharaj finally showed up on the temple roof to throw handfuls of candy to the eager assembly.

The Gaudiya pilgrims and I walked over fifteen miles the next morning, setting out in a northern direction toward the village of Bathain, a favorite "sitting place" used by Krishna and his cowboy friends while they tended the cows. Several of the villagers of Bathain came out of their homes to offer us drinks of fresh buttermilk spiced with salt and roasted cumin seeds. The countryside became more fertile and lush as we drew closer to the Yamuna River, and was covered with bountiful rice fields, flooded with water contained by earthen dikes which divided the fields. The only way to pass through this area was to walk along these narrow dikes, only a foot wide. It was impossible in this terrain to cut a straight line to any particular destination; instead, we had to follow a zigzag course around the square fields. The sunrise that morning was splendid; golden light streamed through the young rice plants, casting them in a bright yellowish green hue. Birds were everywhere and their songs filled the air. We passed two trees full of white-necked storks, and another pair of Saras cranes appeared near our path. The subtle beauty of Braj was slowly enchanting me.

We meandered single file atop the field dikes. The line of colorfully dressed pilgrims against the fertile fields was a striking sight. At one point we encountered the 150 pilgrims riding the horse-drawn tongas. Since the horses could not traverse this terrain, this group was forced to walk across the rice fields. They had arrived at our current destination sometime earlier and were now returning to the tongas. We met in the middle of the fields, which meant that the two groups had to pass each other on the narrow dikes—a nearly impossible task. Many of those riding tongas were from Manipur, since they came from a cool mountain climate and were most troubled by the heat of Braj. Lavender and peach-colored Manipuri sarongs mixed with red and white Bengali saris. The result was chaos! Feet slipped off the dikes into the muddy water below. Reactions varied; some swore, many laughed. Everyone got muddy. After slipping into the water, one Bengali woman reached down, smeared her face with mud, and danced, laughing wildly. Again, pilgrimage is not ethereal religion, is not refined intellectualism, but rather is concrete bodily experience of the material. Characterizing pilgrimage, Niebuhr writes, "Spirit no longer hovers above creation but is sunk deep in matter and being itself."[41] Pilgrims get down and dirty! They do not worship in immaculate churches but in muddy fields. We eventually maneuvered our way around the oncoming group and arrived at the pond of Krishnakund.

Near Krishnakund is an outcrop of boulders. Shuklaji led me into this network of rocks and told me that this area was once the scene of a midnight love dance between Krishna and the gopis. The dance took place on a dark night, creating the need for some kind of illumination. He explained that the rocks we were looking at were once large candles that had sprouted up to provide the dancers with light. Eventually the mounds of melted wax had turned into stone.

Few of the pilgrims showed much interest in this site; they seemed more drawn to the peaceful shores of Krishnakund. A husband-and-wife team who accompanied the pilgrimage to serve tea and potato *pakoras* (a snack dipped in a spicy batter and fried) had somehow packed in their goods and set up shop there. The aroma of the pakoras cooking in mustard oil had attracted a large group of hungry pilgrims. A crowd gathered around the kerosene stove, taking in the scenery while enjoying their food. Shuklaji, who had long since noticed my cameras and had decided this would be a good place for a group photo, bounced to his feet to organize the crowd into a sitting. While framing the group in my camera, I noticed the woman who had held my hand that first night in Mathura; she now had her hand on the bare knee of a young sannyasi.

From Bathain we hiked east to Kosi, a town located on the Delhi-Agra highway. Crossing this busy highway was unnerving; a speeding bus blared its loud horn at us, and we had to wait for a long line of trucks, which belched out clouds of black smoke. These seemed alien to our rural experience. Kosi, which is not associated with any particular lila of Krishna, merely provides a convenient camping site for the pilgrimage. We arrived around noon, established a camp on the eastern side of town, and spent the remainder of the day resting. I went to a nearby well for my daily bath and met two tonga drivers who informed

me that I had made the local news in Mathura. Foreigners rarely perform the Ban-Yatra. The two were impressed enough to take turns
pouring buckets of cold water over my head. I basked in the attention.
"What a glorious morning!" I wrote in my journal the next day. I
wanted so badly to capture in words what I saw and experienced, but
I knew I could not. We were walking along a major irrigation canal to
a site six miles to the north; in fact, this was to be the northernmost
point of our Ban-Yatra circle. Days like this made me understand why
this pilgrimage is to be performed in the rainy season. The sky was
again overcast, intricately textured with dark clouds. The sun rose
with subtle beauty; as it peeked over the horizon, the underside of the
clouds was illuminated with a breathtaking rosy light. We passed a tree
full of white egrets and ibis, which in this light looked more like pink
flamingos. The birds of Braj have an amazing presence; their songs
and chattering continuously fill one's ears. Many expressed the belief
that previously the birds were human saints. Large trees lined the
canal and sprang out randomly in the surrounding countryside. Their
leaves, freshly nurtured by the monsoon rains, shimmered gloriously
in the light. I was again reminded that this pilgrimage is an ecological
celebration. Braj is not simply a space in which Krishna performed
his activities; Vaishnavas claim that Braj itself is a form of Krishna.
The birds, trees, fields, rocks, and ponds are themselves part of a
divine manifestation. "Braj is Krishna, and Krishna is Braj."

We soon came to our destination of the day, Sheshashayi, a small
forest temple on the bank of a wooded lake. Within Sheshashayi, which
means "lying on the cobra," there is a black stone image of Vishnu
lying on his cobra, Shesha. His consort, Lakshmi, sits at his feet,
faithfully massaging his legs. A lotus has sprouted from his navel, upon
which sits a golden image of Brahma, the Lord of Creation. All three
are wrapped in bright decorative cloth. This is the image of Vishnu
arrested just at the moment of creation, which follows a dormant period in which Vishnu has drawn the entire cosmos back into himself,
leaving only a small remainder—(shesha) to support his body as he
rests on the cosmic ocean of milk. Here is the awesome, all-containing
Lord of the universe. It has been installed here because Krishna once
manifested this form to the gopis.

The gopis had had a growing suspicion that Krishna was more than
he seemed and so one day requested him to show his divine form. To
satisfy their desire, Krishna took the form of the cosmic Vishnu and
Balarama took the form of Shesha. The two floated on the nearby lake
(now called Kshir Sagar, the "Milk Ocean") which became the cosmic

ocean of milk. Like Arjuna in the *Bhagavad Gita*,[42] however, the gopis were terrified by this sight and requested that Krishna return to the sweet, attractive human form they knew so well, for this is the form that allows them to approach him with intimacy rather than hesitation. Gracefully, Krishna covered the awesome vision with his previous form. The lesson of this site seems to be that although Krishna is the All-Containing which cannot be contained, he accepts containment in a particularly attractive form that makes love possible. Though the cosmic form is nondifferent from the sweet human form, the gopis, who are the masters of love, are completely unaware of it, a condition which is necessary for the experience of intimate love. Whereas many Indian religious systems view *maya*—that force by which the formless takes form—as a dangerous illusion that must be overcome, in Braj it becomes Yogamaya, the goddess who gives shape to all forms and stages the lilas of Krishna, which make love possible. The image of Vishnu that Krishna revealed to the gopis is the unmanifest god resting behind the manifestation of the world; he is the formless one behind the diversity of forms. But the Krishnaite tradition of Braj judges the unmanifest god unsuitable for the game of love. The gopis desire to caress the diverse surfaces of Krishna's body, they desire a form that they can play around with, and so they beg Krishna to return to his attractive manifest form.

After visiting the temple of Krishna as the reclining Vishnu, we retraced the six miles back to Kosi. The next morning we rose at two o'clock and began a twelve-mile trek east in a light rain. We walked along a roughly paved road lined with wiry trees and tall grass. Lush fields illuminated by a muted moon lay on both sides of the road. A line of tongas galloped past us, followed by the slower-moving bullock carts. The logic of our guides' decision regarding the time of our morning departure escaped me; we arrived at the next campsite by eight. Along the way we visited the village of Phalain, also called Pharen, which is usually said to be derived from the verb *pharna* (to rip open). This name refers to a specific episode which is said to have occurred here.

Prahlad was the son of a demon named Hiranyakashipu. By means of herculean acts of asceticism Hiranyakashipu obtained a boon from Brahma: he would never be killed indoors or outdoors, in the day or in the night, on earth or in the air, by either man, beast, or any being created by Brahma. Thinking that he had thoroughly ensured his immortality, Hiranyakashipu began to take control of the universe with great arrogance and violence. His son, Prahlad, however, was of a very different nature; he was born with an innate devotion to Krishna. This infuriated Hiranyakashipu, who turned on the boy. He first unleashed a host of vicious demons on his son, but when this failed to destroy the child he sought the services of his sister, Holika. Holika, who was known for her ability to survive fire, took Prahlad into a huge bonfire and held him on her lap. This time, however, since Prahlad was protected by Krishna, Holika perished in the fire and Prahlad walked away unharmed. Hiranyakashipu was now incensed. He approached Prahlad with anger, pointed to a pillar and shouted, "If your Lord is everywhere, why is he not present in this pillar?" He grabbed a sword and sprang violently at Prahlad, intending to behead him. At that instant the pillar exploded, and there stood Narasingh, Krishna/Vishnu in the form of a man-lion. This occurred at dusk, the moment between day and night. Narasingh (neither man nor beast) seized Hiranyakashipu and placed him on his lap (neither on the ground nor in the air) and on the threshold of the palace (neither indoors nor outdoors) ripped open his chest. Krishna once again reveals himself in the cracks of all expectations.

A temple to Narasingh and his devotee Prahlad marks the site of this episode in Phalain. This temple is the location of a remarkable event that occurs during the festival of Holi, the very name of which is derived from Holika, Hiranyakashipu's sister who perished in the fire. She is typically understood to be a manifestation of malice, so throughout Braj images of her are burned in huge bonfires during Holi to cleanse the year of any malice that has accrued. The practice of a yearly spring bonfire is old and widespread in India,[43] but in Braj it is now identified with the stories of Krishna and Holika. In Phalain the story of Prahlad and Holika is celebrated in a unique and dramatic manner. Every year at Holi sticks, brush, and cow-dung cakes are gathered on the grounds between the temple of Narasingh and a nearby pond named Prahlad Kund. The year I observed this celebration the circular pile was about thirty-five feet in diameter and fifteen feet high. At a particular moment in the middle of the designated night, the men of the village break into a run around the huge pile, shouting and wielding heavy bamboo sticks while a few of them set fire to the combustible materials. Soon an enormous fire is ablaze; its intensity causes the gathered crowd to reel back. Meanwhile, a priest from the family attending this shrine has been sitting in the temple. For a month he has been preparing himself for this night through meditation and a special diet consisting primarily of milk. As he sits in the temple, he passes his hand through a flame fueled with clarified butter. There is a moment when the flame turns cold; this is the sign that he is to proceed. He immediately goes down to the pond and bathes. Then, dressed only in a wet loincloth and head wrap, he runs barefoot through the raging fire and into the temple of Narasingh. Growse reports that when he witnessed this event in the late nineteenth century, the priest "made a feint of passing through the fire," jumping over some smoldering ashes on the edge.[44] But when I witnessed the event, the priest ran directly through the middle of the fire, with flames shooting well above his head, and came tumbling out the other side. I interviewed him the next day; he showed no signs of burns anywhere on his body. He reported that inside the fire the flames were cool, thus demonstrating the saving power of Krishna.

Our next campsite was set just outside Shergarh, a village located on the bank of the Yamuna River. This town derives its name from a fort built here by Sher Shah, the Afghan ruler who temporarily ousted Babar, the first of the Mughal emperors, and built the road linking the two imperial cities of Delhi and Agra. One of the guides, however, told me that Shergarh had an older name, Khelanaban, the "Forest of Games," since it was here that Krishna and his brother, Balarama, played so intensely with their cowherd friends that they forgot to eat.

We had plenty of time to explore this area. After performing our daily tasks, Umesh and I began wandering the village bazaar. Colorful cloth, brass and copper pots, plastic sandals, and a tangle of prayer beads hung on the walls lining our path. The merchants were very friendly. A cloth dealer insisted on treating us to tea; he was curious to know what the bazaars of America were like. I tried my best to give him a vision of an indoor shopping mall. He seemed puzzled that I might prefer his bazaar. We eventually wound our way through the twisted lanes that lead to the Yamuna River, which was still quite full from the monsoon rains in the distant mountains. The great brown river stretched before us like a broad road of burnished bronze. All the pilgrims seemed delighted to be back by its side. Many approached the river shouting "Yamuna Maiya ki Jai!" (Glory to Mother Yamuna!)

The Yamuna is conceived of in many ways by the residents of Braj, but never simply as a river. For the Vaishnavas of Braj it is a living goddess. Each day, pilgrims offer flowers, milk, and sweets into her sacred body. Vallabha wrote a poem called the *Yamunashtakam*, which is regarded by many as preeminent among his works. This poem, which is recited by many Pushti Margis every day, praises the Yamuna as the drops of perspiration that fell from Krishna's body during lovemaking. It therefore is typically thought to consist of waves of bliss. In a popular poster sold in the bazaars of Braj, Yamuna is pictured as a female form of Krishna. Some say she flows from the sun, a form of Vishnu; others say that while the Ganges flows from the foot of the Lord, the Yamuna flows from the more intimate realm of his heart. Lynch comments: "The river, then, is neither a symbol of nor a metaphor for divinity; rather, she is herself metonymic divinity whom metaphors describe. . . . Thus, bathing in Yamunaji is more than a symbolic act or ritual purification, it is a reactualisation of cosmological events in which pilgrims feel their participation and literally immerse themselves."[45]

Bathing in the Yamuna is considered a transformative experience. Yamuna is said to grant freely all spiritual powers that the yogis spend years striving for. We have already learned of the effect the Yamuna had in transforming the lust of the poet Nandadas and initiating him into the love of Krishna. As we saw earlier in the episode involving Shiva, she has the power to grant the body which allows entrance into the lila. Specifically, the common belief is that Yamuna manifested to bring souls into the lila and grant union with the Lord.

I sat with Umesh on the sandy bank above the brick shell of an old well that had collapsed into the river. An elderly couple made their way down to the shore. They took some water in their hands and, tilting their heads back, sprinkled their faces and dripped the sacred liquid into their mouths. They stood side by side for a few minutes, looking out over the wide expanse of water with their palms joined in prayer, and then left. Umesh turned to me and wondered aloud, "What will our lila be downstream?"

NOTES

1. See, for example, *Rig Veda* x.129 and *Brihadaranyaka Upanishad* 1.4.

2. These two views are represented in a variety of ways in Hindu philosophies. In many ways this involves the creative tension between the ascetics and householders in Hindu traditions. It is also related to the philosophical split between the *vivartavad* schools and the *parinamavad* schools. See also Karl Potter's discussion of progress and leap philosophies in *Presuppositions of India's Philosophies* (Englewood Cliffs, N.J.: Prentice-Hall, 1963).

3. O'Flaherty makes the point that Kamadev is the alter ego of Shiva; see her *Asceticism and Eroticism*, 140-71.

4. Quoted in Vijay, *Braj Bhumi Mohini*, 171.

5. Ibid., 169.

6. Compare Patanjali's *Yoga Sutra* 1.2 with Rupa Goswami's *Bhaktirasa-*

mritasindhu 1.3.4. Rupa uses the term *kama* in a positive sense in his *Bhaktirasamritasindhu*. He defines the highest path as one which follows the passion (kama) of the gopis; see verse 1.2.297.

7. *klim kamadevaya vidmahe puspa-banaya dhimahi tan no'nangah pracodayat.*

8. *Subodini* 10.29.2.

9. *Chaitanya Charitamrita*, Madya-lila 8.138.

10. John Hawley has recorded and translated this play in *At Play with Krishna*, 153–226.

11. *Chaitanya Charitamrita*, Adi-lila 4.164.

12. Hawley, *At Play with Krishna*, 158.

13. Shashibhusan Dasgupta, *Obscure Religious Cults* (Calcutta: Firma KLM, 1976), 135.

14. This story was first told to me by a man on the Pushti Margi pilgrimage. It also appears in Shyam Das, *Ashta Chhap* (Baroda: Shri Vallabha Publications, 1985), 259–67.

15. These three hierarchical positions are sometimes referred to in Braj as, respectively, *ragi, vairagi,* and *vairagi*. A ragi is one who follows the ways of ordinary passion. The ambiguity of the double use of the word *vairagi* has to do with the fact that the Sanskrit prefix *"vi-"* can cause the noun it precedes either to mean its opposite, or it intensifies the meaning of the noun. Thus, in the first case vairagi means one who is dispassionate; in the second case vairagi means one who is extremely passionate. There is a play on this double meaning in Braj, where the gopis are said to be vairagis of the second type.

16. Entwistle, *Braj*, 131.

17. See Sandra P. Robinson, "Hindu Paradigms of Women: Images and Values," in *Women, Religion and Social Change,* ed. Yvonne Yazbeck Haddad and Ellison Banks Findly (Albany: State University of New York Press, 1985), 181–215.

18. *Varaha Purana* 151.38.

19. William James was one of the first among social scientists to analyze the multiple nature of reality; see his *Principles of Psychology,* 2 vols. (New York: Henry Holt, 1890), 2:283–322. See also Alfred Schutz, *Collected Papers I: The Problem of Social Reality,* ed. Maurice Natanson (The Hague: Martins Nijhoff, 1973), 340–47.

20. Clifford Geertz writes: "One of the main methodological problems in writing about religion scientifically is to put aside at once the tone of the village atheist and that of the village preacher, as well as their more sophisticated equivalents, so that the social and psychological implications of particular religious beliefs can emerge in a clear and neutral light" ("Religion as a Cultural System," in *The Interpretation of Cultures* [New York: Basic Books, 1973], 123).

21. Entwistle, *Braj*, 276.

22. This work is one of Vallabha's sixteen short works known collectively as the *Sodashagrantha*.

23. A discussion of these three levels was developed in the philosophical tradition of the Pushti Marg under the respective Sanskrit rubrics: *adhibhautika*, *adhyatmika*, and *adhidaivika*.

24. Richard R. Niebuhr, "Pilgrims and Pioneers," *Parabola* 9, no. 3 (1984): 10–12.

25. Geertz, "Religion as a Cultural System," 112.

26. See, for example, Premdatta Mishra Maithil, "Barsana Vritt," in *Braj Vibhav*, ed. Gopalprasad Vyas (New Delhi: Dilli Hindi Sahitya Sammelan, 1987), 194.

27. Growse, *Mathura*, 42.

28. Ibid., 313.

29. Entwistle, *Braj*, 218.

30. See McKim Marriot, "The Feast of Love," in *Krishna: Myths, Rites, and Attitudes*, ed. Milton Singer (Chicago: University of Chicago Press, 1968), 200–212.

31. I assisted a London crew making a film of Holi. This film, entitled "'Holi' A Festival of Colors," is available from Stein Films Ltd.

32. I witnessed one of these performances while I was with the Pushti Margi pilgrims in Barsana. The lila was enacted by a troupe of actors traveling with the pilgrimage party.

33. *Chaitanya Charitamrita* 2.8.202–4.

34. A version of this episode is told in Vijay, *Braj Bhumi Mohini*, 199.

35. Entwistle, *Braj*, 374.

36. Mukherjee and Habib, "Akbar and the Temples of Mathura."

37. See *Narayana Bhatta Charitamrita* 2.127, and Growse, *Mathura*, 76.

38. Some contemporary sources argue that Abhimanyu was able to touch only a shadow (chaya) form of Radha; see, for example, Krishnadas Baba, *Braj Mandal Darshan*, 89.

39. This is from the title of Turner's major article on pilgrimage, "The Center Out There: Pilgrim's Goal." The destination is an essential feature of pilgrimage for Turner.

40. Growse, *Mathura*, 314–17.

41. Niebuhr, "Pilgrims and Pioneers," 13.

42. See chapter 11 of the *Bhagavad Gita*.

43. Nirmal Kumar Bose, "The Spring Festival of India," in *Cultural Anthropology and Other Essays* (Calcutta: Indian Associated Pub. Co., 1953). Bose maintains that the ancient festivities of spring, in which the god of love was frequently worshiped, were transferred to the celebration of Holi in the sixteenth century (101).

44. Growse, *Mathura*, 93.

45. Lynch, "Pilgrimage with Krishna," 176.

6

Surrender and Return

Return, remain in Vrindavan, I beg you!
Enjoy with those herdgirls the riches of perfect love!
Turn aside from all other tasks,
Bring them joy!

NANDADAS, from *Uddhav's Message*

One cold February at dawn a group of gopis went to the bank of the Yamuna River. As light filtered into the sky, they removed their clothes and entered the icy waters. They were here to perform a vow to the goddess Katyayani, seeking the boon that Krishna would become their lover. While the young ladies were bravely bathing in the Yamuna, Krishna sneaked up on them, snatched their clothes, and climbed quickly into a nearby Kadamba tree, from where he called out gleefully. The women were shocked and remained concealed up to their necks in the cold water. They begged Krishna to return their clothes and leave, but he refused, demanding instead that they come out of the water and take their clothes from him directly. Slowly, they began to surrender to his tease and emerged from the water, ashamedly covering their bodies with their hands. But Krishna would have none of this; he insisted that they honor him by raising joined palms, thereby exposing themselves completely. The gopis stood naked before Krishna, the crooked lover, inadvertently attaining his amorous presence. They had got what they wanted, though not in the form they had in mind.

Much can and has been made of this episode, but Vaishnava interpretations typically include the notion that the gopis represent human souls seeking union with the divine. The clothes represent those fixed ideas and objects that are clung to; they are obstacles that produce the anxiety that keeps one from letting go and plunging into the divine lila. Surrender must be complete, holding nothing back, before the unpredictable Lord who is not bound by human plans or preconceptions.

This famous episode is celebrated on the Ban-Yatra at a site called Chir Ghat, the "Place of Clothes," located about eleven miles downstream from Shergarh. Chir Ghat is a wonderfully peaceful place, situated on the bank of the Yamuna in an isolated stand of Kadamba trees. The Kadamba tree is closely associated with Krishna in the culture of Braj; in the paintings and poetry produced in this region he is commonly pictured sitting on the branch of a Kadamba tree playing his flute. Kadamba trees grow to great heights and produce light-orange, sweet-scented flower balls. Among the Kadamba trees at Chir Ghat stands the "very tree" Krishna climbed after stealing the clothes of the gopis. Beneath this tree is a small shrine of the goddess Katyayani.

Walking to Chir Ghat, I was to undergo an experience which seemed to encapsulate one of the major lessons of this pilgrimage.[1] We had left Shergarh at four-thirty in the morning and headed in a southern direction along the bank of the Yamuna. Soon after our departure it started to drizzle. And then came the rains! The sky opened up as it does only during the monsoons, and dark clouds poured on us relentlessly. As the rain increased, I began to swear. I had looked forward to our walk along the Yamuna, but this was not what I had in mind. "Oh, great!" I thought. "Now what?" I opened my cloth umbrella and tried in vain to keep dry. The rain was cold; I was miserable. I tramped on, grumbling to myself. I overtook Nirmal Ghosh, and as I passed him he turned to me, water pouring down his face, and said, "Oh, David, what bliss this is!" (*Ananda* was the word he used.) I looked at him in disbelief. "I'm sure *you* really mean that," I said sarcastically to myself. "How could anyone be enjoying this?" But I looked at him again, and my smug certainty vanished with a jolt. I realized that he meant it. He was laughing and obviously enjoying himself.

I was once again resisting things as they were, and because of this I was in a state of despair. I wanted desperately for things to be different from what they were. Just ahead the torrential rain had turned the path we were following into a muddy stream. The path soon disappeared into an expanse of water about two feet deep. There was no way to avoid getting wet, yet I tried. I struggled to balance on a high and narrow strip of earth that had not yet been submerged. Suddenly the ridge I was depending on gave way and I slipped into the muddy water, shoes and all. Something inside me burst, and I could hold on no longer. I let go and surrendered to the water. The most wonderful thing then happened. Exploding with laughter, I realized that this *was fun*. I looked around and suddenly became aware that many others were laughing and playing in the rainy water, joyfully shouting, "Radhe! Radhe!" One man fell flat on his ass. He laughed. What a riot!

How often do we as adults allow ourselves to play in the rain? To feel the joy of mud splashing around our feet? We spend so much energy trying to keep clean and dry, but the world often does not cooperate. The muddy water had drenched my clothes, but what did it matter? Why exhaust myself trying to keep them pristine, anyway? What was I saving them for? As long as I resisted the rain and held onto the idea of keeping dry—a fairly impossible task—I was miserable; but after I gave in and surrendered, after I no longer cared, I experienced a playful joy. I had much to learn from the gopis at Chir Ghat, who were forced to let go of the obstacle of their clothing in order to play. I also had much to learn from the rain clouds, which did not expend their forces with an expectation of return. Like the gopis standing naked before Krishna, they held back nothing and destined themselves to complete liquidation.

I met up with Maya. One look at her face told me where she was. We walked on together, splashing and giggling as we went. Shuklaji came sploshing past us and shouted with delight, "Oh look what new experience Radha has given us this time!" We came to the top of a hill and were met by a warm breeze blowing off the Yamuna. Here at Ram Ghat, the river takes a wild turn. This is said to be the result of Balarama dragging it here with his plow after becoming intoxicated with wine and the love of the gopis.[2] A small temple marks the site of this event. Some of the pilgrims sought shelter in the temple of he who commands the water; others continued to play in the rain. Soon the downpour stopped and those around me started peeling off layers of soaked clothing, basking in the golden rays of the morning sun which began streaming through cracks in the dark clouds.

I sat down on a crumbling brick wall near the temple to enjoy the sights around me and reflect on the words just spoken by Shuklaji. This was indeed a wonderful new experience. What a contrast to the scorching heat we had experienced in the beginning of our journey! My own experience also revealed much contrast. In a few short minutes I had slipped from miserable suffering into hilarious joy. What had made the difference? There had been no change in the weather, only in my view of it.

Our lives are based on a hierarchy of experience. We are attached to, or stuck on, certain forms of experience and try desperately to hold onto them while trying equally hard to avoid others. We are happy when certain experiences are present and unhappy when they are absent. We want the weather, for example, to be "just right." But there is no just right. The weather is continually changing. The weatherman's average is a fiction. In an ever-changing world, there is no average, no mean. If we are attached to a certain type of weather, we are bound to be discontent. We are not only cold and wet, but we suffer miserably. Pain is not simply pain, but pain itself becomes a pain; and it is the pain of pain which blocks the experience of bliss.

As long as I wanted things to be different than they were—wanted the rain to stop—I suffered. I certainly could not enjoy the rain in this state. I wanted my experience to come in a very particular form, and when it did not, I was unhappy. But the moment I gave up, surrendered, no longer cared, I slipped into the joyfully playful world of the muddy water. Only then was I able to enjoy the world that was actually before me. Joy—the ananda which the pilgrims talk so much about—comes from surrendering to the ever-changing difference that is lila. Again and again I was told that the aim of this pilgrimage is to experience life as lila. Krishna's lila is an unpredictable play which foils all expectations. We frequently miss much of what is actually there when we become attached to expectations of set, even, unchanging experience. We are stuck on certain forms and unable to "see" the reality that is in continual flux. All life, according to Braj Vaishnavas, is lila, that is, "a kaleidoscope of experience always generating new and polychrome patterns."[3] The experience of joy, then, comes from letting go and being on friendly terms with whatever comes, free to appreciate the next novel experience. The key is to enjoy the differences that make up existence and not be adversely affected by them.

Many journeys are motivated by a quest for some object at the end of the road that promises satisfaction, completion, and wholeness. In this case, experiences along the way are merely endured to reach the final destination. In the Ban-Yatra, however, every experience is to be enjoyed, since it is not being measured against some teleological goal that makes the present seem lacking. The world is not created with a teleological design, according to Braj Vaishnavism. Instead, the motive for creation is lila; the world is created from and for the play of Krishna.

Through my conversations with the guides and other pilgrims—and by slipping off solid ground—I came to realize that I was on the wrong track. By seeing the rain and other difficulties as obstacles in my path I was holding onto the more common view of pilgrimage as a gaining experience. The religion of Braj, however, is eccentric, and from this perspective the experience of rain is as important as any other. This shift in perspective was perhaps best expressed by Mr. Nath, who told me: "In the beginning of this pilgrimage I was hoping to finish in order to make my life different. I was hoping to find something special. But now I am no longer asking for that. I see that everything is special. Whatever Lord Krishna gives me is okay."

The very notion that something is wrong or lacking causes what is to seem problematic, but in a world where everything is Krishna, what is lacking? On the other hand, in an ever-changing reality the concept of a complete wholeness is also suspect. The goal is the pilgrimage itself, not the destination of the pilgrimage. The goal is not the still satisfaction of desire but satisfaction in the movement of desire.

We settled into our tents at Chir Ghat that afternoon. They were pitched on a grassy slope climbing away from the Yamuna and over-looking the stand of Kadamba trees. This was a peaceful haven; many of our previous camps had been placed near noisy roads, but at Chir Ghat I did not hear the sound of a single bus or truck horn, a fairly amazing accomplishment on the plains of northern India. When I reached my tent Umesh was there, along with Renu. Umesh grinned, but Renu complained about the rain. Umesh and I walked to the bank of the Yamuna. As this was the place where the gopis had bathed to attain Krishna, many of the pilgrims were bathing here. Umesh and I joined them. A warm breeze caressed my body, and mud squished between my toes. The water of the Yamuna was warm and inviting. After bathing we returned to camp and saw Shuklaji, who invited us to his tent for lunch. The invitation was offered with profuse apologies for the limitations of a meal prepared in the forest. It was, however, was one of the finest meals I had eaten in weeks. While we were sitting on the ground inside his tent enjoying the chapatis and spiced vegetables that he had prepared, Shuklaji revealed a secret plan that the guides had engineered.

I had become obsessed with the idea of finishing the entire pilgrimage by foot. This obsession had kept me going during those times when I wanted to quit or perhaps should have taken a tonga. I was determined to go the whole way on foot and held to this resolve like a vow. Shuklaji's surprise was this: the next day we were to board boats and float the Yamuna downstream to Belban, one of the twelve forests located on the shore opposite Vrindaban. My initial reaction to this plan was one of resistance. What was I to do with my resolve to walk the entire way? Short of abandoning the pilgrimage party, I had no choice but to go along with the new plan. Vows, Shuklaji told me, were yet another vestige of control which had to be surrendered to keep moving with this pilgrimage. The vow was an obstacle to a free ride offered by Yamuna.

The secret plan of the guides came at a price, however. The bullock carts which carried our tents and luggage would be unable to cross the river and keep up with the boats; they would therefore be returning to Vrindaban. This meant that tonight would be the last camp with the comfort of our tents and bedding. We did not know exactly where we would be sleeping for the next three nights. From here on we would have to carry whatever we needed. I added a blanket and lota to my backpack.

That evening a cold wind began to blow. I joined some bullock-cart drivers who had built a small twig fire in the middle of our camp. Their heads were wrapped in a colorful assortment of cloths, and they puffed quietly on bidis as they huddled close to the fire. Their bullocks and water buffalo were bedded down nearby. They stared silently into the flames, coming out of their lethargy only long enough to light another bidi; everyone seemed pensive on this last night. The moon, only two days from being full, was shining brightly, illuminating the small forest of Kadamba trees that made this place famous. Its golden reflection swam on the moving surface of the Yamuna. I walked away from the fire to enjoy the scent of the fresh air and then went to find Mr. Nath. Since the tongas would also be unable to keep up with the boats, he had decided to return with them to Vrindaban. We made arrangements to meet there in five days and then said good-bye, after which I went to my tent and wrapped myself in a wool blanket for the night.

We were up slightly before sunrise the next morning. Shivering with cold I put on three shirts, thankful I had included a flannel shirt in my trunk, and wrapped a gamcha around my neck as a scarf. I longed for a cup of hot coffee. I turned my trunk over to the bullock-cart drivers and walked toward the river. There were sixteen large wooden boats tied up on the shore of the Yamuna, now crimson from the rising sun. These had been poled twenty miles up the river from Vrindaban, a task that took most of two days. Bamboo oars for the return journey downstream rested in the front of each boat.

The boatmen finished their morning tea and chapatis, stowed their bedding and stoves under the floor of the boats, and received us aboard around six. Most of them were teenage boys, working in teams of two.

About twenty passengers rode in each vessel. Since there were no seats in the boats, we sat cross-legged on the flat wooden decks. Turtles poked their heads out of the water as we started downstream in the gentle morning light. Some of the women on my boat began singing songs to Radha. Nirmal Ghosh added his uninhibited rough voice. The boy at the oars laughed; others merely smiled and hummed along, faces aglow in the early sunlight. Everyone seemed to appreciate this new mode of travel.

Our first stop came four miles downstream on the western bank of the river at a place called Nanda Ghat. We landed and walked inland through harvested fields to a temple housing a tall yellow image of Krishna's adoptive father, Nanda. Here, we were told the story of Nanda's abduction. Nanda once fasted on the eleventh lunar day of the fortnight. The next day, while it was yet dark, he came here to bathe in the Yamuna. Because he did not wait until dawn, he was guilty of a minor ritual infraction and was seized by a servant demon and taken to the abode of Varuna, Lord of the Waters. When the cowherds discovered that Nanda had been taken, they shouted for Krishna. Krishna, who had little regard for rules, plunged into the water to rescue Nanda and confronted Varuna. Once Varuna realized what had happened, he apologized and then rejoiced, declaring that he had unintentionally attained the highest bliss by achieving a vision of the Supreme Lord.

We returned to the boats and were soon pulled into the powerful current of the monsoon-swollen river. A few of the passengers were anxious about the possibility of capsizing. One of the women suggested that we take confidence from the story we had just heard; we would be protected from the demons that might haunt the deep waters below us. A short distance downstream we landed on the eastern shore and walked two miles to Bhadraban, the "Auspicious Forest," the seventh of the twelve forests and perhaps the most pathetic, for there are very few trees left. Still, it is known to be a favorite grazing place for Krishna's cows because of its fine grass. Some say it was here that Krishna killed the demon named Vatsasura, who had taken the form of a calf and joined Krishna's herd. Recognizing him as a demon, Krishna whirled the calf around and around by the tail and sailed him into the trees. This was the first demon Krishna killed after Nanda had moved his clan from their home in Gokul, thinking that it was too close to the town of Mathura. Today there is a small shrine to Krishna on the site. This is also a forest sacred to Shiva, who is present here under a large tree as a lingam called Jhadakhandeshvar, the "Lord of the Forest."

From Bhadraban we walked south for three miles through open fields until we came to the eighth of the twelve forests, Bhandiraban, the "Forest of the Banyan Tree." A huge banyan tree grows in this forest, which is thick with a tangle of vines. Nearby are temples and the adobe buildings of a small village. At least two stories are associated with the banyan tree: here Radha and Krishna were secretly married, and here Krishna's brother, Balarama, fought a demon.

One day Nanda was tending cows among the flowering trees and tender grass.[4] He had brought along his young son Krishna. While Nanda was preoccupied with the cows, Krishna suddenly made the sky grow dark with thick clouds. A fierce wind began to blow; seeing the coming storm, Nanda became concerned for his young son, who had squirmed fearfully into his lap. At this time Radha, beautifully dressed, happened into the forest. Nanda knew that Radha cared for his child and so requested her to take him safely home. Radha was pleased and took the child away. While walking through a dense section of the forest, Radha experienced a great desire for Krishna. Instantly, Krishna changed forms: where there was once a small child there now stood a handsome youth. He led her to a nearby bower, situated beneath this huge banyan tree. Radha surrendered with amazement to Krishna's play, and the two enjoyed each other on a bed of flowers. The god Brahma appeared on the scene and sanctioned their union with a secret marriage. Radha placed a garland of flowers around Krishna's neck, and he placed one around her as the gods showered them with flower petals and sounded celestial music. Suddenly, Krishna resumed the form of a small child, and Radha, in a state of great confusion, returned a hungry infant to Yashoda.

The other story told about this forest involves a demon by the name of Pralamba.[5] Krishna and Balarama were once playing a game here with their cowherd companions. The boys were divided into two teams which were competing in a race to the Bhandira banyan tree. The losers had to carry the winners on their shoulders back to the starting line. While the boys were engaged in this game, the demon Pralamba surreptitiously joined their ranks, assuming the guise of a cowboy. His intention was to kill Krishna and Balarama. Krishna recognized the new boy as a demon and invited him to join his team. The opponents, led by Balarama, won the next round. Pralamba saw this as an opportunity to kill Balarama and volunteered to carry him back to the start.

When Balarama was seated on Pralamba's shoulders, the demon ran off wildly into the surrounding forest, changing back into his true form: a monster with burning eyes and gruesome tusks. Balarama was taken by surprise but recovered his wits in time to bring his fists smashing down on the demon's head. Pralamba fell lifeless to the ground. Balarama was now tired and thirsty, and the others boys were fatigued by the game. To revive them, Krishna stuck his flute into the ground. Fresh sweet water bubbled to the surface.

Venukup, the "Flute Well," is situated in the center of a small cluster of temples within Bhandiraban. The villagers living here say that a drink from this well will quench all desires. There is a temple for Balarama here, and another for the amorous duo, Radha and Krishna. A newly married couple in our party asked me to photograph them before this temple. Tea, fruit, and fried vegetables were available near the well from carts raised on bicycle wheels. We relaxed and filled our stomachs before hiking two miles farther south to where the boats awaited us in the town of Mat.

Mat, according to our guides, derives its name from a large earthen vessel which was used by the cowherds to make yogurt. We were taken to a small shed which protects a large pot sunken in the ground and said to be the very vessel used by Yashoda to make yogurt for Krishna. The pilgrims peered into the pot, tossed in a few coins, and were on their way. On the edge of Mat is a place identified as the spot where Shiva was overcome by the enchanting acts of Vishnu/Krishna. The place is called Rudraviryakhalanaban, the "Forest Where Shiva Dropped His Semen."[6]

In the beginning of this world the gods sought to secure the nectar of immortality, acquired by churning the ocean. Vishnu advised them that this would be an impossible task without the aid of the demons. The gods were afraid, however, that the demons would overpower them and steal the immortal drink. Vishnu had a plan to insure that this did not happen: he would become the enchanting woman Mohini, a form of his own creative power (*maya*) guaranteed to steal the heart of any male, and seduce the nectar away from the demons. Through cooperative effort the gods and demons produced the immortal nectar from the ocean but in the process unfortunately produced a world-endangering poison. The mighty Shiva was persuaded to drink the poison and thus save the world. As predicted, the demons tried to make off with the nectar, but Vishnu, in the guise of the mind-stealing Mohini, bewitched the demons and got it back for the gods. Shiva, still presumably under the influence of the poison, missed the whole show and so later approached Vishnu and requested sight of his enchanting female form. Smiling, Vishnu agreed and then vanished.

Shiva suddenly found himself in a beautiful flowering garden. Before him stood the most beautiful woman he had ever seen. She was dressed in delicate clothing and was playing with a ball, bouncing it high into the air so that her full breasts were alluringly revealed. Her cheeks glowed from the play and were framed by bright dangling earrings. Her dark eyes darted back and forth with the ball. When they caught sight of Shiva she flung him a seductive glance and a coy smile. Shiva lost his mind. Suddenly, a wind came up and blew the ball away from the enchanting woman; it also tore the delicate clothing from her body. Feigning shame, she ran off into the forest. Seeing this ravishing beauty slipping away, Shiva abandoned himself to her pursuit. He followed her through the forest, finally catching hold of her long braid. He drew her tantalizing curves close to his body. The beautiful woman suddenly disappeared, but Shiva had already been aroused and his seed spurted to the ground. Thereupon he regained his senses and realized that he had just been seduced by none other than Vishnu's maya. A stone now marks the site of this erotic emission. Once again in the forests of Braj, Shuklaji pointed out to me, Shiva surrenders his ascetic ways in the play of Krishna.

A large crowd from the town of Mat accompanied us to the spot on the river where the boats were docked. We waved good-bye to them and continued on our journey by water. It was late morning, and the chill of the early hours was left far behind. We now basked in a warm sunlight which illuminated the green fields of the surrounding countryside. The passengers on the boat chatted quietly as we passed a herd of black-and-white cows grazing lazily on the riverbank. A colony of Baya Weaver birds had built nests in a tree overhanging the Yamuna. These small yellow-and-brown birds work together in couples to weave grass into long, graceful hanging baskets, which are entered through tunnels open at the bottom. A dozen or more such baskets hung from the busy tree under which we passed. We soon approached a wooded bank, the site of one of the cowherds' favorite swimming holes. This place, called Kalidah Ghat, is located slightly upstream from Vrindaban and is said to be the place where Krishna subdued the mighty serpent Kaliya.

Krishna was once grazing cows in this area with the other cowboys. It was a scorching summer day, and they became hot and thirsty. The boys discovered a beautiful pool in the Yamuna and dove in for a swim. They all, however, were immediately stunned by poison. After reviving his friends, Krishna discerned that a terrible and enormous multi-hooded cobra inhabited the pool and was poisoning its waters. The snake Kaliya had lived in these waters since he had fled the ocean, pursued by a wrathful Garuda, Vishnu's eagle mount. Krishna climbed a lofty Kadamba tree that grew over the pool and dove deep into the water. The huge serpent gripped Krishna in its coils, and all the boys standing on the bank were sure that he was lost. Krishna remained in the deadly embrace of Kaliya for a long time.

Meanwhile, Nanda and Yashoda had been informed of what was happening. When they arrived and saw their dear child wrapped in the coils of the huge snake, they were horrified. Nanda prepared to dive into the water when Balarama, knowing Krishna's true nature, restrained him. At this moment Krishna expanded his body and broke the hold of the mighty serpent. Krishna then leapt onto the hoods of the cobra and started dancing wildly. His dancing feet crushed the heads of Kaliya, and blood began to ooze from the serpent's mouths. Perceiving that their husband was about to perish, the wives of Kaliya approached Krishna and begged his mercy. Kaliya then surrendered and made an appeal for Krishna's grace, arguing that he was only following the way of snakes, which had, after all, been determined by Krishna himself.

In the end Kaliya was spared; contact with Krishna's feet, even in the dance of destruction, brings salvation. Krishna did not kill Kaliya but instead sent him back to the ocean with the promise that Garuda would no longer harass him, as he now bore the mark of Krishna's feet. Rid of the poisonous snake, the cowboys could now enjoy this pool, and it became one of their favorite swimming holes. As we floated by it, the guides pointed to an old Kadamba tree below the towering red sandstone temple of Madan Mohan, and said that it was the one from which Krishna dove into the pool. A small shrine housing an image of Krishna dancing on the hoods of Kaliya now marks the site of this lila.

The river curved and brought us to the forest of Belban, the ninth of the twelve forests. Here we gathered our belongings, left the boats, and walked inland for perhaps half a mile, following a dirt path which wound through a jungle of twisted shrubs. I immediately noticed the additional weight of my sleeping gear in my pack. The temple spires of Vrindaban were visible in the distance, on the other side of the Yamuna. We soon came to a small temple nestled in a stand of tall trees peacefully removed from any major road or business center. The greenery of this forest is brilliant during the rainy season. The name

Belban refers to a kind of fruit tree sacred to Shiva, and the forest is thus known to be conducive to contemplation. A small stone Shiva lingam set up in the middle of this grove marks it as a place of asceticism, but the temple that stands before it houses an image of the goddess Lakshmi, for this forest is also called Shriban, a name clearly identifying it with Lakshmi. Under a large tree in front of the temple a red sandstone tablet has been erected, on which is chiseled the first Sanskrit verse of the Gopi Gita, a song sung by the gopis in the *Bhagavata Purana* after Krishna disappeared during their amorous moonlight dance in the forest of Vrindaban. In this song the gopis address Krishna: "Glory be to Braj, which is superior to all other places because of your birth, for Lakshmi takes refuge here forever."[7] The story told at Belban accounts for Lakshmi's presence in Braj.

Lakshmi is the Queen of heavenly Vaikuntha. In this position she has it all: wealth, power, and prestige. Most important, she has Vishnu all to herself, competing with no other woman for her wifely place by the side of her lord. But one day, out of a desire for something more, she made a heroic sacrifice and gave up the security of all this.

From a great distance Lakshmi heard the seductive sound of Krishna's flute and experienced a strong desire to join his love dance in the forest of Vrindaban. She came down from her high throne in majestic Vaikuntha to this place, searching for the secret forest of Vrindaban. She soon met some of the local gopis and asked them brusquely where the secret forest was, assuming rather discourteously that if these lowly village women were allowed entrance into Krishna's love dance, then she certainly would be as well. As his wife, she had the sole honor of massaging Lord Vishnu's feet in Vaikuntha, not knowing that in Braj, where the high are low and the low are high, Krishna massages the feet of a gopi. Lakshmi demanded that the women return at night and lead her to Vrindaban. However, because she was unaware of the ways of Braj and would not respect the simple ways of the gopis or adopt the sentiment of the lover (*parakiya*), as opposed to the sentiment of the wife (*svakiya*), the gopis never came back for her. The Yamuna River served as a physical barrier, a sign of her inability to surrender to the strange ways of Braj. Inside Vrindaban proper, there exist no temples for Lakshmi. She remains in this small temple across the river from Vrindaban, engaged in asceticism while contemplating the insecurity—but intensity—of shared love. Krishna's kindness, however, is immense; an image of Krishna stands beside that of Lakshmi in the temple of Belban.

That night we, too, were separated from Vrindaban by the river. Our guides had arranged for food to be brought in from Vrindaban, less than a mile away, but we were to camp out in the grove of Belban. The night was again chilly; I wrapped up in my wool blanket and found a place to lie down under a tree. One day from being full, the moon blessed our camp with a glorious light. Mummylike bundles were strewn everywhere. Lying among the trees of the Belban forest, we saw the lights of Vrindaban. One pilgrim remarked that perhaps we, like Lakshmi, were not yet ready to enter the secret groves of Vrindaban. Seeing Vrindaban so tantalizingly close, yet so removed, caused him to say that his desire for Vrindaban had increased tenfold. From this perspective the pilgrimage seemed to be a departure from Vrindaban just so that one could have the experience of re-entering it; separation generates desire.

The next morning we walked four and a half miles southeast through beautiful mustard fields to Mansarovar, the "Lake of Sulking." Yellow-orange billowy clouds glowed in a cobalt blue sky. As we approached Mansarovar, dark green palm trees pierced this dramatic backdrop. A large lake ringed with lush, dense trees suddenly appeared. White egrets and tall gray herons stalked its shores. Mansarovar is an enchanting place. It is also a sad place, for it was formed by the tears of Radha when she was in a state of *man*, or jealous anger.[8]

Radha had been nervously watching Krishna for a long time, suspiciously looking for signs of another woman. Such thoughts occupied her mind as she waited for him in a dark bower. She waited all night. In the early morning hours, after she was worn out with worry, he finally showed up. The signs she had feared were clearly present; his body was marked by love play with another woman. Sheepishly, he tried to explain, but the burden of jealousy and the strain of the long wait proved to be too much for Radha. She exploded, shouting that he should return to his other lover. She rushed off, making her way to this lonely spot, and collapsed, giving way to a torrent of tears, thereby creating the waters of Mansarovar. A small, charming temple, built by wives of Suraj Mal Singh of Dig and now maintained by Radhavallabhi priests, stands in this grove at the edge of the lake. A raised circular porch with a circular roof supported by eight pillars extends in front of the red-and-white temple, and is used for religious performances and gaining visual access to the shrine. Inside Radha remains alone. The attending priest drew back a gold curtain and revealed the image; only her face was visible through the piles of flowers and red cloth that decorated her.

The pilgrims lingered at Mansarovar for some time, savoring its mood of separation, and then ventured southeast for another six miles to the town of Raya. Raya is not the site of any known lila but served merely as another stopping station. We camped out in the compound of a small college. The compound consisted of a large walled square, surrounded on all sides by arched porches and single-story cement classrooms, all colored with a faded yellow veneer. Local vendors set up temporary stalls in the compound to serve tea, flatbreads, and vegetables to the pilgrims. That night many in our group slept under the arches, but Umesh and I decided to risk inclement weather and spend the night on the roof of one of the buildings. Under the beauty of a full moon, we rolled up in our blankets and went to sleep. Sometime in the night, however, we were awakened by large drops of rain splashing on our faces. Snickering at our fate, we staggered off the roof and went in search of a dry place to sleep. We found only a solid mass of groaning bodies, and no room. A camp cook finally discovered us and led us to a multitiered lecture room where he had set up his pots and kerosene stove. We climbed the stairs and settled down for the remainder of the night under some wooden benches. Umesh made a crack about the lecturer boring us to sleep.

We were up at four the next morning and heading south along the single-lane paved road which stretches for eleven miles between Raya and the next stop, Dauji. A good number in our group were tired and so decided to take a bus. I was urged to join them but found the idea ludicrous at this point in our journey. I had reached a tolerable standoff with my feet and was greatly enjoying our daily hikes. I continued walking.

I walked with Umesh, Shuklaji, and some of Shuklaji's Bengali passengers. Three-quarters of the way to Dauji we came to the village of Bandi. On the western side of the village is a pond and walled garden compound housing the temple of Anandi and Bandi, the family goddesses of Krishna's parents, Nanda and Yashoda. We sat before Ananda Devi, the Goddess of Bliss, talking about the place of ananda in this pilgrimage. Shuklaji again made the point that the purpose of this pilgrimage was to experience bliss. "Ananda is that bliss which spilled out of Krishna and created the world when he looked into the loving eyes of Radha. It is present at all times, although it is 'covered' most of the time for most people." The Ban-Yatra, he explained, is an exercise in uncovering and becoming aware of that ever-present bliss.

We pressed on to Dauji and were overtaken by a vivacious figure dressed in a crisp white turban. He approached us with a quick and powerful gait, and when he spoke his eyes sparkled with energy. He introduced himself as one of the pandas, or guides, of Dauji, and with a slight grin said meaningfully that he would be seeing us later. We watched him fade into the road ahead of us, leaving me wondering what he had meant by this loaded remark.

We reached Dauji, the southernmost point of our journey, around one-thirty, and although we were hot and tired we went immediately to the main temple, an imposing stone structure built in the eighteenth century. A burst of colored flags fluttered atop its main spire. The temple is enclosed with tall, thick, white-plastered stone walls, entered through heavy wooden gates. When we arrived these gates were temporarily closed. Since we had not yet bathed that day, we proceeded to Kshir Sagar, the "Milk Ocean," located adjacent to the temple. I took one look at the slimy green surface of the tank and declared that I would not bathe in it. Umesh and Shuklaji harassed me for being a coward, but after Umesh stuck his foot into the water and it came out covered with a thick slime they joined me for a bath at a nearby well. After bathing we returned to the temple for a sight of the macho hero of Dauji.

Dauji, meaning "older brother," is the name given to the town of Krishna's powerful brother, Balarama. The striking black stone image housed in the main temple is very old, perhaps dating back nearly two thousand years. Standing over six feet tall, this image is the largest in Braj and resembles one of the nagas, or snake deities, once worshiped in this area. It was clothed in bright orange cloth and decorated with huge garlands of flowers. His right hand extends upward into a seven-headed cobra which hoods the entire figure. An opening in the cloth exposed a cup which Balarama holds in his left hand.

According to Vaishnava theology, Balarama is an incarnation of Vishnu's cosmic serpent, Ananta. Scholarly research has shown that the current worship of Balarama is the survival of a much older agrarian cult of a plow-wielding snake deity.[9] Mathura was an important center for this cult of snakes, and Naga temples and anthropomorphic representations of snakes dating back to the third century B.C.E. have been found around the city.[10] The cult of the snake deity Balarama reached its zenith in the Mathura area during the Kushana period (2nd cent. B.C.E.). Over the course of time Balarama was absorbed into the Vaishnava cult and identified with Vishnu's serpent. In Braj he was to take on the character of a rowdy wrestler known for his irreverently direct and forceful ways.

The image of Balarama in the Dauji temple is believed to have been established by Vajranabh to reign over the southern regions of Braj but was later hidden to protect it from Muslim invaders. The local account of its rediscovery is that Gokulnath, one of the seven grandsons of Vallabha, heard from some cowherds that a cow was releasing milk on a stone sticking out of the pond named Kshir Sagar.[11] He went to investigate and discovered the image of Balarama. Gokulnath tried to move the image to Gokul, but it refused to budge, as this was the birthplace of Revati, his consort. Thus, a temple was built for Balarama on the shore of Kshir Sagar; Revati now stands facing him inside the inner chamber of the temple.

The enclosed courtyard of the temple is the scene of the most riotous of all events of the spring festival of Holi. The celebration is inspired by an episode involving Balarama. One day he observed Krishna playing Holi with Radha. Later he approached Radha, desiring also to play with her. Radha danced for Balarama, but as her love was for only Krishna, she and the gopis stripped him and flogged him with his own lust. During Holi this incident is celebrated by flooding the temple with water dyed with baskets of marigold petals. The men of the village enter the temple, following the head priest who is riding a phallus-shaped horse and dancing lewdly. Singing provocative songs, they approach the women of the village who are waiting for them inside the temple, veiled for anonymity. The women attack the crowd of men, tear the shirts from their bodies, and after soaking the torn shirts in the flower-stained water, begin whipping them. What ensues is a hilarious water fight involving an orgy of water and sensual play. This mass bathing of a swarm of bodies in the colored waters of Radha and Krishna is frequently interpreted to be a means of purifying the body and drenching the soul with the love of Krishna.

My group rested in Dauji at the compound of yet another small college. Our rowdy cook, Mohan, surprised us all by making a meal that was actually tasty. We ate lentils and rice cooked with milk and potatoes that were served on the ground on dried leaf plates. After a short rest we returned to the temple. There in the courtyard stood the man wearing the crisp white turban whom we had met on the road to Dauji earlier in the day. He seemed to be waiting for us. He approached me and told me that Dauji's afternoon *bhog*—food enjoyed by the deity and returned to the offerer as prasad—was very special. An oil arati lamp was waved before Balarama, and a large stainless steel bowl was offered at the three o'clock worship. The man in the white turban went forward, received something from the officiating priest, and returned by my side. He handed me a glass full of a green milky liquid. "Take this," he said. "Drink it! It is the prasad of Balarama."

The substance looked strange but tasted sweet. I gulped it down. I was told that many residing in the town of Dauji drink this every day. I could detect milk, sugar, and ground almonds. "It's good," I said. "What is it?" The turbaned guide then informed me, "Every afternoon Balarama enjoys bhang bhog." So this was what was in the cup that Balarama held! In Braj, Balarama is the patron deity of bhang eaters, so fond is he of the intoxicating substance, and Dauji is the center of this cult. I learned that we had just taken bhang in the form of the cooling drink *thandai*. This was to make for a very interesting afternoon.

We left Dauji and headed west toward the Yamuna and into the environs of Mahaban, the tenth of the twelve forests. This area is the site of Krishna's childhood lilas. It seemed oddly appropriate that we would be finishing this pilgrimage, which celebrates the backward god, by visiting the sites of the beginning of Krishna's life in Braj. The walk to the river was relaxing; the road was lined with large shade trees, and the countryside blossomed with beauty. Along the way, two boys riding a single bicycle informed us that there was a mad water buffalo up ahead and that it had already knocked down an elderly woman. She was not seriously injured but had to be taken away in a tonga. Sure enough, we encountered the buffalo after walking another half mile. I was amazed by its erratic movements; for such a bulky animal, it ran surprisingly fast. Maneuvering around this crazy beast, we reached the Yamuna River at a place called Brahmanda Ghat, the site of our next stopping station. Brahmanda literally means the "Egg of Brahma" and refers to the entire universe as revealed to a stunned Yashoda on this site long ago.

One day young Krishna was out in the forest while tending cows and playing with his friends. He reached down, picked up a handful of dirt, and popped it into his mouth. The elder Balarama and the others told Krishna to stop eating dirt. He defiantly refused to heed their words. The boys ran to mother Yashoda to tattle. Yashoda called Krishna to her side and began scolding him. Krishna returned her rough words with a bewildered look and denied the accusation of the elder boys. Suspecting her mischievous son, Yashoda ordered him to open his mouth so that she could determine the truth for herself. Peering inside Krishna's tiny mouth, Yashoda was completely overwhelmed, for there she saw the entire universe.

Yashoda experienced a divine vision; Krishna's awesome glory was revealed to her. But with the dawn of this new awareness, Yashoda lost the ability to love Krishna as a needy child. Love depends on illusion, an illusion which gives form to the formless. Once her illusion was shattered, Yashoda began to worry about the way she had been treating God, questioning the propriety of her actions. She had hit God with a stick, spanked God, yelled at God, scolded God. She became anxious about the entire nature of the illusion she had been living. But this illusion itself is part of Krishna's play, and, moreover, it has a beneficial purpose: it allows love. Yashoda was able to love Krishna so intimately only because of the illusion which made him appear as her baby. The Vaishnava theologians of Braj discuss this distinction at great length. According to them Krishna has two forms: an awesomely majestic form (*aishvarya rupa*), such as that revealed here and to the gopis at Sheshashayi, and an attractive human form (*madhurya* or *manusha rupa*).[12] Though Krishna is never contained by the attractive form, in Braj this form conceals the awesome form, thus enabling the worshiper to approach Krishna with casual intimacy. Krishna appears elsewhere in his awesome form, but he appears to the residents of Braj, who approach him without hesitation, only in his sweet human form.

Removal of her worries and restoration of her beneficial illusion were thus necessary if Yashoda was once again to love Krishna with the intensity of a mother for a child. In the *Bhagavata Purana* it is written that Krishna himself recast the loving illusion over Yashoda.[13] But in Braj a slightly different story is told, once again involving Shiva.

Downstream from Brahmanda Ghat is a small, peaceful grove called Chinta Haran, meaning "Removal of Anxiety." I ventured down to this enchanting forest alone. It was simultaneously one of the most quiet yet noisy places I have ever been. There was little sound of human civilization, yet hundreds of green parrots flashed through the trees, chattering and shrieking a cacophony of sounds. A wiry old Nimbarki sadhu inhabited the forest. I watched him chop fodder with a heavy ax and sweep the forest bed with tree branches bound together as a broom. As he swept with effortless motion, I had the impression that he was preaching a silent sermon; my own anxieties seemed to be swept away in the peace of this place.

I met a Ramanandi priest, his face smeared with bright orange sandalwood paste, who showed me the temple of this forest and narrated its story. After Yashoda's world was shattered by the universal vision inside Krishna's mouth and she was overcome with anxiety, Krishna led her to this forest where resides Chinta Haran Mahadev, Shiva as the Remover of Anxiety. Here there is a weathered Shiva temple housing a single lingam carved so that it comprises 1,008 lingams. According to the attending priest, it was this form of Shiva who took away Yashoda's anxiety and once again cast the net of loving illusion over her. Yashoda emerged from these woods once again able to love.

I returned to Brahmanda Ghat and joined the party of pilgrims resting on stone steps and platforms built along the bank of the river. We passed the remainder of the day relaxing under large shade trees. There comes a subtle joy from simply being in such places. People sat conversing quietly, crows squawked incessantly, and the trees rustled softly in the breeze. The late afternoon sun played on a sandstone structure built over the river. Multicolored saris hung drying on its railing, a gentle breeze inciting them to dance. In the middle of this platform stood a tree, which a local guide claimed marks the exact spot where Krishna ate dirt. The guide demanded a donation for this information. At the top of the stone steps is a temple, looked after by a long-haired Ramandi priest, that celebrates the episode of Krishna eating dirt. Inside is an image of the child Krishna with a butter ball in his hand. Or is it a dirt ball? This question occupied several Bengali men standing beside me, for at the entrance of the temple was a basket of dirt balls, called either "sweets of Brahmanda" or "dirt candy," which could be purchased by the pilgrims as souvenirs. The temple bells clanged loudly as a golden sun began to disappear into the spent monsoon clouds floating in the western sky.

I learned here that those who had ridden the bus from Raya had returned to Vrindaban after quickly viewing the remaining sites. Renu was among them. I never saw her again and was sorry that I did not get a chance to say good-bye to her. A picture of her broad face with strong lines of determination remained in my mind.

Our last night out seemed particularly blessed. Even though I had developed a new blister on my left foot, I was still happy to be here. It was not that my feet had stopped hurting but that somehow blistered feet had become acceptable—at least for a while. I joined Umesh and Shuklaji, who were sitting on the stone steps at the edge of the river. The effects of Balarama's prasad lingered on, heightening our senses. We bathed in the warm water and then sat for three hours watching the sun sink and the evening light slowly fade in the western sky. The shapes and colors of the clouds were fantastic. At one point a cloud appeared which resembled in detail Vishnu lying on his cobra couch. We marveled at the resemblance and then reflected on its possible meaning. We talked without hurry but with some sadness, knowing this was our last night out. Tomorrow we would be returning to our respective responsibilities.

The Vishnu-shaped cloud reminded me of another story, and suddenly I realized that I, too, according to Vaishnava theology, was looking into the mouth of Vishnu. A story is told of the great sage Markandeya, who was blessed with immortality.[14] After the entire universe had been reabsorbed into the body of Vishnu at the end of an era, Markandeya wandered about enjoying himself in the world inside the body of the dreaming god. One day in the course of his wanderings he slipped out of Vishnu's mouth and suddenly found himself swimming in a dreadful sea of darkness. Markandeya was terrified by the sudden annihilation of his world and began splashing about in the silent black water. This aroused the attention of the dormant Vishnu, who seized Markandeya and swallowed him. Markandeya once again found himself in his familiar world and yet now saw it with new eyes.

When Markandeya slipped out of the mouth of Vishnu, he fell out of existence and plunged into the great sea of nothingness, but by so doing gained a greater understanding of reality. It was only by crossing the threshold of Vishnu's mouth—passing from inside to outside, then back again—that Markandeya came to realize that he was living inside the mouth of God. Vaishnavas maintain that we are living continuously inside the body of God but are unaware of this because of its constant presence. Yashoda lived continuously in the presence of Krishna but was unaware of his divinity until she slipped out of the world of ordinary perception. The boundary of Braj is finally an illusory boundary to enable one to see the extraordinary nature of the ordinary; by crossing this boundary the pilgrim becomes aware of things as they really are.

According to Braj Vaishnavism, this entire world is Krishna. He is the beautiful sunset that was enchanting me, the road that blistered my feet, the sun that scorched me, the birds that serenaded me, the trees that whispered to me, and, perhaps most of all, the muddy water I had slipped into on the way to Chir Ghat. He is this very world in all its wonderfully twisted multiplicity of forms. There is no need to tear away the surface for some metaphysical depth; the diverse lila as it appears is it.

The three of us sat watching a multitude of colors drift across the sky until the stars shone brightly. Finally we were hungry, so we moved to a small tea stall perched at the top of the steps. There, under a huge tree, we consumed chapatis, a spicy bean and vegetable mixture, and hot sweet milk. While we ate, a peacock landed to roost for the night on a branch of the tree. Umesh and Shuklaji went to look for a place to sleep in the compound of a Sanskrit school located near Brahmanda Ghat. I wandered along the river. The moon was yet full. The schedule that Narayan Bhatt had designed for the Ban-Yatra had the pilgrimage culminate in a lunar climax. I stood captivated by its incredibly gorgeous reflection in the Yamuna and felt thankful for the experiences I had just gone through. If I were not planning to spend another eight months wandering this area, I think I would have been completely overwhelmed with sadness at the thought that this was the last night of our pilgrimage. Saying good night to it all, I went off to join Umesh and Shuklaji.

The next morning we were up early, and as the sun began to paint another day we marched ahead back into the childhood lilas of Krishna. We would be walking upstream until noon, back to the city of Mathura, winding our way for fourteen miles along a route marked by the play of Krishna in his infancy. On the road from Brahmanda Ghat to the town of Gokul we came first to the site where Yashoda bound Krishna to a large pestle.[15]

Mischievous Krishna was always stealing butter from his mother. One day Yashoda ran to take boiling milk off the fire, leaving Krishna unattended. While she was out of the room, Krishna broke a pot containing some butter she had just made and began eating it. Yashoda caught him in the act and threatened to strike him with a rod. Krishna was so frightened by this that Yashoda threw down the rod and decided instead to tie him to a large pestle so that he could not get into any more mischief. Krishna makes havoc of all boundaries yet exists within them; he is the void beyond all form yet simultaneously is all forms. Regarding that which is beyond all form as her own child, Yashoda continued. She tried binding Krishna with a rope, but the rope was too short. She took another piece of rope and added it to the first, but the combined ropes were still just slightly short of the required length. She added another, then another, and still another, but all ropes combined were too short to bind Krishna. Perceiving that his mother was becoming exhausted, boundless Krishna at last relented and allowed himself to be bound.

Yashoda left Krishna and resumed her household duties. Finding it impossible to stay still and out of mischief, Krishna began to move about, dragging the heavy pestle behind him. The pestle became stuck between two Arjuna trees. Krishna gave a strong tug, and the two trees came crashing to the earth. By this action Krishna released the trapped souls of two men who had been cursed by the ascetic Narada, who had seen them making love with a group of women in naked abandonment and imprisoned them inside the trees. We were shown the remains of the two trees and fragments of the pestle at the small shrine which celebrates this lila.

A little farther up the road, a shallow ravine takes off to the right and leads up a hill to the house of Nanda in Old Gokul. This ravine, the site of another famous lila of Krishna's childhood, is said to have been made by the writhing body of the huge demoness Putana.[16]

Krishna's wicked uncle Kansa had learned that Devaki's eighth child yet lived. Terrified, he sought the aid of one of the most dreaded demons of the area. Putana, whose name means "foul smelling," was a master at killing infants. Kansa sent her to the house of Nanda and Yashoda in Gokul; before arriving, the hideous ogress took the form of a loving nursemaid. Putana captivated the inhabitants of Gokul with her beauty and sweet smile, and soon had worked her way into Nanda's house as a nursemaid for the young Krishna. When everyone in the household had accepted her, she offered her breast to the infant Krishna as an apparent sign of affection. Not knowing that her breast was poisonous, everyone looked on with delightful approval. For a moment it appeared that Putana's mission might be successful. Krishna took her breast in his mouth and began to suck. He sucked, and he sucked, and he sucked, until he began to suck the life right out of her. Perceiving that her life was in danger, Putana threw off her disguise, resumed her huge demonic form, and began flailing about violently. It was this action, Shuklaji told us, that produced the ravine which led to Nanda's house. At the end of the struggle, Putana's colossal body lay lifeless. After recovering their dear child from the enormous breast, the cowherds stared at this body with amazement. They then dismembered and cremated Putana's body, and a strange thing occurred. A sweet fragrance was emitted from the cremation fire. In giving suck to the baby Krishna, Putana had inadvertently achieved salvation.

We climbed Putana's ravine and entered the house of Nanda in Old Gokul. This is the heart of Mahaban, the "Great Forest" which surrounds the cowherds' first encampment where Krishna's earliest lilas in Braj take place. Mahaban was once the site of a fortified Hindu settlement that was attacked and destroyed by the Muslim forces of Sultan Muhmud of Ghazni in 1017. The Hindu prince who ruled here killed his family and then himself to avoid capture.[17] Mahaban became a strategic military headquarters and administrative center for both the Delhi Sultanate and the Mughal empire.

Mahaban is one of the oldest sites associated with the Krishna story in Braj. Sometimes called Old Nandagaon in Braj literature, it is believed to have been the residence of Nanda before he moved to Nandagaon to be farther from the demonic threats of King Kansa. It was here that Balarama was born and the newborn Krishna was carried by Vasudeva across the raging waters of the swollen Yamuna on that dark and rainy night of his birth. The stately structure of Nanda's House was built with eighty pillars from Hindu temples which had been rearranged to construct a mosque during the reign of Aurangzeb. The edifice was later converted back into a Hindu temple. It is one of the few structures still standing in Braj which uses portions of buildings predating the Mughal period. The walls are covered with many colorful paintings depicting episodes from the infancy of Krishna. The priests of this wealthy temple were extremely eager for business with pilgrims. The courtyard of the temple is paved with white marble tiles inscribed with the names of their donors. Inside the main shrine is an image of baby Krishna, wrapped in decorative cloth and jewels and placed in a cradle suspended by ropes. The temple priests encouraged the pilgrims—for a sum of twenty-five rupees—to swing baby Krishna by gently pulling the end of a cord attached to his cradle. While the priests were busy talking with a potential customer, Nirmal Ghosh grabbed the cord, yanked Krishna into motion, and sped out of the temple laughing. I never saw him again. The solemn priests were not amused.

About a mile below Nanda's house in the forest of Mahaban is Gokul. This town, which is situated on the bank of the Yamuna, was our next destination. On the way to Gokul we passed through Raman Reti, an area along the river covered with white sand, where it is believed Krishna played, danced, and made love with the gopis. Here a number of people from our party popped a few grains of this sacred soil into their mouths and then abandoned themselves to several minutes of rolling in the sand. Today Raman Reti is the site of a colony of holy men who live in neat rows of little mud huts covered with thatched roofs; the temple in the center of their colony is dedicated to Radha-Krishna.

Gokul is one of the major centers in Braj of the Pushti Margis, since Vallabha spent time here in the early sixteenth century. The *Chaurasi Baithak Charitra* says that the forgotten location of Gokul was revealed to Vallabha directly by the goddess Yamuna.[18] Three of Vallabha's twenty-two baithaks in Braj are located in Gokul. It was at the first of these, situated under a chonkar tree on the bank of the Yamuna at Govinda Ghat, that he had the vision in which Krishna instructed him to begin initiating disciples. Govinda Ghat is therefore the main focus of pilgrimage activity in Gokul. Since this is the first and most important of the baithaks of Vallabha, some Pushti Margis begin their Ban-Yatra of Braj here.

The site of Gokul was developed considerably by Vallabha's second son, Vitthalnath, who took over the position of central authority soon after his father's death. Vallabha's eldest son, Gopinath, seems to have died early under mysterious circumstances, leaving the way clear for Vitthalnath to assume control of the movement. Though Vitthalnath did not settle in Braj until the reign of Akbar, when he did shift here he began an elaborate expansion of the religious activities of the Pushti Margis in Braj. It was Vitthalnath who expanded and embellished the temple worship of Shri Nathji to include elaborate food offerings, dress, and music which reflected the changing moods of the seasons and times of day. Many in the Pushti Marg consider him an incarnation of Krishna. He was to make Gokul the center of this new presence in Braj.

Vitthalnath obtained a series of imperial farmans from Akbar, giving him the right to settle in Gokul and develop temples. He began constructing temples at this site in the 1570s. In 1577 Akbar made a grant of the town of Gokul to Vitthalnath for the maintenance of his family and his deity, Shri Nathji.[19] Then again in 1581 Akbar granted two more farmans, giving him the right to graze his cows freely in the environs of Gokul.[20] These privileges continued to be supported by the Mughal court under Shah Jahan, who issued two imperial farmans in 1633 confirming these rights for Vitthalnath's great-grandson Vitthalray.[21] The core of Gokul consists of seven temples established by the seven sons of Vitthalnath, who gave each of his sons a special image of Krishna that has been passed down by the seven main lineage holders to the present day. Although these temples still survive in Gokul and remain under the care of the seven recognized descendants of Vitthalnath's sons, only one of the original images, Gokulnath, remains here today. The others were taken out of Gokul during the second half of the seventeenth century in response to the increasingly anti-Hindu policies of Aurangzeb. The temple of Gokulnath, established by the fourth son of Vitthalnath, is currently the most active of the temples in Gokul.

It was in Gokul that I last saw Maya. As we meandered through the twisted lanes of the town of Gokul I saw her enter a Bhajan ashram, an institution established for the support of widows. She turned and smiled a good-bye and then settled down to sing with a group of older widows all dressed in white. She was soon absorbed into an indistinguishable crowd as more and more widows filed into the room. Although I never did understand my connection with her, I was sad to see her go.

We continued our march upstream until we came to Raval, the village of Radha's mother and the site of Radha's birth (though some maintain that Radha was born in Barsana). The story is told that Radha's parents, Brishabhanu and Kirtida, had performed great austerities in a previous life and had received the boon of caring for Radha as an infant. One day Brishabhanu went to the Yamuna to bathe; when he reached the bank he saw a brilliant light coming from the middle of the river. The source of the light turned out to be a lotus flower, and sitting on the luminous flower was a small girl. Brahma appeared to Brishabhanu and informed him that as a result of previous merit this was to be his daughter. Brishabhanu took the beautiful child home to Raval and presented her to his wife, Kirtida. The couple raised Radha with great affection, later moving with her to Barsana. A small white temple, built in the nineteenth century to replace the previous temple that had been washed away in a flood, now marks this site. The temple houses Radha and Krishna as Larliji and Lalji, the same names they assume in Barsana.

Four miles to the north we came to the eleventh and last of the forests before our return to Vrindaban, which is usually numbered twelfth in the series. Lohaban, the "Iron Forest," is so named because here Krishna killed a demon called Lohajangha, "He with Iron Thighs." This demon lived in a deep, dark cave, situated in a dirt mound above a small pond. A crowd of village boys was eager to lead us to this cave. After we reemerged from Lohajangha's cramped cave, they proudly showed us a blackened stone image of the Loha demon, which is set up not far from the entrance to the cave. Although the villagers insist it is the remains of the Loha demon, art historians have pointed out that the folds of cloth on the legs, and the fact that it is made out of red sandstone, indicate it is most likely an old Buddhist statue. Regardless, the figure is broken at the hips; only the lower portion has survived. The top of the image is well worn due to the labor of the villagers who use what remains of Iron Thighs to sharpen their knives and other iron instruments. Our thighs, too, were beginning to feel like iron, but we pushed on, turning west and walking the remaining four miles to the bridge leading into the city of Mathura. Our final destination was Vishram Ghat, the "Resting Place."

For years Kansa had been trying to kill Krishna by whatever means possible. Krishna, however, was destined to survive and kill his wicked uncle Kansa, since one of the reasons Krishna was born was to rid the earth of Kansa and his host of demons. (The other, and more important, reason according to Braj Vaishnavas was to create the experience of love with the inhabitants of Braj, especially Radha.) At last Kansa hit upon a plan which he thought was sure to succeed and bring an end to Krishna; little did he know that it would bring about his own demise.

Upon learning that Krishna was yet alive, Kansa had Vasudeva and Devaki, who were already in prison, shackled with iron fetters. He then had a magnificent wrestling arena built and announced a great festival. The massive and deadly wrestlers Chanura and Mushtika were included in his plan, and a monstrous elephant by the name of Kuvalayapida was stationed at the entrance to the arena. Kansa then sent Akrura to Braj in his chariot to invite Krishna and Balarama to attend the grand wrestling match and bring them back to the court in Mathura. As the two brothers approached the arena, the elephant trainer was to direct the fierce beast to trample them. If that failed, the huge wrestlers were to attack and crush them to death.

On his way to the forests of Braj, Akrura anticipated with delight his meeting with Krishna. Krishna and Balarama received him with much honor, but the gopis accused Akrura (whose name means "not cruel") of great cruelty, since he had come to take their dear one away from Braj. The gopis lamented Krishna's immanent departure with intense sorrow. Krishna promised the gopis that he would return someday and climbed aboard Akrura's chariot. Akrura stopped along the road, entered the Yamuna to bathe, and had the simultaneous vision of Krishna sitting both in the chariot and in the Yamuna, which indicated that from a certain perspective Krishna would never leave Braj.[22] Perhaps Akrura was not as cruel as the gopis had first surmised.

Krishna's entry into the royal city of Mathura was impressive. His sight so confused the women that they were unable even to dress themselves properly. While strolling the streets of Mathura, Krishna met a beautiful hunchbacked woman by the name of Trivakra ("bent in three places"; she is also known as Kubja). She was an attendant of Kansa who served him with scented sandalwood paste. Krishna requested some perfumed paste from her, and she yielded to his charms, painting both his and Balarama's face. Krishna took pity on her and, standing on her toes, straightened her up by lifting her chin with his fingers. As her eyes were raised to meet his, she fell hopelessly in love. She parted with Krishna only after extracting a promise from him that he would join her for an erotic encounter after he had dealt with Kansa. Images of Krishna and the hunchbacked woman are housed in a temple close to where one enters the city of Mathura after crossing the bridge over the Yamuna.

Krishna and Balarama proceeded to the wrestling arena. Kansa's wrestlers marched in amid great pageantry and a flourish of trumpets. The two brothers then entered the arena, and the demonic elephant was unleashed. It charged violently, but Krishna intercepted it and caught it by the tail. He whirled it around and around above his head and then smashed it forcefully to the ground. Seeing that the elephant had failed to stop Krishna and Balarama, the enormous wrestlers Chanura and Mushtika went into action. After a vicious battle Chanura and Mushtika lay lifeless on the ground. Kansa then jumped up on his elevated dais and called for the death of Krishna, Balarama, and all their friends and relatives. Krishna could take no more; he sprang up to the dais, seized Kansa by the hair, and dashed him to the ground. This was the end of the demonic King Kansa.[23]

After this fatiguing battle, Krishna desired to rest. He first released all those who had been imprisoned by Kansa, restored King Ugrasena to the throne, and then made his way down to the refreshing waters of the Yamuna. There he bathed his weary body at a place that came to be known as Vishram Ghat, the "Resting Place." Soon after this, Krishna left Braj.

This is the end of the story; this is the end of the pilgrimage. Our pilgrimage party made its way through the colorfully crowded bazaars of Mathura, passed under the ancient arches standing above Vishram Ghat, and walked down the heavy stone steps leading to the river. We were at the end of our journey and were very tired: what better place to rest one's weary bones than where Krishna himself had rested. The Mathura Mahatmya states that the fatigue caused by the journey to all pilgrimage sites is quickly washed away at Vishram Ghat in Mathura.[24] Everyone celebrated the climax of the journey in their own way. A few of the pilgrims climbed a bell tower on the arches above the ghat and triumphantly planted an orange flag they had carried from the beginning. I chose to sit and soak my feet in the water as a way of honoring them. They had carried me well over two hundred miles in the last twenty-one days.

Vishram Ghat, the final scene of Krishna's activities in Braj, is the traditional destination of the journey through the twelve forests. After resting here, Krishna left Braj for good; so the story goes. This was to be our last day; the circle had closed. The end . . .

. . . And yet Gaudiya pilgrims do not remain in Mathura, the city of purpose. Quite emphatically, the guides warned us not to stay at the resting place too long. "Get back to Vrindaban," they said, "anyway you can!" Mathura, the center of the circle of Braj, was not to be the end of our journey. Umesh and I chose as our mode of return one of the three-wheeled motorized "tempos" that ply the road between Mathura and Vrindaban.

Thus, in a very important sense, the circular journey of the Ban-Yatra has no end. This pilgrimage is about becoming aware of Krishna's lila, becoming aware that life is lila, and this lila is ever new, unique, and changing. It has no end. The lila goes on, and since the lila goes on, the pilgrimage must too. Krishna's players are in perpetual motion. To stop is to be stuck, and to be stuck is to miss the marvelousness that is the lila. To be at rest (the state of ascetic repose is also called *vishram*) is to stop playing. But play is all there is. There is no reason to stop. There is no goal, there is nothing to accomplish; each moment is as full or as empty as the next. The return is then a return without return, without expectation of gain. The "goal" of this pilgrimage is to reject all binding goals, to keep moving freely, to keep playing, to be ever aware of the fresh lila as it presents itself in whatever form.

The Ban-Yatra, then, in a sense has two ends, or more precisely, an end and an endless "end." The pilgrimage ends in Mathura, the story ends in Mathura, but Krishna's pilgrims must get back—any way they can—to Vrindaban, the edgy, unfixed place where the story, the unpredictable lila, never ends.

NOTES

1. In his article on the Ban-Yatra, Owen Lynch identifies what he thinks is the main lesson of this pilgrimage: "In the Pushti Marg cultural construction of reality, pilgrimage is an exercise in seeing the world correctly *(alaukika)* as god's *lila* and experiencing it emotionally as his eternal bliss ("Pilgrimage with Krishna," 180).

2. This story is told in *Bhagavata Purana* 10.65.

3. Lynch, "Pilgrimage with Krishna," 180.

4. I heard an abbreviated form of this story from a local priest during the pilgrimage, which I have fleshed out with Vijay, *Braj Bhumi Mohini*, 326–27.

5. This story appears in *Bhagavata Purana* 10.18.

6. Ibid., 8.6–12.

7. Ibid., 10.31.1.

8. The following account was told to me by Shuklaji.

9. See N. P. Joshi, *Iconography of Balarama* (New Delhi: Abhinav Publications, 1979).

10. Ibid., 17.

11. Growse, *Mathura*, 292; Entwistle, *Braj*, 421–22.

12. These are terms taken from the *Bhagavad Gita* and used by Gaudiya theologians such as Rupa Goswami to analyze the particular relationship the residents of Braj have with Krishna; see my *Acting as a Way of Salvation*, 46–47.

13. *Bhagavata Purana* 10.8.43.

14. This story from the *Matsya Purana* is told by Zimmer, *Myths and Symbols in Indian Art and Civilization*, 35–53.

15. This story appears in *Bhagavata Purana* 10.9–10.

16. This story appears in *Bhagavata Purana* 10.6.

17. Entwistle, *Braj*, 122.

18. *Chaurasi Baithak Charitra*, 1–2.

19. This is the first of the farmans which have been translated in Jhaveri, *Imperial Farmans*.

20. Ibid., see farmans II, III.

21. Ibid., see farmans VI, and VII.

22. This story is told at the end of chapter 1.

23. Although later Vaishnava theologians claim that Kansa's fearful preoccupation with Krishna insured his salvation; see Rupa Goswami, *Bhaktirasamritasindhu* 1.2.275ff.

24. *Varaha Purana* 177.32–33.

Appendix

Itinerary of Brajbasi Ban-Yatra

Date (September)	Campsite (daily destination)	Places Visited Along the Way
3–6	Vrindaban	(preliminary temple rituals)
7	Mathura	Akrura Ghat
8	Madhuban	Talban
9	Shantanukund	Kumudban
10	Radhakund	Bahulaban, Mukharai
11	Govardhan	Kusum Sarovar, Govindakund, Jatipura, Manasi Ganga
12	Dig	Balabhadrakund
13	Khoh	Sudama's house, Burebadri
14	Pasopa	Pashupati, Badrinath
15	Kamaban	Kedarnath, Charan Pahari
16	Kamaban (parikrama)	Vimalakund
17	Barsana	Dehakund, Unchagaon
18	Barsana (parikrama)	Sankari Khor, Gavarban
19	Nandagaon	Sanket, Bathain, Javat, Kokilaban
20	Kosi	Rupa Goswami's meditation hut
21	Kosi (environs north)	Sheshashayi, Khirsagar
22	Shergarh	Phalain, Prahladkund
23	Chir Ghat	Ram Ghat
24	Belban	Bhadraban, Bhandiraban, Mat
25	Raya	Mansarovar
26	Brahmanda Ghat	Anandi Bandi, Dauji
27	Vrindaban	Mahaban, Raman Reti, Gokul, Raval, Lohaban, Vishram Ghat

Based on the itinerary published by the Shri Brajbasi Panda Society of Vrindaban for the 1988 season (Vrindaban: Shri Gadadhargaurhari Press, 1988).

Itinerary of Pushti Margi Ban-Yatra

Date	Campsite
September	
13–14	Mathura
15	Madhuban
16	Kumudban
17	Shantanukund
18	Bahulaban
19	Kusum Sarovar
20–21	Chandra Sarovar
22–29	Jatipura
30	Dig
October	
1	Parmadra
2–4	Kamaban
5–8	Barsana
9–11	Nandagaon
12	Kokilaban
13	Bathain
14	Kotban
15	Sheshashayi
16	Kosi
17	Paigaon
18	Shergarh
19	Chir Ghat
20	Bacchban
21–24	Vrindaban
25	Lohaban
26	Dauji
27–28	Gokul
29	Mathura

Based on the itinerary of Shri Mathuresh Goswami, the Maharaj who led the pilgrimage in 1988. Published in *Braj Parikrama Parishishta* (Mathura: Shri Balabhadra Seva Sansthan, 1988).

Glossary

Abhimanyu   The husband of Radha.

Akbar   The powerful Mughal emperor who ruled northern India from 1556 to 1605. Several of the Hindu officers of Akbar's court were involved in the patronage of the temples of Braj.

ananda   Literally "bliss." Ananda is considered to be the highest aspect of Krishna; theologically it is associated with Radha. It is the resulting experience of the awareness that all life is lila. As such, it is the expressed "goal" of the Ban-Yatra.

arati   An act of worship involving the waving of a lighted lamp in a circular motion before a deity.

Aurangzeb   The Mughal emperor who ruled from 1658 to 1707. Aurangzeb was the great-grandson of Akbar and is credited with altering the policy of tolerance toward Hindus that was initiated by his great-grandfather.

baithak   Literally a "seat." A baithak refers specifically in the Pushti Marg to a shrine built on a particular site to commemorate some significant act that was performed there by Vallabha or some other important saint of the lineage.

Balarama   The elder brother of Krishna. Balarama is considered to be a manifestation of the cosmic serpent Shesha. His main temple in Braj is in the town of Dauji.

ban   A forest. The Ban-Yatra is structured so that the pilgrims visit twelve such forests.

Bhagavata Purana   A major Vaishnava scripture that includes a narration of the story of Krishna. Most scholars date the composition of this text in the ninth century.

bhakti   Typically translated as "devotion." A path in the Hindu tradi-

227

tion which seeks to "enjoy" or consciously "participate in" the highest reality.

bhang   An intoxicating plant related to marijuana.

bhava   An emotional state or power of the imagination that allows a higher perception of reality.

bidi   A small hand-tied cigarette.

bindu   A "point." Refers specifically to that undifferentiated point that is in the center of all that is differentiated.

Chaitanya   The charismatic Bengali saint who inspired the movement which came to be known as Gaudiya Vaishnavism. Chaitanya lived from 1486 to 1533 and is reported to have performed the Ban-Yatra in 1514.

chapati   A circular flatbread made of wheat.

darshan   Literally "seeing." Refers specifically to the act of viewing some image or form of divinity.

dham   A sacred abode.

farman   An imperial order.

gamcha   A piece of cloth that serves as a multipurpose towel.

Gaudiya Vaishnava   A member of a Vaishnava denomination present in Braj who follows the sixteenth-century saint Chaitanya.

ghat   Steps built on the edge of a river or pond to provide easy access.

gopi   A female cowherd lover of Krishna. The gopis are exemplary spiritual figures for the Vaishnava traditions in Braj. One's inner being which is capable of the highest love is typically considered a gopi.

Jatila   Mother of Abhimanyu; mother-in-law of Radha.

Jiva Goswami   One of the six Vrindaban Goswamis. Jiva wrote many important philosophical works and was the nephew of Rupa and Sanatana Goswami.

kama   "Desire" or "passion."

Kansa   The wicked king of Mathura and archenemy of Krishna.

kos   A measurement approximately equal to two miles.

Krishna The chief conception of ultimate reality as celebrated in Braj; the darling of the residents of Braj. As the youthful lover, he is the favorite deity of many Hindus.

Krishnadas Kaviraj A star pupil of the Vrindaban Goswamis; author of the *Chaitanya Charitamrita*, a biographical work about Chaitanya that presents the main philosophical tenents of the Vrindaban Goswamis.

kund A pond or small lake.

kunj A love bower.

Kutila Sister of Abhimanyu; sister-in-law of Radha.

Lalita Foremost of the sakhis, the girlfriends of Radha and Krishna.

lila "Play," both in the sense of "fun" or "game," and in the sense of "drama." In Vaishnava theology lila is understood to be purposeless divine activity.

lingam Literally a "mark" or "sign." The lingam is a common aniconic form found in the center of a Shaivite temple; it represents the undifferentiated, unmanifest aspect of reality.

lota A small metal pot used to carry water.

lungi A long, saronglike cloth tucked round the waist and worn in informal circumstances in northern India.

mandala A "circle"; Braj is typically conceived of as a mandala.

mast A state of being characterized as "laid-back," "carefree," "happy," "intoxicated," or "lusty."

maya That force by which the undifferentiated becomes differentiated. Maya is often translated by the pejorative word "illusion," but in Braj it is frequently identified with the goddess Yogamaya, who creates all forms and stages the lilas, which make love possible.

moksha Literally "liberation." This is the goal of many Hindu ascetics, who aim for a return to that tranquil, undifferentiated reality beyond the realm of passionate multiplicity.

Nanda The adoptive father of Krishna.

Narayan Bhatt The sixteenth-century figure who played a crucial role in the physical development of Braj. He was initiated into the Gaudiya

Vaishnava tradition and is believed to have been the first to establish the Ban-Yatra as the systematic pilgrimage it is today. He is known as the Great Founder of Braj.

Nimbarki   A member of a Vaishnava denomination present in Braj who follows the fourteenth-century saint Nimbark.

panda   A traditional pilgrimage guide.

parikrama   "Circumambulation"; the circling of an object as a way of honoring and experiencing it.

prasad   Literally "grace." Usually refers specifically to edible grace, that is, food given to a worshiper after it has been offered to a deity.

prema   The highest "love."

puja   A Hindu form of "worship."

Purana   A genre of Hindu scripture which contains a wealth of mythology and traditional history. There are eighteen major Puranas: chief among them for the residents of Braj is the *Bhagavata Purana*.

Pushti Margi   A member of a Vaishnava denomination present in Braj who follows the sixteenth-century saint Vallabha.

Radha   Krishna's main consort and chief lover. Theologically, Radha is an aspect of Krishna's own bliss and as such is the source of love.

Radhavallabhi   A member of a Vaishnava denomination present in Braj who follows the sixteenth-century saint Hit Harivams.

Raghunath Das   One of the six Vrindaban Goswamis. Raghunath spent much of his life developing the site of Radhakund.

rasa-lila   The amorous circle dance of Krishna and the gopis; a dramatic form staged in Braj that portrays the stories of Krishna.

Revati   The consort of Balarama.

Rupa Goswami   One of the six Vrindaban Goswamis. Rupa was perhaps the most influential among the group; his major contributions included an analysis of Vaishnava bhakti which utilized classical Indian aesthetic theory.

sadhana   A "means of realization"; religious practice.

sakhi   A "girlfriend" of Radha and Krishna.

samadhi   A state of yogic trance; the tomb of a saint.

samsara   Worldly existence; the experience of differentiated reality.

Sanatana Goswami   One of the six Vrindaban Goswamis. Sanatana was the elder brother of Rupa Goswami and a major force in the early development of Braj.

sannyasi   A person who has "renounced" ordinary life.

shehnai   A reeded wind instrument similar to a clarinet.

Suraj Mal Singh   The powerful Jat king who ruled over the area of Braj during the mid-eighteenth century. Members of Suraj Mal's family were some of the most significant patrons of Braj, particularly of Govardhan.

Surdas   A famous sixteenth-century Braj poet who composed many well-known poems in praise of the love of Radha and Krishna. He is associated with the Pushti Marg.

svarupa   A natural form of God.

tapas or tapasya   Literally "heat"; also commonly understood as "asceticism".

tirtha   A place to "cross over"; a passageway to another world. Many pilgrimages in South Asia are called "tirtha-yatras."

tonga   A wooden horse-drawn cart.

Vaishnavism   A major school of Hinduism that worships Vishnu or Krishna as the supreme reality.

Vajranabh   The great-grandson of Krishna. He is credited by the residents of Braj with founding many important temples.

Vallabha   The inspirational southern Indian saint who founded the movement which came to be known as the Pushti Marg. Vallabha lived from 1479 to 1531 and is reported to have performed the Ban-Yatra in 1494.

vishram, vishranti   Literally "rest"; also ascetic repose.

Vitthalnath   The second son of Vallabha; Vitthalnath assumed the position of head of the Pushti Margis soon after his father's death. He established the seven "seats" of the Pushti Marg through his seven sons.

Yashoda   Krishna's adoptive mother.

yatra   A "journey." Often refers specifically to pilgrimage.

yoga-pitha   A "place of union." Refers specifically to the site of a tryst of Radha and Krishna.

yojana   A measurement approximately equal to eight miles.

Bibliography

Abu-L-Fazl. *The Akbar Nama*. 2 vols. Trans. H. Beveridge. Delhi: Rare Books, 1972.

Agrawal, C. M. *Akbar and His Hindu Officers*. Jalandar: ABS Publishers, 1986.

Banerjea, J. N. "The So-Called Trimurti of Elephanta." *Arts Asiatiques* 2 (1955): 120–26.

Bansal, Naresh C. *Chaitanya Sampradaya: Siddhant aur Sahitya*. Agra: Vinod Pustak Mandir, 1980.

Barz, Richard. *The Bhakti Sect of Vallabhacarya*. Faridabad: Thomas Press, 1976.

Bhagavandas, Manohar Lal. *Braj Yatra*. Mathura: Sitaram Pustakalay, 1984.

Bhagavata Purana. 2 vols. Sanskrit text with English translation by C. L. Goswami. Gorkhapur: Gita Press, 1971.

Bhandarkar, Ramkrishna G. *Vaisnavism, Saivism and Other Religious Systems*. Varanasi: Indological Book House, 1965.

Bharati, Agehananda. "Pilgrimage in the Indian Tradition." *History of Religions* 3, no. 1 (1963): 135–67.

————. "Pilgrimage Sites and Indian Civilization." In *Chapters in Indian Civilization*. Ed. J. W. Elder, 85–126. Dubuque, Ia.: Kendall-Hunt, 1970.

Bhardwaj, Surinder M. *Hindu Places of Pilgrimage in India*. Berkeley: University of California Press, 1973.

Bose, Nirmal Kumar. "The Spring Festival of India." In *Cultural Anthropology and Other Essays*, 73–102. Calcutta: Indian Associated Pub. Co., 1953.

Bowman, Glenn. "Anthropology of Pilgrimage." In *Dimensions of Pilgrimage: An Anthropological Appraisal*. Ed. Makhan Jha, 1–9. New Delhi: Inter-India Publications, 1985.

Brown, C. Mackenzie. "The Theology of Radha in the Purana." In *The Divine Consort: Radha and the Goddesses of India*. Ed. J. S. Hawley and D. M. Wulff, 57–71. Berkeley, Calif.: Graduate Theological Union, 1982.

Bryant, Kenneth E. *Poems to the Child-God: Structures and Strategies in the Poetry of Surdas*. Berkeley: University of California Press, 1978.

Chandra, Kailash. *Braj Yatra Darshan*. Mathura: Bharati Anusandhan Bhavan, 1984.

Clifford, James, and Marcus, George E., eds. *Writing Culture: The Poetics and Politics of Ethnography*. Berkeley: University of California Press, 1986.

Connerton, Paul. *How Societies Remember*. Cambridge, Engl.: Cambridge University Press, 1989.

Corcoran, Maura. "Vrndavana in Vaisnava Braj Literature." Ph.D. diss., School of Oriental and African Studies, University of London, 1980.

Daniel, E. Valentine. *Fluid Signs: Being a Person the Tamil Way.* Berkeley: University of California Press, 1984.

Dasgupta, Shashibhusan. *Obscure Religious Cults.* Calcutta: Firma KLM, 1976.

Datta, Pulinbihari. *Vrindaban Katha.* Calcutta: Manasi Press, 1920.

De, S. K. *Early History of the Vaishnava Faith and Movement in Bengal.* Calcutta: Firma K. L. Mukhopadhyay, 1961.

Dimock, Edward C., Jr. "Lila." *History of Religions* 29, no. 2 (1989): 159–73.

Dumont, Louis. *Religion, Politics, and History in India.* Paris: Mouton, 1970.

———. "World Renunciation in Indian Religions." *Contributions to Indian Sociology* 4 (1960): 33–62.

Eck, Diana L. *Banaras: City of Light.* Princeton, N.J.: Princeton University Press, 1982.

———. "The City as a Sacred Center." *Journal of Developing Societies* 2 (1986): 149–59.

———. *Darsan: Seeing the Divine Image in India.* Chambersburg, Pa.: Anima Publications, 1981.

———. "India's Tirthas: 'Crossings' in Sacred Geography." *History of Religions* 20, no. 2 (1981): 323–44.

Eickelman, Dale. *Moroccan Islam.* Austin: Texas University Press, 1976.

Eliade, Mircea. *The Myth of the Eternal Return.* New York: Bollingen, 1954.

———. *The Sacred and the Profane: The Nature of Religion.* New York: Harcourt Brace, 1959.

Entwistle, Alan. *Braj: Center of Krishna Pilgrimage.* Groningen: Egbert Forsten, 1987.

———. "From Vraja to Braj." In *Re-discovering Braj. International Association of the Vrindaban Research Institute Bulletin* 14 (1988): 14–18.

Freud, Sigmund. "Beyond the Pleasure Principle." In *The Essentials of Psychoanalysis,* 218–68. Middlesex: Penguin Books, 1986.

Geertz, Clifford. "Religion as a Cultural System." In *The Interpretation of Cultures.* New York: Basic Books, 1973.

Gokulnath. *Charasi Baithak Charitra.* Ed. Niranjandev Sharma. Mathura: Shri Govardhan Granthmala Karyalay, 1967.

Gold, Ann G. *Fruitful Journeys: The Ways of Rajasthani Pilgrims.* Berkeley: University of California Press, 1988.

Goswami, Shrivatsa. "Charaiveti! Charaiveti!" In *Shri Ban Yatra,* 5–11. Vrindaban: Shri Chaitanya Prem Sansthan, 1986.

———. "Radha: The Play and Perfection of Rasa." In *The Divine Consort: Radha and the Goddesses of India.* Ed. J. S. Hawley and D. M. Wulff, 72–88. Berkeley, Calif.: Graduate Theological Union, 1982.

Govindadas, Seth. "Braj-Yatra ka Uday aur Vikas." In *Braj aur Braj Yatra.*

Ed. Seth Govindadas and Ram Narayan Agrawal, 85–90. Delhi: Bharatiya Visva Prakashan, 1959.

Grapard, Allan G. "Flying Mountains and Walkers of Emptiness: Toward a Definition of Sacred Space in Japanese Religions." *History of Religions* 21, no. 3 (1982): 195–221.

Gross, Daniel. "Ritual and Conformity: A Religious Pilgrimage to Northeastern Brazil." *Ethnology* 10, no. 2 (1971): 129–48.

Growse, Frederick S. *Mathura: A District Memoir.* New Delhi: Asian Educational Services, 1882.

Gupta, Rakesh. *Braj Guide.* Mathura: Vandana Prakashan, 1988.

Haberman, David L. *Acting as a Way of Salvation: A Study of Raganuga Bhakti Sadhana.* New York: Oxford University Press, 1988.

———. "The Bengali Tradition." In *Textual Sources for the Study of Hinduism.* Ed. Wendy Doniger O'Flaherty, 151–67. Manchester: Manchester University Press, 1988; Chicago: University of Chicago Press, 1990.

———. "On Trial: The Love of the Sixteen Thousand Gopees." *History of Religions* 33, no. 1 (1993): 44–70.

———. "Vraja: A Place in the Heart." In *Re-discovering Braj. International Association of the Vrindaban Research Institute Bulletin* 14 (1988): 19–25.

Hardy, Friedhelm. "Madhavendra Puri: A Link Between Bengal Vaisnavism and South Indian Bhakti." *Journal of the Royal Asiatic Society,* no. 1 (1974): 23–41.

Hawley, John S. *At Play with Krishna: Pilgrimage Dramas from Brindaban.* Princeton, N.J.: Princeton University Press, 1981.

———. "Krishna's Cosmic Victories." *Journal of the American Academy of Religion* 47, no. 2 (1979): 201–21.

———. *Sur Das: Poet, Singer, Saint.* Delhi: Oxford University Press, 1984.

Hein, Norvin. *Miracle Plays of Mathura.* New Haven, Conn.: Yale University Press, 1972.

Hume, Robert E., trans. *The Thirteen Principal Upanishads.* Oxford: Oxford University Press, 1921.

Ikram, S. M. *Muslim Civilization in India.* New York: Columbia University Press, 1964.

Inden, Ronald. *Imagining India.* Oxford: Basil Blackwell, 1990.

Irvine, William. "Ahmad Shah, Abdali, and the Indian Wazir Imad-ul-Mulk. (1756–57)." *Indian Antiquary* 36 (1907): 10–18, 43–51, 55–70.

James, William. *Principles of Psychology.* 2 vols. New York: Henry Holt, 1890.

Jana, Naresh C. *Vrindabaner Choe Goswami.* Calcutta: Calcutta University, 1970.

Janaki Prasad Bhatt. *Narayana Bhatta Charitamrita.* Ed. Krishnadas Baba. Kusum Sarovar: Krishnadas Baba, 1958.

Jhaveri, Krishnalal M. *Imperial Farmans (A.D. 1577 to A.D. 1805) Granted to the Ancestors of His Holiness the Tikayat Maharaj.* Bombay: The News Printing Press, 1928.

Jiva Goswami. *Bhagavata Sandarbha.* Ed. Chinmayi Chatterjee. Calcutta: Jadavpur University, 1972.

Joshi, M. C. *Dig.* New Delhi: Archaeological Survey of India, 1982.

Joshi, N. P. *Iconography of Balarama.* New Delhi: Abhinav Publications, 1979.

Kakar, Sudhir. "Erotic Fantasy: The Secret Passion of Radha and Krishna." In *The Word and the World.* Ed. Veena Das, 75–94. New Delhi: Sage Publications, 1986.

———. *The Inner World: A Psycho-analytic Study of Childhood and Society in India.* Delhi: Oxford University Press, 1981.

Karve, Irawati. "On the Road: A Maharashtrian Pilgrimage." *Journal of Asian Studies* 22 (1962): 13–30.

Kinsley, David R. *The Sword and the Flute: Kali and Krsna, Dark Visions of the Terrible and the Sublime in Hindu Mythology.* Berkeley: University of California Press, 1975.

Kramrisch, Stella. *The Presence of Siva.* Princeton, N.J.: Princeton University Press, 1981.

Krishnadas Baba. *Braj Mandal Darshan.* Kusum Sarovar: Krishnadas Baba, 1958.

Krishnadas Kaviraj. *Chaitanya Charitamrita.* With the commentaries of Sacchidananda Bhaktivinod Thakur and Barshobhanabidayita Das. Calcutta: Gaudiya Math, 1958.

Lemaire, Anika. *Jacques Lacan.* New York: Routledge & Kegan Paul, 1979.

Lynch, Owen M. "The Mastram: Emotion and Person Among Mathura's Chaubes." In *Divine Passions.* Ed. Owen Lynch, 91–115. Berkeley: University of California Press, 1990.

———. "Pilgrimage with Krishna, Sovereign of the Emotions." *Contributions to Indian Sociology* 22, no. 2 (1988): 171–94.

McGregor, R. S. *Nandadas: The Round Dance of Krishna and Uddhav's Message.* London: Luzac & Company, 1973.

Madan, T. V. *Non-Renunciation: Themes and Interpretations of Hindu Culture.* Delhi: Oxford University Press, 1987.

Maithil, Premdatta Mishra. "Barsana Vritt." In *Braj Vibhav.* Ed. Gopalprasad Vyas, 194–99. New Delhi: Dilli Hindi Sahitya Sammelan, 1987.

Marriot, McKim. "The Feast of Love." In *Krishna: Myths, Rites, and Attitudes.* Ed. Milton Singer, 200–212. Chicago: University of Chicago Press, 1968.

Miller, Barbara S. *Love Song of the Dark Lord.* New York: Columbia University Press, 1977.

Mital, Prabhu Dayal. *Braj ka Sanskritik Itihas.* Mathura: Sahitya Sansthan, 1966.

———. *Braj ke Dharm-Sampradayo ka Itihas.* Delhi: National Publishing House, 1968.

Mital, Saraswati Prasad. *Chaurasi Kos ki Braj-Yatra.* Agra: Sanjay Press, n.d.

Mohan Das "Narad Baba." *Sampurna Braj Darshanam*. Vrindaban: Shri Radha Mohan Satsang Mandal, 1987.

Mokashi, D. B. *Palkhi: An Indian Pilgrimage*. Albany: State University of New York Press, 1987.

Morinis, E. Alan. *Pilgrimage in the Hindu Tradition: A Case Study of West Bengal*. Delhi: Oxford University Press, 1984.

Mukherjee, Tarapada, and Habib, Irfan. "Akbar and the Temples of Mathura and Its Environs." Unpublished paper delivered to the annual meeting of the Indian History of Congress, Goa, November 1987. Published in part in *Proceedings of the Indian History Congress* 48 (1987): 234–50.

———. "The Mughal Administration and the Temples of Vrindavan During the Reigns of Jahangir and Shah Jahan." *Proceedings of the Indian History Congress* 49 (1988): 287–300.

———. "Land Rights in the Reign of Akbar: The Evidence of the Sale-deeds of Vrindaban and Aritha." *Proceedings of the Indian History Congress* 50 (1989): 236–55.

Myerhoff, Barbara G. *Peyote Hunt: The Sacred Journey of the Huichol Indians*. Ithaca, N.Y.: Cornell University Press, 1974.

Nabhaji. *Bhaktamala*. With commentary of Priyadasji. Lucknow: Navalkishor, 1977.

Narada Purana (Naradiya Purana). Delhi: Nag Publishers, 1984.

Narahari Chakravarti. *Bhaktiratnakar*. Ed. Navinrishna Paravidyalankar. Calcutta: Gaudiya Math, 1940.

Narayan Bhatt. *Vraja Bhakti Vilasa*. Ed. Krishnadas Baba. Kusum Sarovar: Krishnadas Baba, 1951.

———. *Vrajotsava Chandrika*. Ed. Krishnadas Baba. Kusum Sarovar: Krishnadas Baba, 1960.

Natwar-Singh, K. *Maharaj Suraj Mal*. New Delhi: Vikas Publishing House, 1983.

Navadvipdas. *Shri Radhakund Itihas*. Vrindaban: Shri Krishna Press, n.d.

Niebuhr, Richard R. "Pilgrims and Pioneers." *Parabola* 9, no. 3 (1984): 6–13.

Niradprasad Nath. *Narottam Das o Tahar Rachanavali*. Calcutta: University of Calcutta, 1975.

O'Flaherty, Wendy Doniger. *Asceticism and Eroticism in the Mythology of Shiva*. London: Oxford University Press, 1973.

Padma Purana. 4 vols. Delhi: Nag Publishers, 1984.

Pande, Ram. *Studies in History: The Jats*. Jaipur: Chinmaya Prakashan, 1981.

Pfaffenberger, Bryan. "The Kataragama Pilgrimage: Hindu-Buddhist Interaction and Its Significance in Sri Lanka's Polyethic Social System." *Journal of Asian Studies* 38 (1979): 253–70.

Potter, Karl. *Presuppositions of India's Philosophies*. Englewood Cliffs, N.J.: Prentice-Hall, 1963.

Prasad, Rajiva N. *Raja Man Singh of Amber*. Calcutta: The World Press, 1966.

Purohit, Lalitaprasad. *Braj Chaurasi Parikrama*. Vrindaban: Shri Hari Prakashan, 1982.

Qanungo, Kalika R. *History of the Jats.* Calcutta: M. C. Sarkar & Sons, 1925.

Rasakhan. *Rasakhan-Granthavali.* Edited with a Hindi introduction by Desharajasingh Bhati. Delhi: Ashok Prakashan, 1987.

Redington, James D. *Vallabhacarya on the Love Games of Krsna.* Delhi: Motilal Banarsidass, 1983.

Robinson, Sandra P. "Hindu Paradigms of Women: Images and Values." In *Women, Religion and Social Change.* Ed. Yvonne Yazbeck Haddad and Ellison Banks Findly, 181–215. Albany: State University of New York Press, 1985.

Roy, Ashim K. *History of the Jaipur City.* New Delhi: Manohar Publications, 1978.

Rupa Goswami. *Bhaktirasamritasindhu.* With commentaries of Jiva Goswami, Mukundadas Goswami, and Vishvanatha Chakravarti. Edited with a Bengali translation by Haridas Das. Navadvip: Haribol Kutir, 1945.

———. *Mathura Mahatmya.* Ed. Puridas Mahashay. Vrindaban: Shachinatharay Chaturdhurin, 1946.

———. *Upadeshamrita.* With commentaries of Jiva Goswami and Vishvanatha Chakravarti. Ed. Puridas. Vrindaban: Haridas Sharma, 1954.

Sallnow, M. J. "Communitas Reconsidered: The Sociology of Andean Pilgrimage." *Man* 16 (1981): 163–82.

Sarkar, Jadunath. *History of Aurangzib.* 5 vols. Calcutta: M. C. Sarkar, 1912–24.

Sax, William S. *Mountain Goddess: Gender and Politics in a Himalayan Pilgrimage.* New York: Oxford University Press, 1991.

Schutz, Alfred. *Collected Papers I: The Problem of Social Reality.* Ed. Maurice Natanson. The Hague: Martins Nijhoff, 1973.

Sharma, Ram. *The Religious Policy of the Mughal Emperors.* Bombay: Asia Publishing House, 1972.

Shesh, Chunnilal. "Braj-Yatra ki Parampara." In *Braj aur Braj Yatra.* Ed. Seth Govindadas and Ram Narayan Agrawal, 91–111. Delhi: Bharatiya Visva Prakashan, 1959.

Shyam Das. *Ashta Chhap.* Baroda: Shri Vallabha Publications, 1985.

Siegel, Lee. *Sacred and Profane Dimensions of Love in Indian Traditions as Exemplified in the Gitagovinda of Jayadeva.* Delhi: Oxford University Press, 1978.

Singh, Khushwant. *History of the Sikhs.* 2 vols. Princeton, N.J.: Princeton University Press, 1963, 1966.

Skanda Purana. Delhi: Nag Publishers, 1984.

Smith, Jonathan Z. *Imagining Religion: From Babylon to Jonestown.* Chicago: University of Chicago Press, 1982.

———. "The Wobbling Pivot." In his *Map Is Not Territory*, 88–103. Leiden: E. J. Brill, 1978.

Smith, Vincent A. *Akbar the Great Mogul.* Oxford: Clarendon Press, 1902.

Srinivasan, Dori M. "Vaisnava Art and Iconography at Mathura." In *Mathura: The Cultural Heritage.* Ed. D. M. Srinivasan, 383–92. New Delhi: American Institute of Indian Studies, 1989.

Srivastava, Ashirbadi L. *Akbar the Great.* 2 vols. Agra: Shiva Lal Agarwala, 1972.

Stanley, John M. "Special Time, Special Power: The Fluidity of Power in a Popular Hindu Festival." *Journal of Asian Studies* 37, no. 1 (1977): 27–43.

Statler, Oliver. *Japanese Pilgrimage.* New York: William Morrow, 1983.

Sumption, Jonathan. *Pilgrimage: An Image of Mediaeval Religion.* Totowa, N.J.: Rowman & Littlefield, 1975.

Taylor, Mark C. *Altarity.* Chicago: University of Chicago Press, 1987.

Thapar, Romila. "The Early History of Mathura." In *Mathura: The Cultural Heritage.* Ed. D. M. Srinivasan, 12–18. New Delhi: American Institute of Indian Studies, 1989.

Thoreau, Henry David. "Walking" In *The Writings of Henry David Thoreau* 9: 251–304.New York: Houghton, 1896.

Tiwari, Balji. "Braj Yatra ki Parampara." In *Braj Vaibhav.* Ed. Radheshyam Dvivedi, 297–300. Mathura: Bharati Anusandhan Bhavan, 1972.

Toomey, Paul M. *Food from the Mouth of Krishna: Sacred Food and Pilgrimage at Mount Govardhan.* Ann Arbor, Mich.: University Microfilms, 1986.

Turner, Victor. "The Center Out There: Pilgrim's Goal." *History of Religions* 12, no. 3 (1973): 191–230.

———. "Passages, Margins, and Poverty: Religious Symbols of Communitas." In his *Dramas, Fields, and Metaphors,* 231–71. Ithaca, N.Y.: Cornell University Press, 1974.

———. "Pilgrimage and Communitas." *Studia Missionalia* 23 (1974): 305–27.

———. *The Ritual Process.* Ithaca, N.Y.: Cornell University Press, 1969.

Turner, Victor, and Turner, Edith. *Image and Pilgrimage in Christian Culture.* New York: Columbia University Press, 1978.

Vajpeyi, Krishna Datta. *Braj ka Itihas.* Mathura: Akhil Bharatiya Braj Sahitya Mandal, 1955.

Van Gennep, Arnold. *The Rites of Passage.* Chicago: University of Chicago Press, 1975.

Varaha Purana. Ed. Anad Swarup Gupta. Varanasi: All-India Kashiraj Trust, 1981.

Vaudeville, Charlotte. "Braj, Lost and Found." *Indo-Iranian Journal* 18 (1976): 195–213.

———. "The Cowherd God in Ancient India." In *Pastoralists and Nomads in South Asia.* Ed. L. S. Leshnik and G. D. Sontheimer, 92–116. Wiesbaden: Otto Harrassowitz, 1975.

———. "The Govardhan Myth in Northern India." *Indo-Iranian Journal* 22 (1980): 1–45.

———. "Krishna Gopala, Radha, and the Great Goddess." In *The Divine Consort: Radha and the Goddesses of India,* Ed. J. S. Hawley and D. M. Wulff, 1–12. Berkeley, Calif.: Graduate Theological Union, 1982.

Vidyapati. *The Songs of Vidyapati.* Trans. Subhadra Jha. Banaras: Motilal Banarsidass, 1954.

Vijay. *Braj Bhumi Mohini.* Vrindaban: Shri Prem Hari Press, 1985.

Wulff, Donna M. "A Sanskrit Portrait: Radha in the Plays of Rupa Gosvami." In *The Divine Consort: Radha and the Goddesses of India.* Ed. J. S. Hawley and D. M. Wulff, 27–41. Berkeley, Calif.: Graduate Theological Union, 1982.

Zimmer, Heinrich. *Myths and Symbols in Indian Art and Civilization.* Princeton, N.J.: Princeton University Press, 1972 [1946]).

Index

Lalita, 59, 172, 177
Lila (play), viii, 23, 25, 26, 28, 36,
    40, 57, 61, 74–76, 154–55, 157,
    161, 199, 223
Lohaban, 51, 63, 65, 68, 126, 220
Lynch, Owen, 46, 98 n.69, 125,
    156–57, 193, 223 n.1

Madhavendra Puri, 65, 117–19
Madhuban, 47, 51, 62, 64, 67, 81,
    82, 84, 88, 126
Mahaban, 51, 58, 63, 65, 68, 77, 126,
    140, 212–18
Manasi Ganga, 58, 65, 67, 101,
    115–16, 141
Mansarovar, 67, 208
Man Singh, 33–36, 102
Markandeya, 215
Mat, 204–5
Mathura, 5–6, 40, 53, 58, 62, 67, 76,
    126, 127, 136
    as center, 49, 98 n.79, 223
    as city, 48
    history of, 76–79
    Keshavdev temple, 38, 53, 54,
        77–79
    in Mathura Mahatmya, 50–51
    starting place of Ban-Yatra, 39,
        40, 64
    in stories, 3–4
Mathura Mahatmya, xi, xix, 47,
    50–51, 68, 79, 87, 116, 167, 222
Mughals, xiii, 30–38
    Akbar, 33–36, 60, 78, 116, 121,
        136, 219
    Aurangzeb, 37, 54, 78, 120,
        136–37, 167, 218, 219
    Babar, 30, 192
    Humayun, 31
    Jahangir, 36, 77
    Shah Jahan, 36–37, 219
Mukharai, 93
Moksha, viii, 24–25, 27–28
Mount Kailash, 21, 23, 28, 153

Nanda, 4, 12, 58, 62, 65, 111, 147,
    185–87, 202, 203, 206, 217–28
Nandadas, 120, 164–65, 193
Nandagaon, 63, 65, 67, 129, 174–75,
    185–87, 218
Nanda Ghat, 67, 202
Narada, 52, 53, 56–58, 88, 114
Narayan Bhatt, xii, 25, 52, 81, 90,
    125–26, 172, 177, 182, 216
    as Acharya of Braj, xi, 49, 173
    life story of, 55–61
    systematizer of Ban-Yatra, 61–63
Nature worship, 110, 124–29
Niebuhr, Richard R., 170, 188
Nimbarki, 20, 29, 83, 213

Pandas. *See* Pilgrimage
Phalain, 190–92
Pilgrimage
    guides (pandas), xii, 9–10, 29, 39,
        46–47, 82–83
    reflections on movement and
        meaning, 7, 83, 130, 151, 181,
        184, 188, 199–200
    theoretical works, vii–viii, x, xix
        n.1, 69–76, 97 nn.59, 60, 98 n.65
Prahlad, 190–91
Prema (love), 162–65
Prema Sarovar, 178–80
Puranas. *See also* Mathura Ma-
    hatmya
    Bhagavata, xvi, 6, 36, 52, 83, 93,
        104, 111, 118, 162, 207, 213
    Narada, 51, 52, 68
    Padma, 25, 52
    Skanda, 53, 161
    Varaha, xi, xix, 42 n.38, 47,
        50–51, 68, 79, 116, 167
Pushti Marg (Vallabhacharyas), xviii,
    9, 63, 76, 80, 93, 119–21, 167,
    180–81, 187, 192, 218–19. *See
    also* Vallabha
    ideal pilgrimage, 66–68, 219
Putana, 217

CPSIA information can be obtained at www.ICGtesting.com
Printed in the USA
BVOW05s0848161214

379096BV00006B/1/P